Switching, Routing, and Wireless Essentials Labs and Study Guide (CCNAv7)

Allan Johnson

Cisco Press

221 River St.

Hoboken, NJ 07030 USA

Switching, Routing, and Wireless Essentials Labs and Study Guide (CCNAv7)

Published by:
Cisco Press
221 River St.
Hoboken, NJ 07030 USA

ScoutAutomatedPrintCode

Student ISBNs:

ISBN-13: 978-0-13-663438-6
ISBN-10: 0-13-663438-9

Instructor ISBNs:

ISBN-13: 978-0-13-663440-9
ISBN-10: 0-13-663440-0

Library of Congress Control Number: 2020906044

Printed and bound by CPI Group (UK) Ltd, Croydon, CR0 4YY

Editor-in-Chief
Mark Taub

Director, ITP Product Management
Brett Bartow

Alliances Manager, Cisco Press
Arezou Gol

Senior Editor
James Manly

Managing Editor
Sandra Schroeder

Development Editor
Marianne Bartow

Project Editor
Mandie Frank

Copy Editor
Kitty Wilson

Technical Editor
Dave Holzinger

Editorial Assistant
Cindy Teeters

Designer
Chuti Prasertsith

Composition
codeMantra

Proofreader
Abigail Manheim

Warning and Disclaimer

This book is designed to provide information about the Cisco Networking Academy Switching, Routing, and Wireless Essentials (CCNAv7) course. Every effort has been made to make this book as complete and as accurate as possible, but no warranty or fitness is implied.

The information is provided on an "as is" basis. The authors, Cisco Press, and Cisco Systems, Inc. shall have neither liability nor responsibility to any person or entity with respect to any loss or damages arising from the information contained in this book or from the use of the discs or programs that may accompany it.

The opinions expressed in this book belong to the author and are not necessarily those of Cisco Systems, Inc.

Trademark Acknowledgments

All terms mentioned in this book that are known to be trademarks or service marks have been appropriately capitalized. Cisco Press or Cisco Systems, Inc., cannot attest to the accuracy of this information. Use of a term in this book should not be regarded as affecting the validity of any trademark or service mark.

Special Sales

For information about buying this title in bulk quantities, or for special sales opportunities (which may include electronic versions; custom cover designs; and content particular to your business, training goals, marketing focus, or branding interests), please contact our corporate sales department at corpsales@pearsoned.com or (800) 382-3419.

For government sales inquiries, please contact governmentsales@pearsoned.com.

For questions about sales outside the U.S., please contact intlcs@pearson.com.

Feedback Information

At Cisco Press, our goal is to create in-depth technical books of the highest quality and value. Each book is crafted with care and precision, undergoing rigorous development that involves the unique expertise of members from the professional technical community.

Readers' feedback is a natural continuation of this process. If you have any comments regarding how we could improve the quality of this book, or otherwise alter it to better suit your needs, you can contact us through email at feedback@ciscopress.com. Please make sure to include the book title and ISBN in your message.

We greatly appreciate your assistance.

Americas Headquarters	Asia Pacific Headquarters	Europe Headquarters
Cisco Systems, Inc.	Cisco Systems (USA) Pte. Ltd.	Cisco Systems International BV Amsterdam,
San Jose, CA	Singapore	The Netherlands

Cisco has more than 200 offices worldwide. Addresses, phone numbers, and fax numbers are listed on the Cisco Website at **www.cisco.com/go/offices**.

Cisco and the Cisco logo are trademarks or registered trademarks of Cisco and/or its affiliates in the U.S. and other countries. To view a list of Cisco trademarks, go to this URL: www.cisco.com/go/trademarks. Third party trademarks mentioned are the property of their respective owners. The use of the word partner does not imply a partnership relationship between Cisco and any other company. (1110R)

About the Contributing Author

Allan Johnson entered the academic world in 1999, after 10 years as a business owner/operator, to dedicate his efforts to his passion for teaching. He holds both an M.B.A. and an M.Ed. in training and development. He taught CCNA courses at the high school level for 7 years and has taught both CCNA and CCNP courses at Del Mar College in Corpus Christi, Texas. In 2003, Allan began to commit much of his time and energy to the CCNA Instructional Support Team, providing services to Networking Academy instructors worldwide and creating training materials. He now works full time for Cisco Networking Academy as Curriculum Lead.

About the Technical Reviewer

Dave Holzinger has been a curriculum developer, project manager, author, and technical editor for Cisco Networking Academy in Phoenix since 2001. Dave works on the team that develops Cisco Networking Academy's online curricula, including CCNA, CCNP, and IT Essentials. He has been working with computer hardware and software since 1981. Dave has certifications from Cisco, BICSI, and CompTIA.

Contents at a Glance

Contents

Command Syntax Conventions

The conventions used to present command syntax in this book are the same conventions used in the IOS Command Reference. The Command Reference describes these conventions as follows:

- **Boldface** indicates commands and keywords that are entered literally as shown. In actual configuration examples and output (not general command syntax), boldface indicates commands that are manually input by the user (such as a **show** command).

- *Italic* indicates arguments for which you supply actual values.

- Vertical bars (|) separate alternative, mutually exclusive elements.

- Square brackets ([ ]) indicate an optional element.

- Braces ({ }) indicate a required choice.

- Braces within brackets ([{ }]) indicate a required choice within an optional element.

Introduction

This book supports instructors and students in Cisco Networking Academy, an IT skills and career building program for learning institutions and individuals worldwide. Cisco Networking Academy provides a variety of curricula choices, including the very popular Cisco Certified Network Associate (CCNA) curriculum. It includes three courses oriented around the topics of CCNA certifications.

Switching, Routing, and Wireless Essentials Labs and Study Guide is a supplement to your classroom and laboratory experience with the Cisco Networking Academy. To be successful on the exam and achieve your CCNA certification, you should do everything in your power to arm yourself with a variety of tools and training materials to support your learning efforts. This book provides just such a collection of tools. Used to its fullest extent, it will help you gain the knowledge as well as practice the skills associated with the content area of the Switching, Routing, and Wireless Essentials v7 course. Specifically, this book will help you work on these main areas:

- Configure devices using security best practices.
- Explain how Layer 2 switches forward data.
- Implement VLANs and trunking in a switched network.
- Troubleshoot inter-VLAN routing on Layer 3 devices.
- Explain how STP enables redundancy in a Layer 2 network.
- Troubleshoot EtherChannel on switched links.
- Implement DHCPv4 to operate across multiple LANs.
- Configure dynamic address allocation in IPv6 networks.
- Explain how FHRPs provide default gateway services in a redundant network.
- Explain how vulnerabilities compromise LAN security.
- Implement switch security to mitigate LAN attacks.
- Explain how WLANs enable network connectivity.
- Implement a WLAN using a wireless router and WLC.
- Explain how routers use information in packets to make forwarding decisions.
- Configure IPv4 and IPv6 static routes.
- Troubleshoot static and default route configurations.

Labs and Study Guides similar to this one are also available for the other two courses: Introduction to Networks Labs and Study Guide and Enterprise Networking, Security, and Automation Labs and Study Guide.

Who Should Read This Book

This book's main audience is anyone taking the Switching, Routing, and Wireless Essentials course of the Cisco Networking Academy curriculum. Many Academies use this Labs and Study Guide as a required tool in the course, whereas other Academies recommend the Labs and Study Guide as an additional resource to prepare for class exams and the CCNA certification. The secondary audience for this book is people taking CCNA-related classes from professional training organizations. This book can also be used for college- and university-level networking courses, as well as anyone wanting to gain a detailed understanding of routing. However, the reader should know that the content of this book tightly aligns with the Cisco Networking Academy course. It may not be possible to complete some of the Study Guide sections and Labs without access to the online course. Fortunately, you can purchase the Switching, Routing, and Wireless Essentials v7.0 Companion Guide (ISBN: 9780136729358).

Goals and Methods

The most important goal of this book is to help you pass the 200-301 Cisco Certified Network Associate exam, which is associated with the Cisco Certified Network Associate (CCNA) certification. Passing the CCNA exam shows that you have the knowledge and skills required to manage a small enterprise network. You can view the detailed exam topics online, at http://learningnetwork.cisco.com. They are divided into six broad categories:

- Network Fundamentals
- Network Access
- IP Connectivity
- IP Services
- Security Fundamentals
- Automation and Programmability

The Introduction to Networks v7 course covers introductory material in the first five bullets. The next two courses, Switching, Routing, and Wireless Essentials v7 and Enterprise Networking, Security, and Automation v7, cover the material in more detail. Each chapter of this book is divided into a "Study Guide" section followed by a "Labs and Activities" section. The "Study Guide" section offers exercises that help you learn the concepts, configurations, and troubleshooting skills crucial to your success as a CCNA exam candidate. Each chapter is slightly different and includes some or all of the following types of exercises:

- Concept question exercises
- Skill-building activities and scenarios
- Configuration scenarios
- Packet Tracer exercises
- Troubleshooting scenarios

The "Labs and Activities" sections include all the online course labs and Packet Tracer activity instructions. In some chapters, this section begins with a Command Reference that you will complete to show that you understand all the commands introduced in the chapter.

Packet Tracer and Companion Website

This book includes the instructions for all the Packet Tracer activities in the online course. You need to be enrolled in the Introduction to Networks v7 course to access these Packet Tracer files.

Nine Packet Tracer activities have been created exclusively for this book. You can access these unique Packet Tracer files at this book's companion website.

To get your copy of Packet Tracer software and the nine unique files for this book, please go to the companion website for instructions. To access this companion website, follow these steps:

Step 1. Go to www.ciscopress.com/register and log in or create a new account.

Step 2. Enter the ISBN: 9780136634386.

Step 3. Answer the challenge question as proof of purchase.

Step 4. Click on the Access Bonus Content link in the Registered Products section of your account page to be taken to the page where your downloadable content is available.

How This Book Is Organized

This book corresponds closely to the Cisco Networking Academy Switching, Routing, and Wireless Essentials v7 course and is divided into 16 chapters:

- **Chapter 1, "Basic Device Configuration":** This chapter explains how to configure devices using security best practices. It includes initial switch and router configuration, switch port configuration, remote access configuration, and verification of connectivity between two networks.

- **Chapter 2, "Switching Concepts":** This chapter explains how switches forward data. It includes frame forwarding methods and collision and broadcast domain comparison.

- **Chapter 3, "VLANs":** This chapter explains how to implement VLANs and trunking in a switched network. It includes an explanation of the purpose of VLANs, how VLANs forward frames in a multi-switched environment, VLAN port assignments, trunk configuration, and DTP configuration.

- **Chapter 4, "Inter-VLAN Routing":** This chapter explains how to implement inter-VLAN routing. It includes a description of inter-VLAN routing options, router-on-a-stick configuration, Layer 3 switch inter-VLAN routing, and troubleshooting of common inter-VLAN routing configuration issues.

- **Chapter 5, "STP Concepts":** This chapter explains how STP enables redundancy in a Layer 3 network. It includes an explanation of common problems in redundant Layer 2 networks, STP operation, and Rapid PVST+ operation.

- **Chapter 6, "EtherChannel":** This chapter explains how to implement EtherChannel on switched links. It includes a description of EtherChannel technology, EtherChannel configuration, and EtherChannel troubleshooting.

- **Chapter 7, "DHCPv4":** This chapter explains how to implement DHCPv4 for multiple LANs. It includes an explanation of DHCPv4 operation and how to configure a router as a DHCPv4 server or DHCPv4 client.

- **Chapter 8, "SLAAC and DHCPv6":** This chapter explains how to implement dynamic address allocation in an IPv6 network. It includes an explanation of how an IPv6 host acquires its addressing, SLAAC operation, DHCPv6 operation, and how to configure a router as a stateful or stateless DHCPv6 server.

- **Chapter 9, "FHRP Concepts":** This chapter explains how FHRPs provide default gateway services in a redundant network. It includes an explanation of the purpose of FHRPs and HSRP operation.

- **Chapter 10, "LAN Security Concepts":** This chapter explains how vulnerabilities compromise LAN security. It includes an explanation of how to use endpoint security, how to use AAA and 802.1X for authentication, Layer 2 vulnerabilities, MAC address table attacks, and LAN attacks.

- **Chapter 11, "Switch Security Configuration":** This chapter explains how to configure switch security to mitigate LAN attacks. It covers port security implementation as well as mitigation of VLAN, DHCP, ARP, and STP attacks.

- **Chapter 12, "WLAN Concepts":** This chapter explains how WLANs enable network connectivity for wireless devices. It covers WLAN technology, WLAN components, and WLAN operation. In addition, the chapter discusses how CAPWAP is used to manage multiple APs for a WLC. It includes WLAN channel management and concludes with a discussion of threats to WLANs and how to secure WLANs.

- **Chapter 13, "WLAN Configuration":** This chapter explains how to implement a WLAN by using a wireless router and a WLC. It includes an explanation of wireless router configuration and WLC WLAN configuration for both WPA2 PSK and WPA2-Enterprise authentication. The chapter concludes with a discussion of how to troubleshoot common wireless configuration issues.

- **Chapter 14, "Routing Concepts":** This chapter explains how routers use information in packets to make forwarding decisions. It includes an explanation of path determination, packet forwarding, basic router configuration, routing table structure, and static and dynamic routing concepts.

- **Chapter 15, "IP Static Routing":** This chapter explains how to implement IPv4 and IPv6 static routes. It includes static route syntax, static and default routing configuration, floating static routing configuration, and static host route configuration.

- **Chapter 16, "Troubleshoot Static and Default Routes":** This chapter explains how to troubleshoot static and default route implementations. It covers how a router processes packets when a static route is configured and how to troubleshoot static and default route configuration issues.

CHAPTER 1

Basic Device Configuration

The "Study Guide" portion of this chapter uses a variety of exercises to test your knowledge of the advances in modern network technologies. The "Labs and Activities" portion of this chapter includes all the online curriculum research lab and Packet Tracer activity instructions.

As you work through this chapter, use Chapter 1 in *Switching, Routing, and Wireless Essentials v7 Companion Guide* or use the corresponding Module 1 in the Switching, Routing, and Wireless Essentials online curriculum for assistance.

Study Guide

Configure a Switch with Initial Settings

In this section, you review the switch boot sequence, the **boot system** command, the LED indicators on a Cisco Catalyst 2960, system crash recovery, and switch management configuration.

Switch Boot Sequence

Briefly explain the steps in the switch boot sequence.

After a Cisco switch is powered on, it goes through the following boot sequence:

Step 1. _____

Step 2. _____

Step 3. _____

Step 4. _____

Step 5. _____

The boot system Command

In Example 1-1, the BOOT environment variable is set using the **boot system** global configuration mode command.

Example 1-1   Setting the BOOT Environment Variable

```
S1(config)# boot system flash:/ c2960-lanbasek9-mz.150-2.SE
/c2960-lanbasek9-mz.150-2.SE.bin
S1(config)#
```

In Table 1-1, enter the description for each part of the **boot system** command shown in Example 1-1.

Table 1-1   The *boot system* Command Structure

Command	Definition
boot system	
flash:	
c2960-lanbasek9-mz.150-2.SE/	
c2960-lanbasek9-mz.150-2.SE.bin	

Switch LED Indicators

Figure 1-1 shows the switch LEDs and the Mode button for a Cisco Catalyst 2960 switch.

Figure 1-1   Cisco Catalyst 2960 LEDs and Mode Button

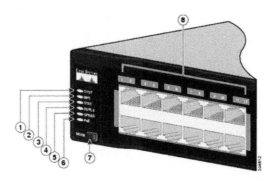

The Mode button (number 7 in Figure 1-1) is used to toggle through port status, port duplex, port speed, and, if supported, the Power over Ethernet (PoE) status of the port LEDs (8 in Figure 1-1). In Table 1-2, briefly describe the meaning of each of the color states for each LED indicator. An LED indicator can be green, amber, or off.

Table 1-2   LED Indicator Meanings

LED Indicator	Meaning
1 SYST	LED is off: _____
	LED is green: _____
	LED is amber: _____
2 RPS (redundant power supply)	LED is off: _____
	LED is green: _____
	LED is blinking green: _____
	LED is amber: _____
	LED is blinking amber: _____
3 STAT	LED is green: _____
	Port LED is off: _____
	LED is green on a port: _____
	LED on a port is blinking green: _____
	Port LED is alternating green/amber: _____
	Port LED is amber: _____
	Port LED is blinking amber: _____

LED Indicator	Meaning
4 DUPLX	LED is green: _____
	Port LED is off: _____
	Port LED is green: _____
5 SPEED	LED is green: _____
	Port LED is off: _____
	Port LED is green: _____
	Port LED is blinking green: _____
6 POE (Power over Ethernet)	LED is off: _____
	LED is blinking amber: _____
	LED is green: _____
	Port LED is off: _____
	Port LED is green: _____
	Port LED is alternating green/amber: _____
	Port LED is blinking amber: _____
	Port LED is amber: _____

Recovering from a System Crash

If the operating system cannot be loaded, use the boot loader command line to access files stored on the switch. Use these steps to access the boot loader:

Step 1. Connect a PC by console cable to the switch console port. Configure terminal emulation software to connect to the switch.

Step 2. Unplug the switch power cord.

Step 3. Reconnect the power cord to the switch and, within 15 seconds, press and hold down the Mode button while the System LED is still flashing green.

Step 4. Continue pressing the Mode button until the System LED turns briefly amber and then solid green; then release the Mode button.

Step 5. The boot loader **switch:** prompt appears in the terminal emulation software on the PC.

In Example 1-2, fill in the missing commands that will show the path of the switch BOOT variable, initialize flash, find the IOS file name, and boot the switch.

Example 1-2   Loading the IOS with Boot Loader

```
switch: _____

BOOT=flash:/c2960-lanbasek9-mz.122-55.SE7/c2960-lanbasek9-mz.122-55.SE7.bin

(output omitted)

switch: _____

Initializing Flash...

flashfs[0]: 2 files, 1 directories

flashfs[0]: 0 orphaned files, 0 orphaned directories

flashfs[0]: Total bytes: 32514048

flashfs[0]: Bytes used: 11838464

flashfs[0]: Bytes available: 20675584

flashfs[0]: flashfs fsck took 10 seconds.

...done Initializing Flash.

switch: _____

Directory of flash:/

    2   -rwx   11834846                   c2960-lanbasek9-mz.150-2.SE8.bin

    3   -rwx   2072                       multiple-fs

switch: _____

switch: _____

BOOT=flash:c2960-lanbasek9-mz.150-2.SE8.bin

(output omitted)

switch: _____
```

Switch Management Access

A console cable is used to connect a switch to a PC so that the switch can be initially configured. In Figure 1-2, the switch virtual interface (SVI) on S1 should be assigned an IP address so that the administrator can remotely access the switch.

Figure 1-2   Console Connection to a Switch

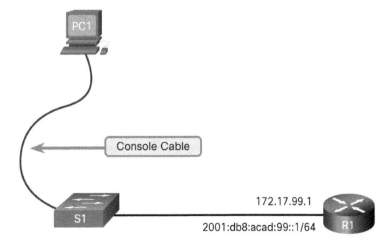

Switch SVI Configuration

In Table 1-3, enter the commands to configure and verify the S1 SVI in Figure 1-2.

Table 1-3   Switch SVI Configuration Example

Task	IOS Commands
Enter global configuration mode.	S1# _____
Enter interface configuration mode for the SVI.	S1(config)# _____
Configure the management interface IPv4 address.	S1(config-if)# _____
Configure the management interface IPv6 address.	S1(config-if)# _____
Enable the management interface.	S1(config-if)# _____
Return to global configuration mode.	S1(config-if)# _____
Configure the default gateway for the switch.	S1(config)# _____
Return to the privileged EXEC mode.	S1(config)# or _____
Save the running config to the startup config.	S1# _____
Verify the IPv4 interface IP address and status.	S1# _____
Verify the IPv6 interface IP address and status.	S1# _____

Configure Switch Ports

In this section, you review duplex modes, physical layer configuration, auto-MDIX, switch verification commands, and troubleshooting of the network access layer.

Duplex Communication

_____ communication, or bidirectional communication, increases bandwidth efficiency by allowing both ends of a connection to transmit and receive data simultaneously. There is no collision domain associated with a switch port operating in this mode. Gigabit Ethernet and 10 Gbps NICs require this mode in order to operate.

_____ communication is unidirectional and creates performance issues because data can flow in only one direction at a time, often resulting in collisions.

Configure Switch Ports at the Physical Layer

In Table 1-4, list the commands to configure the FastEthernet 0/1 port on S1 to operate in full-duplex mode at 100 Mbps.

Table 1-4   Switch Port Physical Layer Configuration Example

Task	IOS Commands
Enter global configuration mode.	S1# _____
Enter interface configuration mode.	S1(config)# _____
Configure the interface duplex.	S1(config-if)# _____
Configure the interface speed.	S1(config-if)# _____
Return to the privileged EXEC mode.	S1(config-if)# _____
Save the running config to the startup config.	S1# _____

What is the default setting for duplex and speed on Cisco Catalyst 2960 and 3560 switches? And why is it set this way?

Auto-MDIX

When auto-MDIX is enabled, the interface automatically detects the required cable connection type (straight-through or crossover) and configures the connection appropriately.

When using auto-MDIX on an interface, what must the interface speed and duplex be set to so that the feature operates correctly?

What is the command, including switch prompt, to enable auto-MDIX on an S1 interface?

What is the command, including switch prompt, to examine the auto-MDIX setting for the fa0/1 interface on S1?

Switch Verification Commands

In Table 1-5, list the syntax for switch verification commands that will achieve each task. If applicable, include both the IPv4 and IPv6 commands.

Table 1-5   Switch Verification Commands

Task	IOS Commands
Display interface status and configuration.	
Display current startup configuration.	
Display current running configuration.	
Display information about flash file system.	
Display system hardware and software status.	
Display history of command entered.	
Display IP information about an interface.	
	or
Display the MAC address table.	
	or

Network Access Layer Issues

The output from the **show interfaces** command is useful for detecting common media issues, as shown in Example 1-3.

Example 1-3   The *show interfaces* Command for Fa0/18

```
S1# show interfaces fastEthernet 0/18
FastEthernet0/18 is up, line protocol is up (connected)
  Hardware is Fast Ethernet, address is 0025.83e6.9092 (bia 0025.83e6.9092)
  MTU 1500 bytes, BW 100000 Kbit/sec, DLY 100 usec,
     reliability 255/255, txload 1/255, rxload 1/255
  Encapsulation ARPA, loopback not set
  Keepalive set (10 sec)
  Full-duplex, 100Mb/s, media type is 10/100BaseTX
  input flow-control is off, output flow-control is unsupported
  ARP type: ARPA, ARP Timeout 04:00:00
  Last input never, output 00:00:01, output hang never
  Last clearing of "show interface" counters never
  Input queue: 0/75/0/0 (size/max/drops/flushes); Total output drops: 0
  Queueing strategy: fifo
  Output queue: 0/40 (size/max)
  5 minute input rate 0 bits/sec, 0 packets/sec
  5 minute output rate 0 bits/sec, 0 packets/sec
     2295197 packets input, 305539992 bytes, 0 no buffer
     Received 1925500 broadcasts (74 multicasts)
     0 runts, 0 giants, 0 throttles
     3 input errors, 3 CRC, 0 frame, 0 overrun, 0 ignored
     0 watchdog, 74 multicast, 0 pause input
     0 input packets with dribble condition detected
     3594664 packets output, 436549843 bytes, 0 underruns
     8 output errors, 1790 collisions, 10 interface resets
     0 unknown protocol drops
     0 babbles, 235 late collision, 0 deferred
```

Based on the output of the **show interfaces** command, possible problems can be fixed as follows:

- If the interface is up and the line protocol is down, what types of problems may exist?

_____

- If the line protocol and the interface are both down, what types of problems may exist?

_____

- If the interface is administratively down, what type of problem exists?

_____

Input errors is the sum of all errors in datagrams that were received on the interface being examined. Output errors is the sum of all errors that prevented the final transmission of datagrams out the interface that is being examined. In Table 1-6, indicate the error type described.

Table 1-6 Interface Input and Output Error Types

Error Type	Description
Input errors	Total number of errors. It includes runts, giants, no buffer, CRC, frame, overrun, and ignored counts.
	Packets that are discarded because they are smaller than the minimum packet size for the medium. For instance, any Ethernet packet that is less than 64 bytes is considered a runt.
	Packets that are discarded because they exceed the maximum packet size for the medium. For example, any Ethernet packet that is greater than 1518 bytes is considered a giant.
	CRC errors are generated when the calculated checksum is not the same as the checksum received.
Output errors	Sum of all errors that prevented the final transmission of datagrams out the interface that is being examined.
	Number of messages retransmitted because of an Ethernet collision.
	Collisions that occur after 512 bits of the frame have been transmitted.

Troubleshooting Network Access Layer Issues

To troubleshoot scenarios involving no connection or a bad connection between a switch and another device, follow the general process shown in Figure 1-3.

Figure 1-3 Troubleshooting Process for Switch Interface Issues

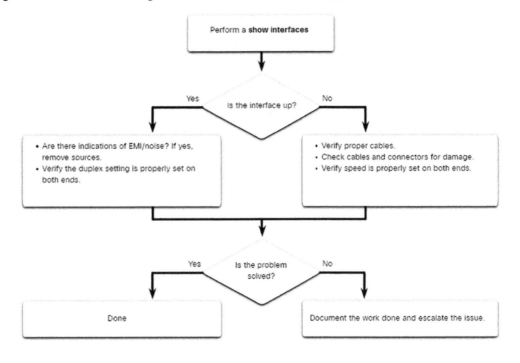

Secure Remote Access

In this section, you review the difference between Telnet and Secure Shell (SSH) remote access. You will then review the configuration and verification of SSH.

Telnet Operation

Telnet uses TCP port 23. Explain why using Telnet is not a recommended method for secure remote access.

SSH Operation

SSH is a secure protocol that uses TCP port 22. Explain why using SSH is the recommended method for secure remote access.

Verify That the Switch Supports SSH

Use the **show version** command, as shown in Example 1-4, to see which IOS version the switch is currently running. An IOS filename that includes the combination "k9" supports cryptographic (encrypted) features and capabilities.

Example 1-4   Verifying That the IOS Version Supports SSH

```
S1# show version
Cisco IOS Software, C2960 Software (C2960-LANBASEK9-M), Version 15.0(2)SE7,
RELEASE SOFTWARE (fc1)
```

Configure SSH

To implement SSH, you need to generate Rivest–Shamir–Adleman (RSA) keys. RSA involves a public key, kept on a public RSA server, and a private key, kept only by the sender and receiver.

To configure a Catalyst 2960 switch as an SSH server, fill in the blanks in the following steps:

Step 1.   Record the command that will verify that the switch supports SSH. If the switch does not support SSH, this command will be unrecognized.

```
S1# _____
SSH Disabled - version 1.99
%Please create RSA keys to enable SSH (and of atleast 768 bits for SSH v2).
<output omitted>
```

Step 2.   Record the command to configure a host domain for S1. Use the domain mydomain.com.

```
S1(config)# _____
```

Step 3.   Record the command to generate an encrypted RSA key pair. Use 1024 as the modulus size.

```
S1(config)# _____
The name for the keys will be: S1.mydomain.com
Choose the size of the key modulus in the range of 360 to 4096 for your
   General Purpose Keys. Choosing a key modulus greater than 512 may take
   a few minutes.

How many bits in the modulus [512]: _____
% Generating 1024 bit RSA keys, keys will be non-exportable...
[OK] (elapsed time was 4 seconds)
*Mar  1 06:04:20.703: %SSH-5-ENABLED: SSH 1.99 has been enabled
```

Step 4.   Record the command to configure the SSH server to authenticate the **admin** user locally with **cisco123!** as the password.

S1(config)# _____

Step 5.   Record the commands to configure all vty lines to allow only SSH access and to use the local database for authentication.

S1(config)# _____

S1(config-line)# _____

S1(config-line)# _____

S1(config-line)# **exit** _____

Step 6.   Record the command to enable SSH version 2.

S1(config)# _____

Verify That SSH Is Operational

To verify that SSH is operational, remotely access the switch using a terminal program configured for SSH access. For example, in Figure 1-4, the administrator on PC1 can use a terminal program, such a PuTTY, to remotely access S1.

Figure 1-4   Using SSH to Remotely Access S1

Packet Tracer Exercise 1-1: Configure Secure Access

Now you are ready to use Packet Tracer to apply your knowledge about SSH. Download and open the file LSG02-0101.pka from the companion website for this book. Refer to the Introduction of this book for specifics on accessing files.

Note: The following instructions are also contained in the Packet Tracer Exercise.

In this Packet Tracer activity, you will configure the switch for secure remote access using SSH. Use the commands you have documented in this chapter as you complete the activity.

Requirements

Access Sw1 with the privileged EXEC password class. Configure Sw1 with the following requirements:

- Configure the hostname for S1.
- Configure S1 to use mydomain.com.
- Generate an encrypted RSA key pair and use a 1024 modulus.
- Configure **admin** as the user with **cisco123!** as the password.
- Configure the vty lines for SSH only, using the local database for authentication.
- Enable SSHv2.
- At the command prompt for PC1, use the command **ssh -l admin 172.17.99.11** to verify secure remote access (where **-l** is a lowercase *L*, not a 1).

Your completion percentage should be 100%. If it is not, click Check Results to see which required components are not yet completed.

Basic Router Configuration

In this section, you review how to configure a router with its basic configuration, including dual stack addressing and loopback interfaces

Configure Basic Router Settings

Basic router settings include the device name, passwords, and setting a banner, as shown in Example 1-5. Be sure you always save your configuration after making changes.

Example 1-5   Sample Basic Router Configuration

```
Router# configure terminal
Enter configuration commands, one per line.  End with CNTL/Z.
Router(config)# hostname R1
R1(config)# enable secret class
R1(config)# line console 0
R1(config-line)# password cisco
R1(config-line)# login
R1(config-line)# exit
R1(config)# line vty 0 4
R1(config-line)# password cisco
R1(config-line)# login
R1(config-line)# exit
R1(config)# service password-encryption
R1(config)# banner motd $Authorized Access Only$
R1# copy running-config startup-config
Destination filename [startup-config]?
Building configuration...
[OK]

R1#
```

Dual Stack Topology

The dual stack topology in Figure 1-5 is used to demonstrate the configuration of router IPv4 and IPv6 interfaces.

Figure 1-5   Dual Stack Topology

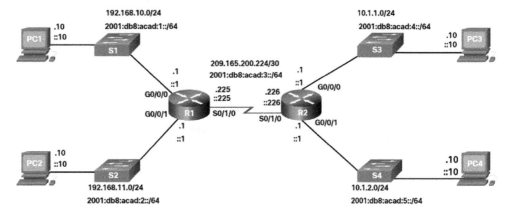

Configure Router Interfaces

In Example 1-6, record the missing commands to configure and activate the interfaces for R1.

Example 1-6 R1 Interface Configuration

```
R1(config)# ipv6 unicast-routing
R1(config)# _____
R1(config-if)# _____
R1(config-if)# _____
R1(config-if)# description Link to LAN 1
R1(config-if)# _____
R1(config-if)# exit
R1(config)# _____
R1(config-if)# _____
R1(config-if)# _____
R1(config-if)# description Link to LAN 2
R1(config-if)# _____
R1(config-if)# exit
R1(config)# _____
R1(config-if)# _____
R1(config-if)# _____
R1(config-if)# description Link to R2
R1(config-if)# _____
R1(config-if)# exit
R1(config)#
```

IPv4 Loopback Interfaces

Loopback interfaces are commonly used in lab environments to create additional interfaces. For example, you can create multiple loopback interfaces on a router to simulate more networks for configuration practice and testing purposes.

The IPv4 address for each loopback interface must be unique and unused by any other interface, as shown in the configuration of loopback interface 0 on R1 in Example 1-7.

Example 1-7   Loopback Interface Configuration

```
R1(config)# interface loopback 0
R1(config-if)# ip address 10.0.0.1 255.255.255.0
R1(config-if)# exit
R1(config)#
%LINEPROTO-5-UPDOWN: Line protocol on Interface Loopback0, changed state to up
```

Packet Tracer Exercise 1-2: Basic Router Configuration

Now you are ready to use Packet Tracer to apply your knowledge of basic router configuration. Download and open the file LSG02-0102.pka from the companion website for this book. Refer to the Introduction of this book for specifics on accessing files.

Note: The following instructions are also contained in the Packet Tracer Exercise.

In this Packet Tracer activity, you will configure the R1 router with basic configurations and dual stack addressing. You will then verify that PC1 and PC2 can ping each other using IPv4 and IPv6 addresses. Use the topology in Figure 1-5 and the commands you documented in the section "Basic Router Configuration."

Requirements

Configure R1 with the following settings:

- The name of the router is **R1**.

- The privileged EXEC password is **class**.

- The line password is **cisco**.

- The message of the day is **Authorized Access Only**.

- Enable IPv6 routing with the **ipv6 unicast-routing** command.

- Configure and activate the R1 LAN interfaces according to Figure 1-5.

- Save the configurations.

- Verify IPv4 and IPv6 connectivity between PC1 and PC2.

Your completion percentage should be 100%. If it is not, click Check Results to see which required components are not yet completed.

Verify Directly Connected Networks

Several **show** commands can be used to verify the operation and configuration of an interface. In this section you use the topology in Figure 1-5 to review the verification of router interface settings.

Verify Interface Status

In Example 1-8, record the commands used to display abbreviated IPv4 and IPv6 interface information.

Example 1-8   Verify Interface Status

```
R1# _____
Interface              IP-Address       OK? Method Status                Protocol
GigabitEthernet0/0/0   192.168.10.1     YES manual up                    up
GigabitEthernet0/0/1   192.168.11.1     YES manual up                    up
Serial0/1/0            209.165.200.225  YES manual up                    up
Serial0/1/1            unassigned       YES unset  administratively down  down
R1# _____
GigabitEthernet0/0/0      [up/up]
    FE80::7279:B3FF:FE92:3130
    2001:DB8:ACAD:1::1
GigabitEthernet0/0/1      [up/up]
    FE80::7279:B3FF:FE92:3131
    2001:DB8:ACAD:2::1
Serial0/1/0               [up/up]
    FE80::7279:B3FF:FE92:3130
    2001:DB8:ACAD:3::1
Serial0/1/1               [down/down]      Unassigned
R1#
```

Verify IPv6 Link-Local and Multicast Addresses

In Example 1-9, record the command to display the detailed information for this IPv6 interface.

Example 1-9   Verify IPv6 Link-Local and Multicast Addresses

```
R1# _____
GigabitEthernet0/0/0 is up, line protocol is up
  IPv6 is enabled, link-local address is FE80::7279:B3FF:FE92:3130
  No Virtual link-local address(es):
  Global unicast address(es):
    2001:DB8:ACAD:1::1, subnet is 2001:DB8:ACAD:1::/64
  Joined group address(es):
    FF02::1
    FF02::1:FF00:1
    FF02::1:FF92:3130
  MTU is 1500 bytes
  ICMP error messages limited to one every 100 milliseconds
  ICMP redirects are enabled
  ICMP unreachables are sent
  ND DAD is enabled, number of DAD attempts: 1
  ND reachable time is 30000 milliseconds (using 30000)
  ND advertised reachable time is 0 (unspecified)
  ND advertised retransmit interval is 0 (unspecified)
```

```
   ND router advertisements are sent every 200 seconds
   ND router advertisements live for 1800 seconds
   ND advertised default router preference is Medium
R1#
```

Verify Interface Configuration

In Example 1-10, record the command that will display only the part of the running configuration that shows the G0/0/0 interface configuration.

Example 1-10   Verify Interface Configuration

```
R1 _____
Building configuration...
Current configuration : 158 bytes
!
interface GigabitEthernet0/0/0
 description Link to LAN 1
 ip address 192.168.10.1 255.255.255.0
 negotiation auto
 ipv6 address 2001:DB8:ACAD:1::1/64
end
R1#
```

Verify Routes

In Example 1-11, record the commands to view the complete IPv4 and IPv6 routing tables.

Example 1-11   Verify Routes

```
R1# _____
Codes: L - local, C - connected, S - static, R - RIP, M - mobile, B - BGP

Gateway of last resort is not set
      192.168.10.0/24 is variably subnetted, 2 subnets, 2 masks
C        192.168.10.0/24 is directly connected, GigabitEthernet0/0/0
L        192.168.10.1/32 is directly connected, GigabitEthernet0/0/0
      192.168.11.0/24 is variably subnetted, 2 subnets, 2 masks
C        192.168.11.0/24 is directly connected, GigabitEthernet0/0/1
L        192.168.11.1/32 is directly connected, GigabitEthernet0/0/1
      209.165.200.0/24 is variably subnetted, 2 subnets, 2 masks
C        209.165.200.224/30 is directly connected, Serial0/1/0
L        209.165.200.225/32 is directly connected, Serial0/1/0
```

```
R1# _____

IPv6 Routing Table - default - 7 entries

Codes: C - Connected, L - Local, S - Static, U - Per-user Static route


C   2001:DB8:ACAD:1::/64 [0/0]

      via GigabitEthernet0/0/0, directly connected

L   2001:DB8:ACAD:1::1/128 [0/0]

      via GigabitEthernet0/0/0, receive

C   2001:DB8:ACAD:2::/64 [0/0]

      via GigabitEthernet0/0/1, directly connected

L   2001:DB8:ACAD:2::1/128 [0/0]

      via GigabitEthernet0/0/1, receive

C   2001:DB8:ACAD:3::/64 [0/0]

      via Serial0/1/0, directly connected

L   2001:DB8:ACAD:3::1/128 [0/0]

      via Serial0/1/0, receive

L   FF00::/8 [0/0]

      via Null0, receive

R1#
```

Filter Show Command Output

Another very useful feature that improves the user experience at the command-line interface (CLI) is the filtering of **show** output. Filtering commands can be used to display specific sections of output. To enable a filtering command, enter a pipe (I) character after the **show** command and then enter a filtering parameter and a filtering expression.

Example 1-12 shows examples of using the **section**, **include**, **exclude**, and **begin** filtering commands.

Example 1-12   Filter Show Command Output

```
R1# show running-config | section line vty
line vty 0 4
 password 7 110A1016141D
 login
 transport input all
R1# show ip interface brief | include up
GigabitEthernet0/0/0    192.168.10.1    YES manual up                    up
GigabitEthernet0/0/1    192.168.11.1    YES manual up                    up
Serial0/1/0             209.165.200.225 YES manual up                    up
```

```
R1# show ip interface brief | exclude unassigned
Interface              IP-Address      OK? Method Status              Protocol
GigabitEthernet0/0/0   192.168.10.1    YES manual up                  up
GigabitEthernet0/0/1   192.168.11.1    YES manual up                  up
Serial0/1/0            209.165.200.225 YES manual up                  up
R1# show ip route | begin Gateway
Gateway of last resort is not set
      192.168.10.0/24 is variably subnetted, 2 subnets, 2 masks
C        192.168.10.0/24 is directly connected, GigabitEthernet0/0/0
L        192.168.10.1/32 is directly connected, GigabitEthernet0/0/0
      192.168.11.0/24 is variably subnetted, 2 subnets, 2 masks
C        192.168.11.0/24 is directly connected, GigabitEthernet0/0/1
L        192.168.11.1/32 is directly connected, GigabitEthernet0/0/1
      209.165.200.0/24 is variably subnetted, 2 subnets, 2 masks
C        209.165.200.224/30 is directly connected, Serial0/1/0
L        209.165.200.225/32 is directly connected, Serial0/1/0
R1#
```

Command History Feature

The command history feature is useful because it temporarily stores the list of executed commands to be recalled.

What two methods can you use to quickly recall commands in the history buffer?

_____

The command output begins with the most recent command. Repeat the key sequence to recall successively older commands. What two methods can you use to return to more recent commands in the history buffer?

_____

Repeat the key sequence to recall successively more recent commands. What is the default amount of command lines stored in the history buffer?

_____

What command shows the commands stored in the history buffer?

_____

What command, including router prompt, can you use to increase the size of the history buffer to the last 100 commands?

_____

Check Your Understanding—Verify Directly Connected Networks

Check your understanding of verifying directly connected networks by choosing the BEST answer to each of the following questions.

1. Which command displays a summary of all IPv6-enabled interfaces on a router that includes the IPv6 address and operational status?

   a. show ip interface brief

   b. show ipv6 route

   c. show running-config interface

   d. show ipv6 interface brief

2. When verifying routes, what code is used to identify directly connected routes in the routing table?

   a. C

   b. D

   c. L

   d. R

3. Which command displays packet flow counts, collisions, and buffer failures on an interface?

   a. show interface

   b. show ip interface

   c. show running-config interface

4. An IPv6-enabled interface is required to have which type of address?

   a. loopback

   b. global unicast

   c. link-local

   d. static

5. What character is used to enable the filtering of commands?

   a. pipe: |

   b. comma: ,

   c. colon: :

   d. semicolon: ;

6. Which filtering expression shows all output lines starting from the line matching the filtering expression?

   a. section

   b. begin

   c. include

   d. exclude

Labs and Activities

Command Reference

In Table 1-7, record the command, including the correct router or switch prompt, that fits each description.

Table 1-7 Commands for Chapter 1, "Basic Device Configuration"

Command	Description
	The command to enter interface configuration mode for VLAN 99 on switch S1.
	The command to configure 172.17.99.11/24 as the management interface IPv4 address.
	The command to configure 2001:db8:acad:99::1/64 as the management interface IPv6 address.
	The command to enable the management interface.
	The command to configure the default gateway for switch S1 as 172.17.99.1.
	The command to configure an interface on switch S1 for full-duplex.
	The command to configure an interface on switch S1 for 100 Mbps.
	The command to configure an interface on switch S1 for auto-MDIX.
	The command to verify SSH is enabled on switch S1.
	The command to configure switch S1 with mydomain.com
	The command to configure switch S1 to generate an encrypted RSA key pair
	The command to configure switch S1 with admin as a user and cisco123! as the password.
	In line configuration mode for the vty lines, the command to configure SSH as the only allowed remote access.
	The command to configure the lines to use the local database for authentication.
	The command to configure switch S1 to use SSHv2.
	In interface configuration mode, the command to configure the router R1 interface to use 10.10.10.1/24 as the IPv4 address.

Command	Description
	In interface configuration mode, the command to configure the router R1 interface to use 2001:db8:acad:1::1/64 as the IPv6 address.
	The command to view an abbreviated listing of the status of IPv4 interfaces on R1.
	The command to view an abbreviated listing of the status of IPv6 interfaces on R1.
	The command to view all the IPv4 routes on R1.
	The command to view all the IPv6 routes on R1.
	The command to view the command history buffer on R1.
	The command to change the command history buffer to 50 on R1.

1.1.7 Lab—Basic Switch Configuration

Topology

Addressing Table

Device	Interface	IP Address / Prefix
S1	VLAN 99	192.168.1.2 /24
		2001:db8:acad::2 /64
		fe80::2
PC-A	NIC	192.168.1.10 /24
		2001:db8:acad:3 /64
		fe80::3

Objectives

Part 1: Cable the Network and Verify the Default Switch Configuration

Part 2: Configure Basic Network Device Settings

- Configure basic switch settings.

- Configure the PC IP address.

Part 3: Verify and Test Network Connectivity

- Display device configuration.

- Test end-to-end connectivity with ping.

- Test remote management capabilities with Telnet.

Part 4: Manage the MAC Address Table

- Record the MAC address of the host.

- Determine the MAC addresses that the switch has learned.

- List the **show mac address-table** command options.

- Set up a static MAC address.

Background / Scenario

Cisco switches can be configured with a special IP address known as the switch virtual interface (SVI). The SVI, or management address, can be used for remote access to the switch to display or configure settings. If the VLAN 1 SVI is assigned an IP address, by default all ports in VLAN 1 have access to the SVI IP address.

In this lab, you will build a simple topology using Ethernet LAN cabling and access a Cisco switch using the console and remote access methods. You will examine default switch configurations before configuring basic switch settings. These basic switch settings include device name, interface description, local passwords, message of the day (MOTD) banner, IP addressing, and static MAC address. You will also demonstrate the use of a management IP address for remote switch management. The topology consists of one switch and one host using only Ethernet and console ports.

Note: The switches used are Cisco Catalyst 2960s with Cisco IOS Release 15.2(2) (lanbasek9 image). Other switches and Cisco IOS versions can be used. Depending on the model and Cisco IOS version, the commands available and output produced might vary from what is shown in the labs.

Note: Make sure that the switches have been erased and have no startup configurations. If you are unsure, contact your instructor. Refer to Appendix A for the procedures to initialize and reload a switch.

The **default bias** template used by the Switch Database Manager (SDM) does not provide IPv6 address capabilities. Verify that SDM is using either the **dual-ipv4-and-ipv6** template or the **lanbase-routing** template. The new template will be used after reboot even if the configuration is not saved.

```
S1# show sdm prefer
```

Use the following commands to assign the **dual-ipv4-and-ipv6** template as the default SDM template.

```
S1# configure terminal
S1(config)# sdm prefer dual-ipv4-and-ipv6 default
S1(config)# end
S1# reload
```

Required Resources

- 1 Switch (Cisco 2960 with Cisco IOS Release 15.2(2) lanbasek9 image or comparable)
- 1 PC (Windows with terminal emulation program, such as Tera Term)
- 1 Console cable to configure the Cisco IOS device via the console port
- 1 Ethernet cable as shown in the topology

Part 1: Cable the Network and Verify the Default Switch Configuration

In Part 1, you will set up the network topology and verify default switch settings.

Step 1:   Cable the network as shown in the topology.

    a.   Connect the console cable as shown in the topology. Do not connect the PC-A Ethernet cable at this time.

Note: If you are using Netlab, shut down F0/6 on S1. This has the same effect as not connecting PC-A to S1.

---

    b.   Connect to the switch from PC-A using Tera Term or other terminal emulation program.

       Question:

       Why must you use a console connection to initially configure the switch? Why is it not possible to connect to the switch via Telnet or SSH?

Step 2:   Verify the default switch configuration.

    In this step, you will examine the default switch settings, such as current switch configuration, IOS information, interface properties, VLAN information, and flash memory.

You can access all the switch IOS commands in privileged EXEC mode. Access to privileged EXEC mode should be restricted by password protection to prevent unauthorized use because it provides direct access to global configuration mode and commands used to configure operating parameters. You will set passwords later in this lab.

The privileged EXEC mode command set includes those commands contained in user EXEC mode, as well as the **configure** command through which access to the remaining command modes is gained. Use the **enable** command to enter privileged EXEC mode.

a.   Assuming the switch had no configuration file stored in nonvolatile random-access memory (NVRAM), a console connection using Tera Term or other terminal emulation program will place you at the user EXEC mode prompt on the switch with a prompt of Switch>. Use the **enable** command to enter privileged EXEC mode.

Notice that the prompt changed in the configuration to reflect privileged EXEC mode.

Verify that there is a clean default configuration file on the switch by issuing the **show running-config** privileged EXEC mode command. If a configuration file was previously saved, it must be removed. Depending on the switch model and IOS version, your configuration may look slightly different. However, there should be no configured passwords or IP address. If your switch does not have a default configuration, erase and reload the switch.

Note: Appendix A details the steps to initialize and reload a switch.

b.   Examine the current running configuration file.

Questions:

How many FastEthernet interfaces does a 2960 switch have?

_____

How many Gigabit Ethernet interfaces does a 2960 switch have?

_____

What is the range of values shown for the vty lines?

_____

c.   Examine the startup configuration file in NVRAM.

Question:

Why does this message appear?

_____

d.   Examine the characteristics of the SVI for VLAN 1.

Questions:

Is there an IP address assigned to VLAN 1?

_____

What is the MAC address of this SVI? Answers will vary.

_____

Is this interface up?

_____

e. Examine the IP properties of the SVI VLAN 1.

Question:

What output do you see?

_____

f. Connect an Ethernet cable from PC-A to port 6 on the switch and examine the IP properties of the SVI VLAN 1. Allow time for the switch and PC to negotiate duplex and speed parameters.

Note: If you are using Netlab, enable interface F0/6 on S1.

Question:

What output do you see?

_____

g. Examine the Cisco IOS version information of the switch.

Questions:

What is the Cisco IOS version that the switch is running?

_____

What is the system image filename?

_____

What is the base MAC address of this switch?

_____

h. Examine the default properties of the FastEthernet interface used by PC-A.

Switch# **show interface f0/6**

Question:

Is the interface up or down?

_____

What event would make an interface go up?

_____

What is the MAC address of the interface?

_____

What is the speed and duplex setting of the interface?

_____

i. Examine the default VLAN settings of the switch.

Question:

What is the default name of VLAN 1?

_____

Which ports are in VLAN 1?

_____

Is VLAN 1 active?

_____

What type of VLAN is the default VLAN?

_____

j. Examine flash memory.

Issue one of the following commands to examine the contents of the flash directory.

```
Switch# show flash
Switch# dir flash:
```

Files have a file extension, such as .bin, at the end of the filename. Directories do not have a file extension.

Question:

What is the filename of the Cisco IOS image?

_____

Part 2: Configure Basic Network Device Settings

In Part 2, you will configure basic settings for the switch and PC.

Step 1:   Configure basic switch settings.

a. Copy the following basic configuration and paste it into S1 while in global configuration mode.

```
no ip domain-lookup
hostname S1
service password-encryption
enable secret class
banner motd #
Unauthorized access is strictly prohibited. #
```

b. Set the SVI IP address of the switch. This allows remote management of the switch.

Before you can manage S1 remotely from PC-A, you must assign the switch an IP address. The default configuration on the switch is to have the management of the switch controlled through VLAN 1. However, a best practice for basic switch configuration is to change the management VLAN to a VLAN other than VLAN 1.

For management purposes, use VLAN 99. The selection of VLAN 99 is arbitrary and in no way implies that you should always use VLAN 99.

First, create the new VLAN 99 on the switch. Then set the IP address of the switch to 192.168.1.2 with a subnet mask of 255.255.255.0 on the internal virtual interface VLAN 99. The IPv6 address can also be configured on the SVI interface. Use the IPv6 addresses listed in the Addressing Table.

Notice that the VLAN 99 interface is in the down state even though you entered the **no shutdown** command. The interface is currently down because no switch ports are assigned to VLAN 99.

c. Assign all user ports to VLAN 99.

To establish connectivity between the host and the switch, the ports used by the host must be in the same VLAN as the switch. Notice in the above output that the VLAN 1 interface goes down because none of the ports are assigned to VLAN 1. After a few seconds, VLAN 99 comes up because at least one active port (F0/6 with PC-A attached) is now assigned to VLAN 99.

d. Issue the **show vlan brief** command to verify that all ports are in VLAN 99.

e. Configure the default gateway for S1. If no default gateway is set, the switch cannot be managed from a remote network that is more than one router away. Although this activity does not include an external IP gateway, assume that you will eventually connect the LAN to a router for external access. Assuming that the LAN interface on the router is 192.168.1.1, set the default gateway for the switch.

f. Console port access should also be restricted with a password. Use **cisco** as the console login password in this activity. The default configuration is to allow all console connections with no password needed. To prevent console messages from interrupting commands, use the **logging synchronous** option.

```
S1(config)# line con 0
S1(config-line)# logging synchronous
```

g. Configure the virtual terminal (vty) lines for the switch to allow telnet access. If you do not configure a vty password, you will not be able to telnet to the switch.

Question:

Why is the **login** command required?

Step 2: Configure an IP address on PC-A.

Assign the IP address and subnet mask to the PC as shown in the Addressing Table. An abbreviated version of the procedure is described here. A default gateway is not required for this topology; however, you can enter **192.168.1.1** and **fe80::1** to simulate a router attached to S1.

1) Navigate to the **Control Panel.**

2) In the Category view, select **View network status and tasks.**

3) Click **Change adapter settings** on the left panel.

4) Right-click an **Ethernet** interface, and choose **Properties.**

5) Choose **Internet Protocol Version 4 (TCP/IPv4)** and click **Properties.**

6) Click the **Use the following IP address** radio button and enter the IP address and subnet mask and click **OK.**

7) Select **Internet Protocol Version 6 (TCP/IPv6)** and click **Properties.**

8) Click the **Use the following IPv6 address** radio button and enter the IPv6 address and prefix and click **OK** to continue

9) Click **OK** to exit the Properties window.

Part 3: Verify and Test Network Connectivity

In Part 3, you will verify and document the switch configuration, test end-to-end connectivity between PC-A and S1, and test the switch's remote management capability.

Step 1: Display the switch configuration.

Use the console connection on PC-A to display and verify the switch configuration. The **show run** command displays the entire running configuration, one page at a time. Use the spacebar to advance paging.

a. A sample configuration is shown here. The settings you configured are highlighted in yellow. The other configuration settings are IOS defaults.

```
S1# show run
Building configuration...

Current configuration : 2206 bytes
!
version 15.2
no service pad
service timestamps debug datetime msec
service timestamps log datetime msec
service password-encryption
!
hostname S1
!
boot-start-marker
boot-end-marker
!
enable secret 5 $1$mtvC$6NC.1VKr3p6bj7YGE.jNg0
!
```

```
no aaa new-model
system mtu routing 1500
!
!
no ip domain-lookup
!
<output omitted>
!
interface FastEthernet0/24
 switchport access vlan 99
!
interface GigabitEthernet0/1
 switchport access vlan 99
!
interface GigabitEthernet0/2
 switchport access vlan 99
!
interface Vlan1
 no ip address
 no ip route-cache
!
interface Vlan99
 ip address 192.168.1.2 255.255.255.0
 ipv6 address FE80::2 link-local
 ipv6 address 2001:DB8:ACAD::2/64
!
ip default-gateway 192.168.1.1
ip http server
ip http secure-server
!
banner motd ^C
Unauthorized access is strictly prohibited. ^C
!
line con 0
 password 7 00071A150754
 logging synchronous
 login
line vty 0 4
 password 7 121A0C041104
 login
line vty 5 15
 password 7 121A0C041104
 login
!
end
```

b. Verify the management VLAN 99 settings.

`S1# show interface vlan 99`

Questions:

What is the bandwidth on this interface?

_____

What is the VLAN 99 state?

_____

What is the line protocol state?

_____

Step 2:   Test end-to-end connectivity with ping.

a. From the command prompt on PC-A, ping the address of PC-A first.

`C:\> ping 192.168.1.10`

b. From the command prompt on PC-A, ping the SVI management address of S1.

`C:\> ping 192.168.1.2`

Because PC-A needs to resolve the MAC address of S1 through ARP, the first packet may time out. If ping results continue to be unsuccessful, troubleshoot the basic device configurations. Check both the physical cabling and logical addressing.

Step 3:   Test and verify remote management of S1.

You will now use Telnet to remotely access the switch. In this lab, PC-A and S1 reside side by side. In a production network, the switch could be in a wiring closet on the top floor while your management PC is located on the ground floor. In this step, you will use Telnet to remotely access switch S1 using its SVI management address. Telnet is not a secure protocol; however, you will use it to test remote access. With Telnet, all information, including passwords and commands, are sent across the session in plain text. In subsequent labs, you will use SSH to remotely access network devices.

a. Open Tera Term or other terminal emulation program with Telnet capability.

b. Select the Telnet server and provide the SVI management address to connect to S1. The password is **cisco**.

c. After entering the password **cisco**, you will be at the user EXEC mode prompt. Access privileged EXEC mode using the **enable** command and providing the secret password **class**.

d. Save the configuration.

e. Type **exit** to end the Telnet session.

Part 4: Manage the MAC Address Table

In Part 4, you will determine the MAC addresses that the switch has learned, set up a static MAC address on one interface of the switch, and then remove the static MAC address from that interface.

Step 1: Record the MAC address of the host.

Open a command prompt on PC-A and issue the **ipconfig /all** command to determine and record the Layer 2 (physical) addresses of the NIC.

_____

Step 2: Determine the MAC addresses that the switch has learned.

Display the MAC addresses using the **show mac address-table** command.

```
S1# show mac address-table
```

Questions:

How many dynamic addresses are there?

_____

How many MAC addresses are there in total?

_____

Does the dynamic MAC address match the MAC address of PC-A?

_____

Step 3: List the **show mac address-table** options.

  a. Display the MAC address table options.

```
S1# show mac address-table ?
```

Question:

How many options are available for the **show mac address-table** command?

_____

  b. Issue the **show mac address-table dynamic** command to display only the MAC addresses that were learned dynamically.

```
S1# show mac address-table dynamic
```

Question:

How many dynamic addresses are there?

_____

  c. View the MAC address entry for PC-A. The MAC address formatting for the command is xxxx.xxxx.xxxx.

```
S1# show mac address-table address <PC-A MAC here>
```

Step 3: Set up a static MAC address.

  a. Clear the MAC address table.

To remove the existing MAC addresses, use the **clear mac address-table dynamic** command in privileged EXEC mode.

```
S1# clear mac address-table dynamic
```

b. Verify that the MAC address table was cleared.

```
S1# show mac address-table
```

Question:

How many static MAC addresses are there?

_____

How many dynamic addresses are there?

_____

c. Examine the MAC table again.

More than likely, an application running on your PC has already sent a frame out the NIC to S1. Look at the MAC address table again in privileged EXEC mode to see if S1 has relearned the MAC address of PC-A.

```
S1# show mac address-table
```

Questions:

How many dynamic addresses are there?

_____

Why did this change from the last display?

_____

If S1 has not yet relearned the MAC address for PC-A, ping the VLAN 99 IP address of the switch from PC-A, and then repeat the **show mac address-table** command.

d. Set up a static MAC address.

To specify which ports a host can connect to, one option is to create a static mapping of the host MAC address to a port.

Set up a static MAC address on F0/6 using the address that was recorded for PC-A in Part 4, Step 1. The MAC address 0050.56BE.6C89 is used as an example only. You must use the MAC address of PC-A, which is different than the one given here as an example.

```
S1(config)# mac address-table static 0050.56BE.6C89 vlan 99 interface
fastethernet 0/6
```

e. Verify the MAC address table entries.

```
S1# show mac address-table
```

Questions:

How many total MAC addresses are there?

_____

How many static addresses are there?

_____

f. Remove the static MAC entry. Enter global configuration mode and remove the command by putting a **no** in front of the command string.

Note: The MAC address 0050.56BE.6C89 is used in the example only. Use the MAC address for PC-A.

```
S1(config)# no mac address-table static 0050.56BE.6C89 vlan 99 interface
fastethernet 0/6
```

    g. Verify that the static MAC address has been cleared.

```
S1# show mac address-table
```

Question:

How many total static MAC addresses are there?

Reflection Questions

    1. Why should you configure the vty password for the switch?

    2. Why change the default VLAN 1 to a different VLAN number?

    3. How can you prevent passwords from being sent in plain text?

    4. Why configure a static MAC address on a port interface?

Appendix A: Initialize and Reload a Switch

    a. Console into the switch and enter privileged EXEC mode.

```
Switch> enable
Switch#
```

    b. Use the **show flash** command to determine if any VLANs have been created on the switch.

```
Switch# show flash

Directory of flash:/

    2  -rwx     1919 Mar 1 1993 00:06:33 +00:00   private-config.text
    3  -rwx     1632 Mar 1 1993 00:06:33 +00:00   config.text
    4  -rwx    13336 Mar 1 1993 00:06:33 +00:00   multiple-fs
    5  -rwx 11607161 Mar 1 1993 02:37:06 +00:00   c2960-lanbasek9-mz.150-2.SE.bin
    6  -rwx      616 Mar 1 1993 00:07:13 +00:00   vlan.dat

32514048 bytes total (20886528 bytes free)
```

    c. If the **vlan.dat** file was found in flash, then delete this file.

```
Switch# delete vlan.dat
Delete filename [vlan.dat]?
```

d. You are prompted to verify the filename. If you have entered the name correctly, press Enter; otherwise, you can change the filename.

You are prompted to confirm deletion of this file. Press Enter to confirm.

```
Delete flash:/vlan.dat? [confirm]

Switch#
```

e. Use the **erase startup-config** command to erase the startup configuration file from NVRAM. You are prompted to remove the configuration file. Press Enter to confirm.

```
Switch# erase startup-config

Erasing the nvram filesystem will remove all configuration files! Continue?
[confirm]

[OK]

Erase of nvram: complete

Switch#
```

f. Reload the switch to remove any old configuration information from memory. You will then receive a prompt to confirm reloading of the switch. Press Enter to proceed.

```
Switch# reload

Proceed with reload? [confirm]
```

Note: You may receive a prompt to save the running configuration prior to reloading the switch. Respond by typing **no** and press Enter.

```
System configuration has been modified. Save? [yes/no]: no
```

g. After the switch reloads, you should see a prompt to enter the initial configuration dialog. Respond by entering **no** at the prompt and press Enter.

```
Would you like to enter the initial configuration dialog? [yes/no]: no

Switch>
```

1.3.6 Packet Tracer—Configure SSH

Addressing Table

Device	Interface	IP Address	Subnet Mask
S1	VLAN 1	10.10.10.2	255.255.255.0
PC1	NIC	10.10.10.10	255.255.255.0

Objectives

Part 1: Secure Passwords

Part 2: Encrypt Communications

Part 3: Verify SSH Implementation

Background

SSH should replace Telnet for management connections. Telnet uses insecure plain text communications. SSH provides security for remote connections by providing strong encryption of all transmitted data between devices. In this activity, you will secure a remote switch with password encryption and SSH.

Instructions

Part 1: Secure Passwords

a. Using the command prompt on **PC1**, Telnet to **S1**. The user EXEC and privileged EXEC password is **cisco**.

b. Save the current configuration so that any mistakes you might make can be reversed by toggling the power for **S1**.

c. Show the current configuration and note that the passwords are in plain text. Enter the command that encrypts plain text passwords:

```
S1(config)# service password-encryption
```

d. Verify that the passwords are encrypted.

Part 2: Encrypt Communications

Step 1:   Set the IP domain name and generate secure keys.

It is generally not safe to use Telnet, because data is transferred in plain text. Therefore, use SSH whenever it is available.

a. Configure the domain name to be **netacad.pka**.

b. Secure keys are needed to encrypt the data. Generate the RSA keys using a 1024 key length.

Step 2:   Create an SSH user and reconfigure the VTY lines for SSH-only access.

    a.   Create an **administrator** user with **cisco** as the secret password.

    b.   Configure the VTY lines to check the local username database for login credentials and to only allow SSH for remote access. Remove the existing vty line password.

Step 3:   Verify SSH Implementation

    a.   Exit the Telnet session and attempt to log back in using Telnet. The attempt should fail.

    b.   Attempt to log in using SSH. Type **ssh** and press **Enter** without any parameters to reveal the command usage instructions.

Hint: The **-l** option is the letter "L", not the number 1.

---

    c.   Upon successful login, enter privileged EXEC mode and save the configuration. If you were unable to successfully access **S1**, toggle the power and begin again at Part 1.

Packet Tracer
☐ Activity

1.4.7 Packet Tracer—Configure Router Interfaces

Addressing Table

Device	Interface	IP Address/Prefix	Default Gateway
R1	G0/0	172.16.20.1 /25	N/A
	G0/1	172.16.20.129 /25	N/A
	S0/0/0	209.165.200.225 /30	N/A
PC1	NIC	172.16.20.10 /25	172.16.20.1
PC2	NIC	172.16.20.138 /25	172.16.20.129
R2	G0/0	2001:db8:c0de:12::1/64	N/A
	G0/1	2001:db8:c0de:13::1/64	N/A
	S0/0/1	2001:db8:c0de:11::1/64	N/A
		fe80::2	N/A
PC3	NIC	2001:db8:c0de:12::a/64	fe80::2
PC4	NIC	2001:db8:c0de:13::a/64	fe80::2

Objectives

Part 1: Configure IPv4 Addressing and Verify Connectivity

Part 2: Configure IPv6 Addressing and Verify Connectivity

Background

Routers R1 and R2 each have two LANs. Your task is to configure the appropriate addressing on each device and verify connectivity between the LANs.

Note: The user EXEC password is cisco. The privileged EXEC password is class.

Instructions

Part 1: Configure IPv4 Addressing and Verify Connectivity

Step 1:   Assign IPv4 addresses to R1 and LAN devices.

Referring to the **Addressing Table**, configure IP addressing for **R1** LAN interfaces, **PC1** and **PC2**. The serial interface has already been configured.

Step 2:   Verify connectivity.

PC1 and PC2 should be able to ping each other and the **Dual Stack Server**.

Part 2: Configure IPv6 Addressing and Verify Connectivity

Step 1:   Assign IPv6 addresses to R2 and LAN devices.

Referring to the **Addressing Table**, configure IP addressing for **R2 LAN interfaces**, **PC3** and **PC4**. The serial interface is already configured.

Step 2:   Verify connectivity.

PC3 and PC4 should be able to ping each other and the **Dual Stack Server**.

1.5.10 Packet Tracer—Verify Directly Connected Networks

Addressing Table

Device	Interface	IP Address / Prefix	Default Gateway
R1	G0/0/0	172.16.20.1/25	N/A
	G0/0/1	172.16.20.129/25	N/A
	S0/1/0	209.165.200.225/30	N/A
PC1	NIC	172.16.20.10/25	172.16.20.1
PC2	NIC	172.16.20.138/25	172.16.20.129
R2	G0/0/0	2001:db8:c0de:12::1/64	N/A
	G0/0/1	2001:db8:c0de:13::1/64	N/A
	S0/1/1	2001:db8:c0de:11::1/64	N/A
		fe80::2	N/A
PC3	NIC	2001:db8:c0de:12::a/64	fe80::2
PC4	NIC	2001:db8:c0de:13::a/64	fe80::2

Objectives

- Verify IPv4 Directly Connected Networks
- Verify IPv6 Directly Connected Networks
- Troubleshoot connectivity issues.

Background

Routers R1 and R2 each have two LANs. Your task is to verify the addressing on each device and verify connectivity between the LANs.

Note: The user EXEC password is **cisco**. The privileged EXEC password is **class**.

Instructions

Part 1: Verify IPv4 Directly Connected Networks

Step 1:   Verify IPv4 addresses and port status on R1.

   a.   Check the status of the configured interfaces by filtering the output.

   ```
   R1# show ip interface brief | exclude unassigned
   ```

   b.   Based on the output, correct any port status problems that you see.

   c.   Refer to the **Addressing Table** and verify the IP addresses configured on R1. Make any corrections to addressing if necessary.

   d.   Display the routing table by filtering to start the output at the word **Gateway**.

Note: Terms that are used to filter output can be shortened to match text as long as the match is unique. For example, Gateway, Gate, and Ga will have the same effect. G will not. Filtering is case-sensitive

```
R1# show ip route | begin Gate
```
Question:

What is the Gateway of last resort address?

_____

e. Display interface information and filter for **Description** or **connected**.

Note: When using **include** or **exclude** multiple searches can be performed by separating the search strings with a pipe symbol (|)

```
R1# show interface | include Desc|conn
```
Question:

What is the Circuit ID displayed from your output?

_____

f. Display specific interface information for G0/0/0 by filtering for **duplex**.

Question:

What is the duplex setting, speed, and media type?

_____

Step 2:   Verify connectivity.

PC1 and PC2 should be able to ping each other and the **Dual Stack Server**. If not, verify the status of the interfaces and the IP address assignments.

Part 2: Verify IPv6 Directly Connected Networks

Step 1:   Verify IPv6 addresses and port status on R2.

a. Check the status of the configured interfaces.

```
R2# show ipv6 int brief
```
Question:

What is the status of the configured interfaces?

_____

b. Refer to the **Addressing Table** and make any corrections to addressing as necessary.

Note: When changing an IPv6 address it is necessary to remove the incorrect address since an interface is capable of supporting multiple IPv6 networks.

```
R2(config)# int g0/0/1
R2(config-if)# no ipv6 address 2001:db8:c0de:14::1/64
```

Question:

Configure the correct address on the interface.

_____

c. Display the IPv6 routing table.

_____

Note: Filtering commands do not presently work with the IPv6 commands.

d. Display all IPv6 addressing configured on interfaces by filtering the output of the **running-config**.

Filter the output on **R2** for **ipv6** or **interface**.

```
R2# sh run | include ipv6|interface
```

Question:

How many addresses are configured on each Gigabit interface?

_____

Step 2:   Verify connectivity.

PC3 and **PC4** should be able to ping each other and the **Dual Stack Server.** If not, verify the interface status and IPv6 address assignments.

1.6.1 Packet Tracer—Implement a Small Network

Addressing Table

Device	Interface	Address	Subnet Mask	Default Gateway
RTA	G0/0	10.10.10.1	255.255.255.0	N/A
	G0/1	10.10.20.1	255.255.255.0	N/A
SW1	VLAN1	10.10.10.2	255.255.255.0	
SW2	VLAN1	10.10.20.2	255.255.255.0	
PC-1	NIC		255.255.255.0	
PC-2	NIC		255.255.255.0	

Objectives

Part 1: Create the Network Topology

Part 2: Configure Devices and Verify Connectivity

Instructions

Part 1: Create the Network Topology

Step 1:   Obtain the required devices.

    a.   Click the **Network Devices** icon in the bottom tool bar.

    b.   Click the router icon in the submenu.

    c.   Locate the **1941** router icon. Click and drag the icon for the 1941 router into the topology area.

    d.   Click the switch entry in the submenu.

    e.   Locate the **2960** switch icon. Click and drag the icon for the 2960 switch into the topology area.

    f.   Repeat the step above so that there are **two** 2960 switches in the topology area.

    g.   Click the **End Devices** icon.

    h.   Locate the PC icon. Drag **two** PCs to the topology area.

    i.   Arrange the devices into a layout that you can work with by clicking and dragging.

Step 2:   Name the devices.

The devices have default names that you will need to change. You will name the devices as shown in the Addressing Table. You are changing the display names of the devices. This is the text label that appears below each device. Your display names must match the information in the Addressing Table **exactly**. If a display name does not match, you will not be scored for your device configuration.

    a.   Click the device display name that is below the device icon. A text field should appear with a flashing insertion point. If the configuration window for the device appears, close it and try again, clicking a little further away from the device icon.

b. Replace the current display name with the appropriate display name from the Addressing Table.

c. Repeat until all devices are named.

Step 3: Connect the devices.

a. Click the orange lightning bolt connections icon in the bottom toolbar.

b. Locate the Copper Straight-Through cable icon. It looks like a solid black diagonal line.

c. To connect the device, click the Copper Straight-Through cable icon and then click the first device that you want to connect. Select the correct port and then click the second device. Select the correct port and the devices will be connected.

d. Connect the devices as specified in the table below.

From Device	Port	To Device	Port
RTA	G0/0	SW1	G0/1
	G0/1	SW2	G0/1
SW1	F0/1	PC-1	Fastethernet0
SW2	F0/1	PC-2	Fastethernet0

Part 2: Configure Devices

Record the PC addressing and gateway addresses in the addressing table. You can use any available address in the network for PC-1 and PC-2.

Step 1: Configure the router.

a. Configure basic settings.

1) Hostname as shown in the Addressing Table.

2) Configure **Ciscoenpa55** as the encrypted password.

3) Configure **Ciscolinepa55** as the password on the lines.

4) All lines should accept connections.

5) Configure an appropriate message of the day banner.

b. Configure interface settings.

1) Addressing.

2) Descriptions on the interfaces.

3) Save your configuration.

Step 2:   Configure switch SW1 and SW2.

    a.   Configure the default management interface so that it will accept connections over the network from local and remote hosts. Use the values in the addressing table.

    b.   Configure an encrypted password using the value in step 1a above.

    c.   Configure all lines to accept connections using the password from step 1a above.

    d.   Configure the switches so that they can send data to hosts on remote networks.

    e.   Save your configuration.

Step 3:   Configure the hosts.

Configure addressing on the hosts. If your configurations are complete, you should be able to ping all devices in the topology.

1.6.2 Lab—Configure Basic Router Settings

Topology

Addressing Table

Device	Interface	IP Address / Prefix	Default Gateway
R1	G0/0/0	192.168.0.1 /24	N/A
		2001:db8:acad::1 /64	
		fe80::1	
	G0/0/1	192.168.1.1 /24	
		2001:db8:acad:1::1 /64	
		fe80::1	
	Loopback0	10.0.0.1 /24	
		2001:db8:acad:2::1 /64	
		fe80::1	
PC-A	NIC	192.168.1.10 /24	192.168.1.1
		2001:db8:acad:1::10 /64	fe80::1
PC-B	NIC	192.168.0.10 /24	192.168.0.1
		2001:db8:acad::10 /64	fe80::1

Objectives

Part 1: Set Up the Topology and Initialize Devices

- Cable equipment to match the network topology.

- Initialize and restart the router and switch.

Part 2: Configure Devices and Verify Connectivity

- Assign static IPv4 and IPv6 information to the PC interfaces.

- Configure basic router settings.

- Configure the router for SSH.

- Verify network connectivity.

Part 3: Display Router Information

- Retrieve hardware and software information from the router.

- Interpret the output from the startup configuration.

- Interpret the output from the routing table.

- Verify the status of the interfaces.

Background / Scenario

This is a comprehensive lab to review previously covered IOS router commands. In Parts 1 and 2, you will cable the equipment and complete basic configurations and interface settings on the router.

In Part 3, you will use SSH to connect to the router remotely and utilize the IOS commands to retrieve information from the device to answer questions about the router.

For review purposes, this lab provides the commands necessary for specific router configurations.

Note: The routers used with CCNA hands-on labs are Cisco 4221 with Cisco IOS XE Release 16.9.4 (universalk9 image). The switches used in the labs are Cisco Catalyst 2960s with Cisco IOS Release 15.2(2) (lanbasek9 image). Other routers, switches, and Cisco IOS versions can be used. Depending on the model and Cisco IOS version, the commands available and the output produced might vary from what is shown in the labs. Refer to the Router Interface Summary Table at the end of the lab for the correct interface identifiers.

Note: Make sure that the router and switch have been erased and have no startup configurations. Consult with your instructor for the procedure to initialize and reload a router and switch.

Required Resources

- 1 Router (Cisco 4221 with Cisco IOS XE Release 16.9.4 universal image or comparable)

- 1 Switch (Cisco 2960 with Cisco IOS Release 15.2(2) lanbasek9 image or comparable)

- 2 PCs (Windows with a terminal emulation program, such as Tera Term)

- Console cables to configure the Cisco IOS devices via the console ports

- Ethernet cables as shown in the topology

Note: The Gigabit Ethernet interfaces on Cisco 4221 routers are autosensing and an Ethernet straight-through cable may be used between the router and PC-B. If using another model Cisco router, it may be necessary to use an Ethernet crossover cable.

Instructions

Part 1: Set Up the Topology and Initialize Devices

Step 1:   Cable the network as shown in the topology.

    a.   Attach the devices as shown in the topology diagram, and cable as necessary.

    b.   Power on all the devices in the topology.

Step 2:   Initialize and reload the router and switch.

Part 2: Configure Devices and Verify Connectivity

Step 1:   Configure the PC interfaces.

    a.   Configure the IP address, subnet mask, and default gateway settings on PC-A.

    b.   Configure the IP address, subnet mask, and default gateway settings on PC-B.

Step 2:   Configure the router.

   a.   Console into the router and enable privileged EXEC mode.

   b.   Enter configuration mode.

   c.   Assign a device name to the router.

   d.   Set the router's domain name as ccna-lab.com.

   e.   Disable DNS lookup to prevent the router from attempting to translate incorrectly entered commands as though they were host names.

   f.   Encrypt the plaintext passwords.

   g.   Configure the system to require a minimum 12-character password.

   h.   Configure the username **SSHadmin** with an encrypted password of **55Hadm!n2020.**

   i.   Generate a set of crypto keys with a 1024 bit modulus.

   j.   Assign the privileged EXEC password to **$cisco!PRIV***

   k.   Assign **$cisco!!CON*** as the console password, configure sessions to disconnect after four minutes of inactivity, and enable login.

   l.   Assign **$cisco!!VTY*** as the vty password, configure the vty lines to accept SSH connections only, configure sessions to disconnect after four minutes of inactivity, and enable login using the local database.

   m.   Create a banner that warns anyone accessing the device that unauthorized access is prohibited.

   n.   Enable IPv6 Routing

   o.   Configure all three interfaces on the router with the IPv4 and IPv6 addressing information from the addressing table above. Configure all three interfaces with descriptions. Activate all three interfaces.

   p.   The router should not allow vty logins for two minutes if three failed login attempts occur within 60 seconds.

   q.   Set the clock on the router.

   r.   Save the running configuration to the startup configuration file.

   Question:

   What would be the result of reloading the router prior to completing the **copy running-config startup-config** command?

   _____

Step 3:   Verify network connectivity.

   a.   Using the command line at PC-A, ping the IPv4 and IPv6 addresses for PC-B.

   Note: It may be necessary to disable the PC's firewall.

   Question:

   Were the pings successful?

   _____

b. Remotely access R1 from PC-A using the Tera Term SSH client.

Using Tera Term on PC-A, open an SSH session to the R1 Loopback interface IPv4 address. Ensure that the **SSH** radio button is selected and then click **OK** to connect to the router. Log in as **SSHadmin** with the password **55Hadm!n2020**.

Question:

Was remote access successful?

_____

Using Tera Term on PC-A, open an SSH session to the R1 Loopback interface IPv6 address. Ensure that the **SSH** radio button is selected and then click **OK** to connect to the router. Log in as **SSHadmin** with the password **55Hadm!n2020**.

Note: The IPv6 address should be surrounded with square brackets, i.e. [*IPv6 address*]

Questions:

Was remote access successful?

_____

Why is the Telnet protocol considered to be a security risk?

_____

Part 3: Display Router Information

In Part 3, you will use **show** commands from an SSH session to retrieve information from the router.

Step 1:   Establish an SSH session to R1.

Using Tera Term on PC-B, open an SSH session to the R1 Loopback interface IPv6 address and log in as **SSHadmin** with the password **55Hadm!n2020**.

Step 2:   Retrieve important hardware and software information.

a. Use the **show version** command to answer questions about the router.

Questions:

What is the name of the IOS image that the router is running?

_____

How much non-volatile random-access memory (NVRAM) does the router have?

_____

How much Flash memory does the router have?

_____

    b. The **show** commands often provide multiple screens of outputs. Filtering the output allows a user to display certain sections of the output. To enable the filtering command, enter a pipe (|) character after a **show** command, followed by a filtering parameter and a filtering expression. You can match the output to the filtering statement by using the **include** keyword to display all lines from the output that contain the filtering expression. Filter the **show version** command, using **show version | include register** to answer the following question.

    What is the boot process for the router on the next reload?

Step 3: Display the startup configuration.

    Use the **show startup-config** command on the router to answer the following questions.

    How are passwords presented in the output?

    Use the **show startup-config | section vty** command.

    What is the result of using this command?

Step 4: Display the routing table on the router.

    Use the **show ip route** command on the router to answer the following questions.

    Questions:

    What code is used in the routing table to indicate a directly connected network?

    How many route entries are coded with a C code in the routing table?

Step 5: Display a summary list of the interfaces on the router.

    a. Use the **show ip interface brief** command on the router to answer the following question.

    Question:

    What command changed the status of the Gigabit Ethernet ports from administratively down to up?

---

    b. Use the **show ipv6 int brief** command to verify IPv6 settings on R1.

    Question:

    What is the meaning of the [up/up] part of the output?

---

   c. On PC-B, change its configuration so that it no longer has a static IPv6 address. You may have to reboot the machine. Then, issue the **ipconfig** command on PC-B to examine the IPv6 configuration.

Questions:

What is the IPv6 address assigned to PC-B?

_____

What is the default gateway assigned to PC-B?

_____

Issue a ping from PC-B to the R1 default gateway link local address. Was it successful?

_____

Issue a ping from PC-B to the R1 IPv6 unicast address 2001:db8:acad::1. Was it successful?

_____

Reflection Questions

1. In researching a network connectivity issue, a technician suspects that an interface was not enabled. What **show** command could the technician use to troubleshoot this issue?

_____

2. In researching a network connectivity issue, a technician suspects that an interface was assigned an incorrect subnet mask. What **show** command could the technician use to troubleshoot this issue?

_____

Router Interface Summary Table

Router Model	Ethernet Interface #1	Ethernet Interface #2	Serial Interface #1	Serial Interface #2
1800	Fast Ethernet 0/0 (F0/0)	Fast Ethernet 0/1 (F0/1)	Serial 0/0/0 (S0/0/0)	Serial 0/0/1 (S0/0/1)
1900	Gigabit Ethernet 0/0 (G0/0)	Gigabit Ethernet 0/1 (G0/1)	Serial 0/0/0 (S0/0/0)	Serial 0/0/1 (S0/0/1)
2801	Fast Ethernet 0/0 (F0/0)	Fast Ethernet 0/1 (F0/1)	Serial 0/1/0 (S0/1/0)	Serial 0/1/1 (S0/1/1)
2811	Fast Ethernet 0/0 (F0/0)	Fast Ethernet 0/1 (F0/1)	Serial 0/0/0 (S0/0/0)	Serial 0/0/1 (S0/0/1)
2900	Gigabit Ethernet 0/0 (G0/0)	Gigabit Ethernet 0/1 (G0/1)	Serial 0/0/0 (S0/0/0)	Serial 0/0/1 (S0/0/1)
4221	Gigabit Ethernet 0/0/0 (G0/0/0)	Gigabit Ethernet 0/0/1 (G0/0/1)	Serial 0/1/0 (S0/1/0)	Serial 0/1/1 (S0/1/1)
4300	Gigabit Ethernet 0/0/0 (G0/0/0)	Gigabit Ethernet 0/0/1 (G0/0/1)	Serial 0/1/0 (S0/1/0)	Serial 0/1/1 (S0/1/1)

Note: To find out how the router is configured, look at the interfaces to identify the type of router and how many interfaces the router has. There is no way to effectively list all the combinations of configurations for each router class. This table includes identifiers for the possible combinations of Ethernet and Serial interfaces in the device. The table does not include any other type of interface, even though a specific router may contain one. An example of this might be an ISDN BRI interface. The string in parenthesis is the legal abbreviation that can be used in Cisco IOS commands to represent the interface.

Switching Concepts

The "Study Guide" portion of this chapter uses a variety of exercises to test your knowledge of how Layer 2 switches forward data. There are no labs or Packet Tracer activities in this chapter.

As you work through this chapter, use Chapter 2 in *Switching, Routing, and Wireless Essentials v7 Companion Guide* or use the corresponding Module 2 in the Switching, Routing, and Wireless Essentials online curriculum for assistance.

Study Guide

Frame Forwarding

In this section, you review switching concepts, including ingress and egress ports, the Media Access Control (MAC) address table, and switch forwarding methods. This section concludes with an activity where you build a MAC address table.

Switching in Networking

The decision on how a switch forwards traffic is made based on the flow of that traffic. What are the two terms associated with frames entering and leaving an interface?

- ■ _____ This is the port where a frame enters the device.

- ■ _____ This is the port that frames use when leaving the device.

With a LAN switch, there is only one master switching table that describes a strict association between MAC addresses and ports; therefore, an Ethernet frame with a given destination MAC address always exits the same egress port, regardless of the ingress port it enters.

True or false: It is possible for an Ethernet frame to be forward out the same port on which it was received.

_____

The Switch MAC Address Table

What address does a switch use to make forwarding decisions?

_____

Where is the MAC address table stored?

_____

How does a switch populate its MAC address table?

_____

The Switch Learn and Forward Method

Briefly explain the two steps of the learn and forward method that switches use for every Ethernet frame that enters the switch.

Step 1.   Learn: _____

_____

_____

Step 2.   Forward: _____

_____

_____

Switching Forwarding Methods

Describe the two methods Layer 2 switches use to forward frames.

- Store-and-forward switching: _____

   _____

- Cut-through switching: _____

   _____

Store-and-Forward Switching

What does a store-and-forward switch use to ensure that a frame is free of physical and data-link errors?

_____

In what buffering scenario must a switch use the store-and-forward method?

_____

What does a store-and-forward switch do with a frame that does not pass the FCS check?

_____

Cut-Through Switching

The cut-through switching method may forward invalid frames because no FCS check is performed. However, cut-through switching has the ability to perform rapid frame switching.

Briefly explain fragment-free switching.

_____

_____

In Table 2-1, indicate which method matches each descriptions.

Table 2-1   Identify the Frame Forwarding Method

Description	Store-and-Forward	Cut-Through
Checks the frame for errors before releasing it out of its switch ports. If the full frame was not received, the switch discards it.		
Low-latency switch method used by high-performance computing (HPC) applications requiring process-to-process latencies of 10 microseconds or less.		
No error checking on frames is performed by the switch before releasing the frame out of its ports.		
Buffers frames until the full frame has been received by the switch.		
ASICs-capable switch function; allows frames to be filtered and forwarded after the first 14 bytes and an additional 40 bytes in the frame header have been received.		

Activity—Build the MAC Address Table

Assume that the switch in Figure 2-1 was just installed and powered on. The MAC address table is empty. Answer the following questions and complete Table 2-2 as the switch would build it.

Figure 2-1   Switch Topology with Two LANs

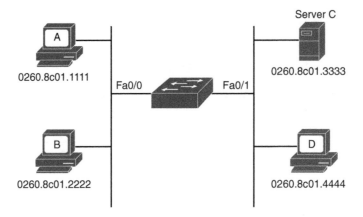

Table 2-2   MAC Address Table

Port	MAC Address

1. Host A sends a unicast frame to Host B. What entry, if any, will the switch enter in its MAC address table?

   What will the switch do with the frame?

2. Host B responds to Host A with a unicast frame. What entry, if any, will the switch enter in its MAC address table?

   What will the switch do with the frame?

3. Host D attempts to log in to Server C. What entry, if any, will the switch enter in its MAC address table?

   What will the switch do with the frame?

4. Server C responds to the login attempt by Host D. What entry, if any, will the switch enter in its MAC address table?

What will the switch do with the frame?

5. Server C sends out a broadcast frame, announcing its services to all potential clients. What entry, if any, will the switch enter in its MAC address table?

What will the switch do with the frame?

Switching Domains

In this section, you review collision and broadcast domains and what methods can be used to alleviate network congestion.

Collision Domains

What is a collision domain?

Why do collisions occur?

What is the difference between half-duplex and full-duplex as it relates to collisions?

What is the default duplex mode on Ethernet switch ports?

Broadcast Domains

What device can segment a broadcast domain?

What is a Layer 2 broadcast domain?

What does a switch do with a broadcast frame?

What happens to a broadcast domain if two switches, each with five hosts connected, are connected together?

Alleviate Network Congestion

By default, interconnected switch ports attempt to establish a link in full-duplex, thereby eliminating collision domains. Switches interconnect LAN segments, use a MAC address table to determine egress ports, and can reduce or eliminate collisions entirely. Characteristics of switches that alleviate network congestion include the following:

- **Fast port speeds:** Switches with faster port speeds cost more but can reduce congestion.

- **Fast internal switching:** Switches use a fast internal bus or shared memory to provide high performance.

- **Large frame buffers:** Switches use large memory buffers to temporarily store more received frames before having to start dropping them.

- **High port density:** High port density switches help keep traffic local, which helps alleviate congestion.

Check Your Understanding—Switching Domains

Check your understanding of switching domains by choosing the BEST answer to each of the following questions.

1. Which port speed will be autonegotiated between a host with a 1 Gbps NIC connecting to a Cisco Catalyst 2960 switch with a 100 Mbps port?

   a. 10 Mbps

   b. 100 Mbps

   c. 1 Gbps

   d. 10 Gbps

2. Which device separates broadcast domains?

   a. access point

   b. hub

   c. router

   d. switch

3. Which two special characteristics do LAN switches use to alleviate network congestion? (Choose two.)

   a. fast port speeds

   b. fast internal switching

   c. low port densities

   d. small frame buffers

Labs and Activities

There are no labs or Packet Tracer activities for this chapter.

VLANs

The "Study Guide" portion of this chapter uses a variety of exercises to test your knowledge and skills of implementing virtual LANs (VLANs) and trunking in a switched network. The "Labs and Activities" portion of this chapter includes all the online curriculum labs and Packet Tracer activity instructions.

As you work through this chapter, use Chapter 3 in *Switching, Routing, and Wireless Essentials v7 Companion Guide* or use the corresponding Module 3 in the Switching, Routing, and Wireless Essentials online curriculum for assistance.

Study Guide

Overview of VLANs

In this section, you review the purpose of VLANs in a switched network, including what a VLAN is, the benefits of a VLAN, and types of VLANs.

VLAN Definitions

VLANs are based on logical connections instead of physical connections. VLANs allow an administrator to segment networks based on factors such as function, team, or application, without regard for the physical location of the users or devices. Each VLAN is considered a separate logical network. Unicast, broadcast, and multicast packets are forwarded and flooded only to end devices within the VLAN where the packets are sourced. Packets destined for devices that do not belong to the VLAN must be forwarded to a routing device.

By using VLANs, network administrators can implement access and security policies according to specific groupings of users. Each switch port can be assigned to only one VLAN (except for a port connected to an IP phone or to another switch).

Benefits of VLAN Design

In Table 3-1, briefly describe each of the benefits of designing a network with VLANs.

Table 3-1   VLAN Benefits

Benefit	Description
Smaller broadcast domains	
Improved security	
Improved IT efficiency	
Reduced cost	
Better performance	
Simpler project and application management	

Types of VLANs

VLANs are used for different reasons in modern networks. Some VLAN types are defined by traffic classes. Other types of VLANs are defined by the specific function that they serve. In Table 3-2, indicate the VLAN type that is described.

Table 3-2 VLAN Types

VLAN Type	Description
	VLAN 1 on a Cisco switch. All ports are assigned to this VLAN unless explicitly configured to be in another VLAN.
	VLANs for groups of users or devices. Voice and network management traffic should not be allowed on this VLAN type.
	A VLAN that is used to transport untagged traffic across a trunk link. By default, the native VLAN uses VLAN 1. But it is a best practice to configure another, unused, VLAN to be the native VLAN.
	A VLAN that is specifically used for network management traffic. By default, VLAN 1 is configured as this VLAN.
	A VLAN that is assigned to traffic that needs assured bandwidth, transmission priority, special routing treatment, and delay of less than 150 ms across the network.

Check Your Understanding—Overview of VLANs

Check your understanding of VLANs by choosing the BEST answer to the each of following questions.

1. True or false: VLANs improve network performance by segmenting broadcast domains.

    a. true

    b. false

2. True or false: VLANs can improve security by isolating sensitive data from the rest of the network.

    a. true

    b. false

3. Which type of VLAN is assigned to 802.1Q trunk ports to carry untagged traffic?

    a. default

    b. native

    c. data

    d. management

4. True or false: It is a best practice to configure the native VLAN as VLAN 1.

    a. true

    b. false

5. Which is true of VLAN 1? (Choose all that apply.)

    a. All switch ports are assigned to VLAN 1 by default.

    b. The native VLAN is VLAN 1 by default.

    c. The management VLAN is VLAN 1 by default.

    d. VLAN 1 cannot be renamed or deleted.

VLANs in a Multi-Switched Environment

In this section, you review how a switch forwards frames based on VLAN configuration in a multi-switched environment, including what a VLAN trunk is, tagging VLANs, and voice VLAN tagging.

Defining VLAN Trunks

A trunk is a point-to-point link between two network devices that carries more than one VLAN. VLAN trunks allow VLAN traffic to propagate between switches. This enables devices connected to different switches but in the same VLAN to communicate without going through a router.

Cisco supports IEEE 802.1Q for coordinating trunks on Fast Ethernet, Gigabit Ethernet, and 10-Gigabit Ethernet interfaces. A VLAN trunk does not belong to a specific VLAN. Instead, it is a conduit for multiple VLANs between switches and routers.

Network Without VLANs

When a switch receives a broadcast frame on one of its ports, it forwards the frame out all other ports except the port where the broadcast was received. In a switched network without VLANs, the broadcast is propagated to all connected switches, as shown in Figure 3-1, where PC1 sends out a Layer 2 broadcast.

Figure 3-1   Layer 2 Broadcast Example Without VLANs

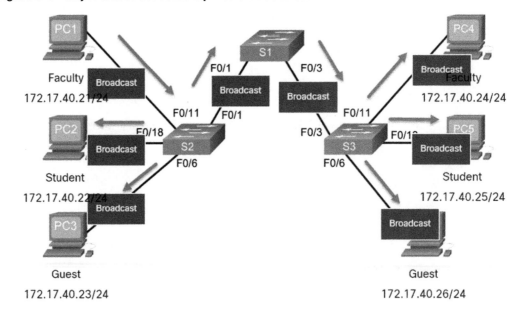

Network with VLANs

In Figure 3-2, the network from Figure 3-1 has now been segmented using two VLANs. The Guest network is not shown. Faculty devices are assigned to VLAN 10, and student devices are assigned to VLAN 20. When a broadcast frame is sent from the faculty computer, PC1, to switch S2, the switch forwards that broadcast frame to the switch ports configured to support VLAN 10. The trunks have been configured to support all the VLANs in the network.

Figure 3-2   Layer 2 Broadcast Example with VLANs

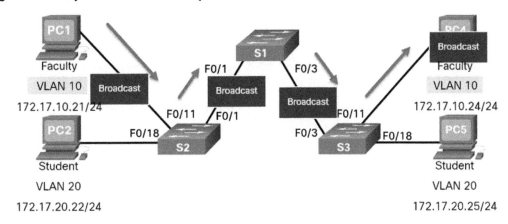

VLAN Identification with a Tag

When Ethernet frames are placed on a trunk, information about the VLANs to which they belong must be added. This process, called *tagging*, is accomplished by using the IEEE 802.1Q header. The switch inserts the tag, which includes the 12-bit VLAN identification number (VID) between the Source MAC address and Type/Length fields, as shown in Figure 3-3.

Figure 3-3   Tagging a Frame with the VLAN ID

Dst MAC	Src MAC	Type/Length	Data	FCS

Dst MAC	Src MAC	Tag	Type/Length	Data	FCS

Type (0x8100)	Pri	CFI	VID
2 Bytes	3 Bits	1 Bit	12 Bits

Native VLANs and 802.1Q Tagging

The IEEE 802.1Q standard specifies a native VLAN for trunk links, which defaults to VLAN 1. When an untagged frame arrives on a trunk port, it is assigned to the native VLAN. Management frames sent between switches is an example of traffic that is typically untagged.

Control traffic sent on the native VLAN should not be tagged. If an 802.1Q trunk port receives a tagged frame with the VLAN ID that is the same as the native VLAN, it drops the frame. However, when a Cisco switch trunk port receives untagged frames (which are unusual in a well-designed network), it forwards those frames to the native VLAN. If there are no devices associated with the native VLAN (which is not unusual) and there are no other trunk ports (which is not unusual), then the frame is dropped.

In Figure 3-4, PC1 sends untagged traffic, which the switches associate with the native VLAN configured on the trunk ports and forward accordingly. This scenario reflects poor network design for several reasons: It uses a hub, it has a host connected to a trunk link, and it implies that the switches have access ports assigned to the native VLAN. It also illustrates the motivation for the IEEE 802.1Q specification for native VLANs as a means of handling legacy scenarios.

Figure 3-4   Poorly Designed Switched Network with Hub and Default Native VLAN Assigned to Access Ports

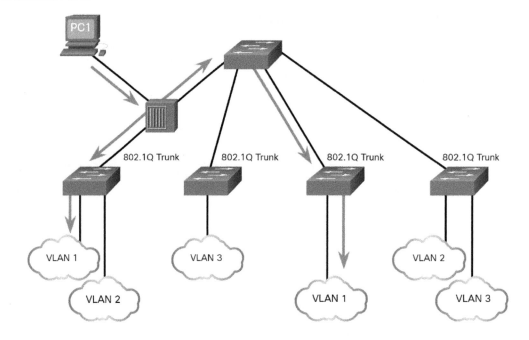

Voice VLAN Tagging

A separate voice VLAN is required to support Voice over IP (VoIP). This enables quality of service (QoS) and security policies to be applied to voice traffic.

A Cisco IP phone connects directly to a switch port. An IP host can connect to the IP phone to gain network connectivity as well. The access port connected to the Cisco IP phone can be configured to use two separate VLANs. One VLAN is for voice traffic and the other is a data VLAN to support the host traffic. The link between the switch and the IP phone simulates a trunk link to carry both voice VLAN traffic and data VLAN traffic.

In Figure 3-5, PC5 is attached to a Cisco IP phone, and the phone is attached to switch S3. VLAN 150 is designed to carry voice traffic, and PC5 is in VLAN 20, which is used for data.

Figure 3-5 Example of a Cisco IP Phone and PC Connected to the Same Switch Port

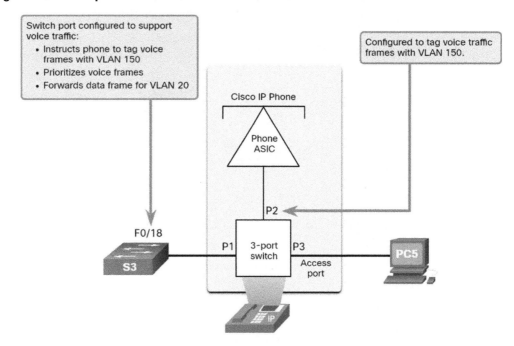

Check Your Understanding—VLANs in a Multi-Switched Environment

1. Refer to the topology in Figure 3-6. PC1 sends an Address Resolution Protocol (ARP) broadcast frame. Which PC will receive the ARP broadcast frame? (Choose all that apply.)

Figure 3-6 Question 1 Topology

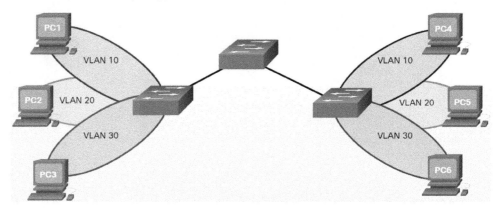

   a. PC2

   b. PC3

   c. PC4

   d. PC5

   e. PC6

2. Refer to the topology in Figure 3-7. PC2 sends an ARP broadcast frame. Which PCs will receive the ARP broadcast frame? (Choose all that apply.)

Figure 3-7   Question 2 Topology

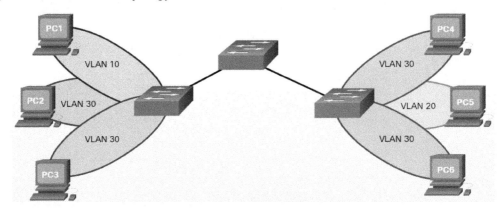

a. PC1

b. PC3

c. PC4

d. PC5

e. PC6

3. Refer to the topology in Figure 3-8. PC3 sends an ARP broadcast frame. Which PC will receive the ARP broadcast frame?

Figure 3-8   Question 3 Topology

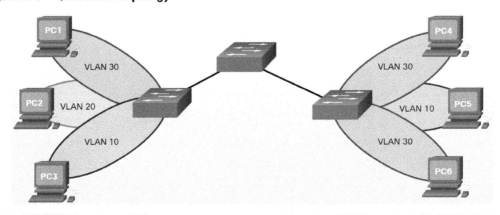

a. PC1

b. PC2

c. PC4

d. PC5

e. PC6

VLAN Configuration

In this section, you review how to assign a switch port to a VLAN based on requirements including VLAN ranges, VLAN creation, VLAN port assignments, data and voice VLANs, verifying VLAN information, and modifying VLANs.

VLAN Ranges on Catalyst Switches

Answer the following questions about VLAN ranges.

1. For VLAN numbers, what is the normal range on 2960 and 2650 Series switches?

   _____

2. For VLAN numbers, what is the extended range on 2960 and 2650 Series switches?

   _____

3. What command can you use to quickly check the default VLANs on a 2960 Series switch?

   _____

4. What are the numbers of the default VLANs?

   _____

In Table 3-3, indicate whether each characteristic applies to normal range VLANs or extended range VLANs.

Table 3-3   Characteristics of Normal and Extended Range VLANs

Characteristic	Normal Range	Extended Range
Configurations are stored in the switch flash memory in a VLAN database file called vlan.dat.		
These VLANs are identified by a VLAN ID between 1 and 1005.		
Configurations are saved, by default, in the running configuration.		
IDs 1 and 1002 to 1005 are automatically created and cannot be removed.		
These VLANs are used by service providers to service multiple customers and by large global enterprises		
These VLANs are identified by a VLAN ID between 1006 and 4094.		
These VLANs support fewer VLAN features than the other range of VLANs.		
These VLANs are used in all small- and medium-sized business and enterprise networks.		

VLAN Creation and Port Assignment Exercise

Use the information in Figure 3-9 to answer the following questions related to configuring and verifying VLANs and port assignments.

Figure 3-9 Data and Voice VLAN Configuration Topology

Finance
192.168.15.21/24
VLAN 15

Voice VLAN 200

F0/5

S2

Enter the commands, including the switch prompts, to configure the VLANs on S2.

_____

_____

_____

_____

_____

Enter the commands, including the switch prompts, to assign the data and voice VLANs to the FastEthernet 0/5 port.

_____

_____

_____

_____

_____

Packet Tracer 3-1: VLAN Creation and Port Assignment

Now you are ready to use Packet Tracer to apply your documented configuration. Download and open the file LSG01-0301.pka from the companion website for this book. Refer to the Introduction of this book for specifics on accessing files.

Note: The following instructions are also contained in the Packet Tracer Exercise.

In this Packet Tracer activity, you will create data and voice VLANs on S2 and assign them to a port. Use the commands you documented in the section "VLAN Creation and Port Assignment Exercise."

Requirements

Configure S2 as follows:

- Create the Finance VLAN 15 and the Voice VLAN 200. Names are case-sensitive.

- Configure the interface connected to the IP phone as an access port.

- Assign the VLANs to the port.

- Configure QoS.

Your completion percentage should be 100%, and all the connectivity tests should show a status of "successful." If not, click Check Results to see which required components are not yet completed.

Verify VLAN Information

Enter the commands that display the following output to verify the configuration on S2.

```
S2# _____

VLAN Name                             Status    Ports
---- -------------------------------- --------- -------------------------------
1    default                          active    Fa0/1,  Fa0/2,  Fa0/3,  Fa0/4
                                                Fa0/6,  Fa0/7,  Fa0/8,  Fa0/9
                                                Fa0/10, Fa0/11, Fa0/12, Fa0/13
                                                Fa0/14, Fa0/15, Fa0/16, Fa0/17
                                                Fa0/18, Fa0/19, Fa0/20, Fa0/21
                                                Fa0/22, Fa0/23, Fa0/24, Gig0/1
                                                Gig0/2
15   Finance                          active    Fa0/5
200  Voice                            active    Fa0/5
1002 fddi-default                     active
1003 token-ring-default               active
1004 fddinet-default                  active
1005 trnet-default                    active
S2# _____
Number of existing VLANs         : 7
Number of existing VTP VLANs     : 7
Number of existing extended VLANS : 0


S2# _____
Name: Fa0/5
Switchport: Enabled
Administrative Mode: static access
Operational Mode: static access
Administrative Trunking Encapsulation: dot1q
Operational Trunking Encapsulation: native
Negotiation of Trunking: Off
Access Mode VLAN: 15 (Finance)
Trunking Native Mode VLAN: 1 (default)
Voice VLAN: 200
<output omitted>
S2#
```

Modify VLANs and Port Assignments

If a switch access port has been incorrectly assigned to a VLAN, then simply reenter the **switchport access vlan** *vlan-id* interface configuration command with the correct VLAN ID.

To change the membership of a port back to the default VLAN 1, use the **no switchport access vlan** interface configuration mode command. Note that VLANs will still be active even though no ports are assigned to them.

To delete a VLAN from the VLAN database, use the **no vlan** *vlan-id* global configuration mode command.

What happens if you delete the VLAN for ports assigned to it but do not reassign the ports to a different VLAN?

_____

To delete the entire VLAN database, use the **delete vlan.dat** privileged EXEC mode command.

VLAN Trunks

In this section, you review how to configure a trunk port on a LAN switch, including trunk configuration and verification commands and how to reset a trunk to its default state.

Trunk Configuration Commands

In Table 3-4, enter the syntax for each of the trunk configuration commands.

Table 3-4   Trunk Configuration Commands

Description	Syntax
Force the link to be a trunk link.	S1(config-if)# _____
Specify a native VLAN for untagged 802.1Q trunks.	S1(config-if)# _____
Specify the list of VLANs to be allowed on the trunk link.	S1(config-if)# _____

On S1, enter the commands to configure GigabitEthernet 0/1 to be an 802.1Q trunk. Use VLAN 99 as the native VLAN.

S1(config)# _____

S1(config-if)# _____

S1(config-if)# _____

What command will display the switch port status of the new trunk port shown in Example 3-1?

Example 3-1   Verifying a Trunk Configuration

```
S1# _____
Name: Gig0/1
Switchport: Enabled
Administrative Mode: trunk
Operational Mode: trunk
Administrative Trunking Encapsulation: dot1q
Operational Trunking Encapsulation: dot1q
Negotiation of Trunking: On
Access Mode VLAN: 1 (default)
Trunking Native Mode VLAN: 99 (Management)
Administrative Native VLAN tagging: enabled
Voice VLAN: none
Administrative private-vlan host-association: none
Administrative private-vlan mapping: none
Administrative private-vlan trunk native VLAN: none
Administrative private-vlan trunk Native VLAN tagging: enabled
Administrative private-vlan trunk encapsulation: dot1q
Administrative private-vlan trunk normal VLANs: none
Administrative private-vlan trunk associations: none
Administrative private-vlan trunk mappings: none
Operational private-vlan: none
Trunking VLANs Enabled: ALL
Pruning VLANs Enabled: 2-1001
Capture Mode Disabled
Capture VLANs Allowed: ALL

Protected: false
Unknown unicast blocked: disabled
Unknown multicast blocked: disabled
Appliance trust: none
S1#
```

Packet Tracer Exercise 3-2: VLAN and Trunk Configuration

Now you are ready to use Packet Tracer to apply your knowledge about VLAN configuration. Download and open the file LSG02-0302.pka from the companion website for this book. Refer to the Introduction of this book for specifics on accessing files.

Note: The following instructions are also contained in the Packet Tracer Exercise.

In this Packet Tracer activity, you will configure and verify VLANs and trunking. Use the commands you documented in the "VLAN Configuration" section and this section to complete the activity.

Requirements

Configure the following:

- Configure interface VLAN 99 on each switch.

- Create and name VLANs on each switch. Names are case-sensitive.

- Assign ports to the correct VLANs.

- Configure trunking between the switches and assign VLAN 99 as the native VLAN.

- Verify that PCs on the same VLAN can ping each other.

- Verify that switches can ping each other.

Your completion percentage should be 100%. If it is not, click Check Results to see which required components are not yet completed.

Reset the Trunk to the Default State

On S1, enter the commands to reset the GigabitEthernet 0/1 interface to its default state with no native VLAN or allowed VLANs.

```
S1(config)# _____

S1(config-if)# _____

S1(config-if)# _____
```

Dynamic Trunking Protocol

In this section, you review how to configure Dynamic Trunking Protocol (DTP), including what it is, how to negotiate interface modes, and how to configure and verify DTP.

Introduction to DTP

DTP is a Cisco-proprietary protocol that negotiates both the status of trunk ports and the trunk encapsulation of trunk ports. To enable trunking from a Cisco switch to a device that does not support DTP, use the _____ and _____ interface configuration mode commands. This causes the interface to become a trunk but not generate DTP frames.

Negotiated Interface Modes

A switch port on a Cisco Catalyst switch supports a number of trunking modes. In Table 3-5, identify the parameters for the **switchport mode** command that can be used to configure a switch port.

Table 3-5   Modes for a Switch Port

Mode	Description
	Puts the interface into permanent nontrunking mode and negotiates to convert the link into a nontrunk link.
	Enables the interface to convert the link to a trunk link. The interface becomes a trunk interface if the neighboring interface is set to trunk or desirable mode. This is the default switchport mode for all Ethernet interfaces.

Mode	Description
	Causes the interface to actively attempt to convert the link to a trunk link. The interface becomes a trunk interface if the neighboring interface is set to trunk, desirable, or auto mode.
	Puts the interface into permanent trunking mode and negotiates to convert the neighboring link into a trunk link. The interface becomes a trunk interface even if the neighboring interface is not a trunk interface.

The _____ command prevents the interface from generating DTP frames. You can use this command only when the interface switchport mode is _____ or _____. You must manually configure the neighboring interface as a trunk interface to establish a trunk link.

Results of a DTP Configuration

In Table 3-6, the arguments for the switchport mode command are listed for the local side of the link down the first column and for the remote side of the link across the first row. Indicate whether the link will transition to access mode or trunk mode after the two switches have sent DTP messages.

Table 3-6 Trunk Negotiation Combinations

	Dynamic Auto	Dynamic Desirable	Trunk	Access
Dynamic auto				
Dynamic desirable				
Trunk				Limited connectivity
Access			Limited connectivity	

In Figure 3-10, indicate which DTP combinations between two switches will become trunk links and which will become access links.

Figure 3-10 Predict DTP Behavior

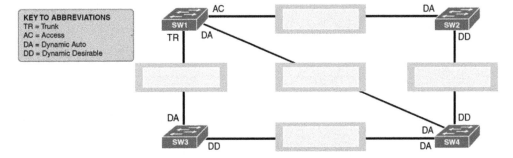

Verify DTP Mode

To determine the DTP mode of interface FastEthernet 0/1, what command would you use in Example 3-2?

Example 3-2   DTP Mode Verification

```
S1# _____

DTP information for FastEthernet0/1:

  TOS/TAS/TNS:                                ACCESS/AUTO/ACCESS

  TOT/TAT/TNT:                                NATIVE/802.1Q/NATIVE

  Neighbor address 1:                         C4F7D5FA0B85

  Neighbor address 2:                         000000000000

  Hello timer expiration (sec/state):         10/RUNNING

  Access timer expiration (sec/state):        never/STOPPED

  Negotiation timer expiration (sec/state):   never/STOPPED

  Multidrop timer expiration (sec/state):     never/STOPPED

  FSM state:                                  S2:ACCESS

  # times multi & trunk                       0

  Enabled:                                    yes

  In STP:                                     no


  Statistics

  ----------

  2645 packets received (2645 good)

  0 packets dropped

      0 nonegotiate, 0 bad version, 0 domain mismatches,

      0 bad TLVs, 0 bad TAS, 0 bad TAT, 0 bad TOT, 0 other

  5288 packets output (5288 good)

      2644 native, 2644 software encap isl, 0 isl hardware native

  0 output errors

  0 trunk timeouts

  1 link ups, last link up on Mon Mar 01 1993, 00:02:57

  0 link downs


S1#
```

Check Your Understanding—Dynamic Trunking Protocol

Check your understanding of Dynamic Trunking Protocol by choosing the BEST answer to each of the following questions.

1. True or false: DTP is an open standard IEEE protocol that specifies autonegotiation of switch trunk links.

    a. true

    b. false

2. What is the default switchport mode for Cisco Catalyst switches?

  a. access

  b. trunk

  c. dynamic auto

  d. dynamic desirable

3. True or false: Two switchports on a link both configured as dynamic auto will success-fully negotiate a trunk.

  a. true

  b. false

4. Which two DTP modes will form a trunk with an interface that is configured as dynamic auto? (Choose two.)

  a. access

  b. trunk

  c. dynamic auto

  d. dynamic desirable

Labs and Activities

Command Reference

In Table 3-7, record the command, including the correct router or switch prompt, that fits each description.

Table 3-7   Commands for Chapter 3, "VLANs"

Command	Description
	Create VLAN 75.
	Assign the name Admin to a VLAN.
	Assign a switch interface to use VLAN 75.
	Display abbreviated output of configured VLANs.
	Display information for VLAN 75.
	Display information for VLAN Admin.
	Display a summary of VLAN information.
	Verify the VLAN configurations on Fa0/10.
	Configure a port to trunk.
	Configure VLAN 86 as the native trunking VLAN.
	Configure a trunk to allow VLANs 75 and 86.
	Display the status of all trunk ports.
	Configure an interface into a permanent nontrunking mode.
	Configure an interface into a permanent trunking mode.
	Configure an interface to actively attempt to convert a link to a trunk.
	Configure an interface to convert to a trunk if the other side of the link is set to trunk or desirable.
	Disable DTP on an interface.

3.1.4 Packet Tracer—Who Hears the Broadcast?

Objectives

Part 1: Observe Broadcast Traffic in a VLAN Implementation

Part 2: Complete Review Questions

Scenario

In this activity, a 24-port Catalyst 2960 switch is fully populated. All ports are in use. You will observe broadcast traffic in a VLAN implementation and answer some reflection questions.

Instructions

Step 1: Use ping to generate traffic.

    a. Click **PC0** and click the **Desktop** tab> **Command Prompt**.

    b. Enter the **ping 192.168.1.8** command. The ping should succeed.

    Unlike a LAN, a VLAN is a broadcast domain created by switches. Using Packet Tracer **Simulation** mode, ping the end devices within their own VLAN. Based on your observation, answer the questions in Step 2.

Step 2: Generate and examine broadcast traffic in a VLAN implementation.

    a. Switch to **Simulation** mode.

    b. Click **Edit Filters** in the Simulation Panel. Uncheck the **Show All/None** checkbox. Check the **ICMP** checkbox.

    c. Click the **Add Complex PDU** tool. This is the open envelope icon on the right toolbar.

    d. Float the mouse cursor over the topology and the pointer changes to an envelope with a plus (+) sign.

    e. Click **PC0** to serve as the source for this test message and the **Create Complex PDU** dialog window opens. Enter the following values:

        ■ Destination IP Address: 255.255.255.255 (broadcast address)

        ■ Sequence Number: 1

        ■ One Shot Time: 0

    Within the PDU settings, the default for **Select Application:** is PING.

    Question:

    What are at least 3 other applications available for use?

    f. Click **Create PDU**. This test broadcast packet now appears in the **Simulation Panel Event List**. It also appears in the PDU List window. It is the first PDU for Scenario 0.

g. Click **Capture/Forward** twice.

Question:

What happened to the packet?

_____

h. Repeat this process for **PC8** and **PC16**.

Reflection Questions

1. If a PC in VLAN 10 sends a broadcast message, which devices receive it?

_____

2. If a PC in VLAN 20 sends a broadcast message, which devices receive it?

_____

3. If a PC in VLAN 30 sends a broadcast message, which devices receive it?

_____

4. What happens to a frame sent from a PC in VLAN 10 to a PC in VLAN 30?

_____

5. Which ports on the switch light up if a PC connected to port 11 sends a unicast message to a PC connected to port 13?

_____

6. Which ports on the switch light if a PC connected to port 2 sends a unicast message to a PC connected to port 23?

_____

7. In terms of ports, what are the collision domains on the switch?

_____

8. In terms of ports, what are the broadcast domains on the switch?

_____

3.2.8 Packet Tracer—Investigate a VLAN Implementation

Addressing Table

Device	Interface	IP Address	Subnet Mask	Default Gateway
S1	VLAN 99	172.17.99.31	255.255.255.0	N/A
S2	VLAN 99	172.17.99.32	255.255.255.0	N/A
S3	VLAN 99	172.17.99.33	255.255.255.0	N/A
PC1	NIC	172.17.10.21	255.255.255.0	172.17.10.1
PC2	NIC	172.17.20.22	255.255.255.0	172.17.20.1
PC3	NIC	172.17.30.23	255.255.255.0	172.17.30.1
PC4	NIC	172.17.10.24	255.255.255.0	172.17.10.1
PC5	NIC	172.17.20.25	255.255.255.0	172.17.20.1
PC6	NIC	172.17.30.26	255.255.255.0	172.17.30.1
PC7	NIC	172.17.10.27	255.255.255.0	172.17.10.1
PC8	NIC	172.17.20.28	255.255.255.0	172.17.20.1
PC9	NIC	172.17.30.29	255.255.255.0	172.17.30.1

Objectives

Part 1: Observe Broadcast Traffic in a VLAN Implementation

Part 2: Observe Broadcast Traffic without VLANs

Background

In this activity, you will observe how broadcast traffic is forwarded by the switches when VLANs are configured and when VLANs are not configured.

Instructions

Part 1: Observe Broadcast Traffic in a VLAN Implementation

Step 1:   Ping from PC1 to PC6.

   a.   Wait for all the link lights to turn to green. To accelerate this process, click **Fast Forward Time** located in the bottom tool bar.

   b.   Click the **Simulation** tab and use the **Add Simple PDU** tool. Click **PC1**, and then click **PC6**.

c. Click the **Capture/Forward** button to step through the process. Observe the ARP requests as they traverse the network. When the Buffer Full window appears, click the **View Previous Events** button.

Questions:

Were the pings successful? Explain.

_____

Look at the Simulation Panel, where did **S3** send the packet after receiving it?

_____

In normal operation, when a switch receives a broadcast frame on one of its ports, it forwards the frame out all other ports. Notice that **S2** only sends the ARP request out F0/1 to **S1**. Also notice that **S3** only sends the ARP request out **F0/11** to **PC4**. **PC1** and **PC4** both belong to VLAN 10. **PC6** belongs to VLAN 30. Because broadcast traffic is contained within the VLAN, **PC6** never receives the ARP request from **PC1**. Because **PC4** is not the destination, it discards the ARP request. The ping from **PC1** fails because **PC1** never receives an ARP reply.

Step 2:   Ping from PC1 to PC4.

a. Click the **New** button under the Scenario 0 dropdown tab. Now click on the **Add Simple PDU** icon on the right side of Packet Tracer and ping from **PC1** to **PC4**.

b. Click the **Capture/Forward** button to step through the process. Observe the ARP requests as they traverse the network. When the Buffer Full window appears, click the **View Previous Events** button.

Question:

Were the pings successful? Explain.

_____

c. Examine the Simulation Panel.

Question:

When the packet reached **S1**, why does it also forward the packet to **PC7**?

_____

Part 2: Observe Broadcast Traffic without VLANs

Step 1:   Clear the configurations on all three switches and delete the VLAN database.

a. Return to **Realtime** mode.

b. Delete the startup configuration on all 3 switches.

Questions:

What command is used to delete the startup configuration of the switches?

_____

Where is the VLAN file stored in the switches?

c. Delete the VLAN file on all 3 switches.

Question:

What command deletes the VLAN file stored in the switches?

Step 2: Reload the switches.

Use the **reload** command in privileged EXEC mode to reset all the switches. Wait for the entire link to turn green. To accelerate this process, click **Fast Forward Time** located in the bottom yellow tool bar.

Step 3: Click Capture/Forward to send ARP requests and pings.

a. After the switches reload and the link lights return to green, the network is ready to forward your ARP and ping traffic.

b. Select **Scenario 0** from the drop-down tab to return to Scenario 0.

c. From **Simulation** mode, click the **Capture/Forward** button to step through the process. Notice that the switches now forward the ARP requests out all ports, except the port on which the ARP request was received. This default action of switches is why VLANs can improve network performance. Broadcast traffic is contained within each VLAN. When the **Buffer Full** window appears, click the **View Previous Events** button.

Reflection Questions

1. If a PC in VLAN 10 sends a broadcast message, which devices receive it?

2. If a PC in VLAN 20 sends a broadcast message, which devices receive it?

3. If a PC in VLAN 30 sends a broadcast message, which devices receive it?

4. What happens to a frame sent from a PC in VLAN 10 to a PC in VLAN 30?

5. In terms of ports, what are the collision domains on the switch?

6. In terms of ports, what are the broadcast domains on the switch?

3.3.12 Packet Tracer—VLAN Configuration

Addressing Table

Device	Interface	IP Address	Subnet Mask	VLAN
PC1	NIC	172.17.10.21	255.255.255.0	10
PC2	NIC	172.17.20.22	255.255.255.0	20
PC3	NIC	172.17.30.23	255.255.255.0	30
PC4	NIC	172.17.10.24	255.255.255.0	10
PC5	NIC	172.17.20.25	255.255.255.0	20
PC6	NIC	172.17.30.26	255.255.255.0	30

Objectives

Part 1: Verify the Default VLAN Configuration

Part 2: Configure VLANs

Part 3: Assign VLANs to Ports

Background

VLANs are helpful in the administration of logical groups, allowing members of a group to be easily moved, changed, or added. This activity focuses on creating and naming VLANs, and assigning access ports to specific VLANs.

Part 1: View the Default VLAN Configuration

Step 1: Display the current VLANs.

On S1, issue the command that displays all VLANs configured. By default, all interfaces are assigned to VLAN 1.

Step 2: Verify connectivity between PCs on the same network.

Notice that each PC can ping the other PC that shares the same subnet.

- PC1 can ping PC4

- PC2 can ping PC5

- PC3 can ping PC6

Pings to hosts on other networks fail.

Question:

What benefits can VLANs provide to the network?

Part 2: Configure VLANs

Step 1:   Create and name VLANs on S1.

  a.   Create the following VLANs. Names are case-sensitive and must match the requirement exactly:

  - VLAN 10: Faculty/Staff

```
S1#(config)# vlan 10

S1#(config-vlan)# name Faculty/Staff
```

  b.   Create the remaining VLANS.

  - VLAN 20: Students

  - VLAN 30: Guest(Default)

  - VLAN 99: Management&Native

  - VLAN 150: VOICE

Step 2:   Verify the VLAN configuration.

Question:

Which command will only display the VLAN name, status, and associated ports on a switch?

_____

Step 3:   Create the VLANs on S2 and S3.

Use the same commands from Step 1 to create and name the same VLANs on S2 and S3.

Step 4:   Verify the VLAN configuration.

Part 3: Assign VLANs to Ports

Step 1:   Assign VLANs to the active ports on S2.

  a.   Configure the interfaces as access ports and assign the VLANs as follows:

  - VLAN 10: FastEthernet 0/11

  b.   Assign the remaining ports to the appropriate VLAN.

  - VLAN 20: FastEthernet 0/18

  - VLAN 30: FastEthernet 0/6

Step 2:   Assign VLANs to the active ports on S3.

S3 uses the same VLAN access port assignments as S2. Configure the interfaces as access ports and assign the VLANs as follows:

- VLAN 10: FastEthernet 0/11

- VLAN 20: FastEthernet 0/18

- VLAN 30: FastEthernet 0/6

Step 3:   Assign the VOICE VLAN to FastEthernet 0/11 on S3.

As shown in the topology, the S3 FastEthernet 0/11 interface connects to a Cisco IP Phone and PC4. The IP phone contains an integrated three-port 10/100 switch. One port on the phone is labeled Switch and connects to F0/4. Another port on the phone is labeled PC and connects to PC4. The IP phone also has an internal port that connects to the IP phone functions.

The S3 F0/11 interface must be configured to support user traffic to PC4 using VLAN 10 and voice traffic to the IP phone using VLAN 150. The interface must also enable QoS and trust the Class of Service (CoS) values assigned by the IP phone. IP voice traffic requires a minimum amount of throughput to support acceptable voice communication quality. This command helps the switchport to provide this minimum amount of throughput.

```
S3(config)# interface f0/11
S3(config-if)# mls qos trust cos
S3(config-if)# switchport voice vlan 150
```

Step 4:   Verify loss of connectivity.

Previously, PCs that shared the same network could ping each other successfully.

Study the output of from the following command on **S2** and answer the following questions based on your knowledge of communication between VLANS. Pay close attention to the Gig0/1 port assignment.

```
S2# show vlan brief

VLAN Name                         Status    Ports
---- ---------------------------- --------- ---------------------------
1    default                      active    Fa0/1, Fa0/2, Fa0/3, Fa0/4
                                            Fa0/5, Fa0/7, Fa0/8, Fa0/9
                                            Fa0/10, Fa0/12, Fa0/13, Fa0/14
                                            Fa0/15, Fa0/16, Fa0/17, Fa0/19
                                            Fa0/20, Fa0/21, Fa0/22, Fa0/23
                                            Fa0/24, Gig0/1, Gig0/2
10   Faculty/Staff                active    Fa0/11
20   Students                     active    Fa0/18
30   Guest(Default)               active    Fa0/6
99   Management&Native            active
150  VOICE                        active
```

Try pinging between PC1 and PC4.

Questions:

Although the access ports are assigned to the appropriate VLANs, were the pings successful? Explain.

_____

What could be done to resolve this issue?

_____

3.4.5 Packet Tracer—Configure Trunks

Addressing Table

Device	Interface	IP Address	Subnet Mask	Switch Port	VLAN
PC1	NIC	172.17.10.21	255.255.255.0	S2 F0/11	10
PC2	NIC	172.17.20.22	255.255.255.0	S2 F0/18	20
PC3	NIC	172.17.30.23	255.255.255.0	S2 F0/6	30
PC4	NIC	172.17.10.24	255.255.255.0	S3 F0/11	10
PC5	NIC	172.17.20.25	255.255.255.0	S3 F0/18	20
PC6	NIC	172.17.30.26	255.255.255.0	S3 F0/6	30

Objectives

Part 1: Verify VLANs

Part 2: Configure Trunks

Background

Trunks are required to pass VLAN information between switches. A port on a switch is either an access port or a trunk port. Access ports carry traffic from a specific VLAN assigned to the port. A trunk port by default is a member of all VLANs. Therefore, it carries traffic for all VLANs. This activity focuses on creating trunk ports and assigning them to a native VLAN other than the default.

Instructions

Part 1: Verify VLANs

Step 1:   Display the current VLANs.

    a.   On **S1**, issue the command that will display all VLANs configured. There should be ten VLANs in total. Notice that all 26 access ports on the switch are assigned to VLAN 1.

    b.   On **S2** and **S3**, display and verify that all the VLANs are configured and assigned to the correct switch ports according to the **Addressing Table**.

Step 2:   Verify loss of connectivity between PCs on the same network.

Ping between hosts on the same the VLAN on the different switches. Although **PC1** and **PC4** are on the same network, they cannot ping one another. This is because the ports connecting the switches are assigned to VLAN 1 by default. In order to provide connectivity between the PCs on the same network and VLAN, trunks must be configured.

Part 2: Configure Trunks

Step 1: Configure trunking on S1 and use VLAN 99 as the native VLAN.

    a. Configure G0/1 and G0/2 interfaces on S1 for trunking.

```
S1(config)# interface range g0/1 - 2
S1(config-if)# switchport mode trunk
```

    b. Configure VLAN 99 as the native VLAN for G0/1 and G0/2 interfaces on S1.

```
S1(config-if)# switchport trunk native vlan 99
```

The trunk port takes about a short time to become active due to Spanning Tree Protocol. Click **Fast Forward Time** to speed the process. After the ports become active, you will periodically receive the following syslog messages:

```
%CDP-4-NATIVE_VLAN_MISMATCH: Native VLAN mismatch discovered on
GigabitEthernet0/2 (99), with S3 GigabitEthernet0/2 (1).

%CDP-4-NATIVE_VLAN_MISMATCH: Native VLAN mismatch discovered on
GigabitEthernet0/1 (99), with S2 GigabitEthernet0/1 (1).
```

You configured VLAN 99 as the native VLAN on S1. However, S2 and S3 are using VLAN 1 as the default native VLAN as indicated by the syslog message.

Question:

Although you have a native VLAN mismatch, pings between PCs on the same VLAN are now successful. Explain.

_____

Step 2: Verify trunking is enabled on S2 and S3.

On **S2** and **S3**, issue the **show interface trunk** command to confirm that DTP has successfully negotiated trunking with S1 on S2 and S3. The output also displays information about the trunk interfaces on S2 and S3. You will learn more about DTP later in the course.

Question:

Which active VLANs are allowed to cross the trunk?

_____

Step 3: Correct the native VLAN mismatch on S2 and S3.

    a. Configure VLAN 99 as the native VLAN for the appropriate interfaces on S2 and S3.

    b. Issue the **show interface trunk** command to verify the correct native VLAN configuration.

Step 4: Verify configurations on S2 and S3.

    a. Issue the **show interface** _interface_ **switchport** command to verify that the native VLAN is now 99.

    b. Use the **show vlan** command to display information regarding configured VLANs.

Question:

Why is port G0/1 on S2 no longer assigned to VLAN 1?

_____

3.4.6 Lab—Configure VLANs and Trunking

Topology

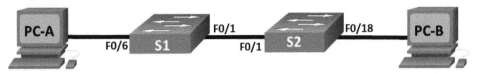

Addressing Table

Device	Interface	IP Address	Subnet Mask	Default Gateway
S1	VLAN 1	192.168.1.11	255.255.255.0	N/A
S2	VLAN 1	192.168.1.12	255.255.255.0	N/A
PC-A	NIC	192.168.10.3	255.255.255.0	192.168.10.1
PC-B	NIC	192.168.10.4	255.255.255.0	192.168.10.1

Objectives

Part 1: Build the Network and Configure Basic Device Settings

Part 2: Create VLANs and Assign Switch Ports

Part 3: Maintain VLAN Port Assignments and the VLAN Database

Part 4: Configure an 802.1Q Trunk between the Switches

Part 5: Delete the VLAN Database

Background / Scenario

Modern switches use virtual local-area networks (VLANs) to improve network performance by separating large Layer 2 broadcast domains into smaller ones. VLANs can also be used as a security measure by controlling which hosts can communicate. In general, VLANs make it easier to design a network to support the goals of an organization.

VLAN trunks are used to span VLANs across multiple devices. Trunks allow the traffic from multiple VLANS to travel over a single link, while keeping the VLAN identification and segmentation intact.

In this lab, you will create VLANs on both switches in the topology, assign VLANs to switch access ports, verify that VLANs are working as expected, and then create a VLAN trunk between the two switches to allow hosts in the same VLAN to communicate through the trunk, regardless of which switch the host is actually attached to.

Note: The switches used with CCNA hands-on labs are Cisco Catalyst 2960s with Cisco IOS Release 15.2(2) (lanbasek9 image). Other routers, switches, and Cisco IOS versions can be used. Depending on the model and Cisco IOS version, the commands available and the output produced might vary from what is shown in the labs. Refer to the Router Interface Summary Table at the end of the lab for the correct interface identifiers.

Note: Ensure that the routers and switches have been erased and have no startup configurations. If you are unsure contact your instructor.

Required Resources

- 2 Switches (Cisco 2960 with Cisco IOS Release 15.2(2) lanbasek9 image or comparable)
- 2 PCs (Windows with a terminal emulation program, such as Tera Term)
- Console cables to configure the Cisco IOS devices via the console ports
- Ethernet cables as shown in the topology

Instructions

Part 1: Build the Network and Configure Basic Device Settings

In Part 1, you will set up the network topology and configure basic settings on the PC hosts and switches.

Step 1:   Cable the network as shown in the topology.

Attach the devices as shown in the topology diagram, and cable as necessary.

Step 2:   Configure basic settings for each switch.

    a.   Console into the switch and enable privileged EXEC mode.

    b.   Enter configuration mode.

    c.   Assign a device name to the switch.

    d.   Disable DNS lookup to prevent the router from attempting to translate incorrectly entered commands as though they were host names.

    e.   Assign **class** as the privileged EXEC encrypted password.

    f.   Assign **cisco** as the console password and enable login.

    g.   Assign **cisco** as the VTY password and enable login.

    h.   Encrypt the plaintext passwords.

    i.   Create a banner that warns anyone accessing the device that unauthorized access is prohibited.

    j.   Configure the IP address listed in the Addressing Table for VLAN 1 on the switch.

    k.   Shut down all interfaces that will not be used.

    l.   Set the clock on the switch.

    m.   Save the running configuration to the startup configuration file.

Step 3:   Configure PC hosts.

Refer to the Addressing Table for PC host address information.

Step 4:   Test connectivity.

Verify that the PC hosts can ping one another.

Note: It may be necessary to disable the PC's firewall to ping between PCs.

Questions:

Can PC-A ping PC-B?

Can PC-A ping S1?

Can PC-B ping S2?

Can S1 ping S2?

If you answered no to any of the above questions, why were the pings unsuccessful?

Part 2: Create VLANs and Assign Switch Ports

In Part 2, you will create Management, Operations, Parking_Lot, and Native VLANs on both switches. You will then assign the VLANs to the appropriate interface. The **show vlan** command is used to verify your configuration settings.

Step 1:   Create VLANs on the switches.

a.   Create the VLANs on S1.

```
S1(config)# vlan 10
S1(config-vlan)# name Operations
S1(config-vlan)# vlan 20
S1(config-vlan)# name Parking_Lot
S1(config-vlan)# vlan 99
S1(config-vlan)# name Management
S1(config-vlan)# vlan 1000
S1(config-vlan)# name Native
S1(config-vlan)# end
```

b.   Create the same VLANs on S2.

c.   Issue the **show vlan brief** command to view the list of VLANs on S1.

```
S1# show vlan brief

VLAN Name                             Status    Ports
---- -------------------------------- --------- -------------------------------
1    default                          active    Fa0/1, Fa0/2, Fa0/3, Fa0/4
                                                Fa0/5, Fa0/6, Fa0/7, Fa0/8
                                                Fa0/9, Fa0/10, Fa0/11, Fa0/12
                                                Fa0/13, Fa0/14, Fa0/15, Fa0/16
```

```
                                                     Fa0/17, Fa0/18, Fa0/19, Fa0/20
                                                     Fa0/21, Fa0/22, Fa0/23, Fa0/24
                                                     Gi0/1, Gi0/2
```

```
10    Operations                active
20    Parking_Lot               active
99    Management                active
1000  Native                    active
1002  fddi-default              act/unsup
1003  token-ring-default        act/unsup
1004  fddinet-default           act/unsup
1005  trnet-default             act/unsup
```

Questions:

What is the default VLAN?

_____

What ports are assigned to the default VLAN?

_____

Step 2:   Assign VLANs to the correct switch interfaces.

    a. Assign VLANs to the interfaces on S1.

        1) Assign PC-A to the Operation VLAN.

```
S1(config)# interface f0/6
S1(config-if)# switchport mode access
S1(config-if)# switchport access vlan 10
```

        2) Move the switch IP address VLAN 99.

```
S1(config)# interface vlan 1
S1(config-if)# no ip address
S1(config-if)# interface vlan 99
S1(config-if)# ip address 192.168.1.11 255.255.255.0
S1(config-if)# end
```

    b. Issue the **show vlan brief** command and verify that the VLANs are assigned to the correct interfaces.

    c. Issue the **show ip interface brief** command.

Question:

What is the status of VLAN 99? Explain.

_____

    d. Assign PC-B to the Operations VLAN on S2.

    e. Remove the IP address for VLAN 1 on S2.

    f. Configure an IP address for VLAN 99 on S2 according to the Addressing Table.

g. Use the **show vlan brief** command to verify that the VLANs are assigned to the correct interfaces.

Questions:

Is S1 able to ping S2? Explain.

_____

Is PC-A able to ping PC-B? Explain.

_____

Part 3: Maintain VLAN Port Assignments and the VLAN Database

In Part 3, you will change VLAN assignments to ports and remove VLANs from the VLAN database.

Step 1: Assign a VLAN to multiple interfaces.

    a. On S1, assign interfaces F0/11–24 to VLAN99.

```
S1(config)# interface range f0/11-24
S1(config-if-range)# switchport mode access
S1(config-if-range)# switchport access vlan 99
S1(config-if-range)# end
```

    b. Issue the **show vlan brief** command to verify VLAN assignments.

    c. Reassign F0/11 and F0/21 to VLAN 10.

    d. Verify that VLAN assignments are correct.

Step 2: Remove a VLAN assignment from an interface.

    a. Use the **no switchport access vlan** command to remove the VLAN 99 assignment to F0/24.

```
S1(config)# interface f0/24
S1(config-if)# no switchport access vlan
S1(config-if)# end
```

    b. Verify that the VLAN change was made.

Question:

Which VLAN is F0/24 now associated with?

_____

Step 3: Remove a VLAN ID from the VLAN database.

    a. Add VLAN 30 to interface F0/24 without issuing the global VLAN command.

```
S1(config)# interface f0/24
S1(config-if)# switchport access vlan 30
% Access VLAN does not exist. Creating vlan 30
```

Note: Current switch technology no longer requires that the **vlan** command be issued to add a VLAN to the database. By assigning an unknown VLAN to a port, the VLAN will be created and added to the VLAN database.

b. Verify that the new VLAN is displayed in the VLAN table.

Question:

What is the default name of VLAN 30?

_____

c. Use the **no vlan 30** command to remove VLAN 30 from the VLAN database.

```
S1(config)# no vlan 30
S1(config)# end
```

d. Issue the **show vlan brief** command. F0/24 was assigned to VLAN 30.

Question:

After deleting VLAN 30 from the VLAN database, what VLAN is port F0/24 assigned to? What happens to the traffic destined to the host attached to F0/24?

_____

e. Issue the **no switchport access vlan** command on interface F0/24.

f. Issue the **show vlan brief** command to determine the VLAN assignment for F0/24.

Questions:

To which VLAN is F0/24 assigned?

_____

_____

Note: Before removing a VLAN from the database, it is recommended that you reassign all the ports assigned to that VLAN.

Why should you reassign a port to another VLAN before removing the VLAN from the VLAN database?

_____

Part 4: Configure an 802.1Q Trunk Between the Switches

In Part 4, you will configure interface F0/1 to use the Dynamic Trunking Protocol (DTP) to allow it to negotiate the trunk mode. After this has been accomplished and verified, you will disable DTP on interface F0/1 and manually configure it as a trunk.

Step 1: Use DTP to initiate trunking on F0/1.

The default DTP mode of a 2960 switch port is dynamic auto. This allows the interface to convert the link to a trunk if the neighboring interface is set to trunk or dynamic desirable mode.

a. Set F0/1 on S1 to negotiate trunk mode.

```
S1(config)# interface f0/1
S1(config-if)# switchport mode dynamic desirable
```

```
Sep 19 02:51:47.257: %LINEPROTO-5-UPDOWN: Line protocol on Interface
FastEthernet0/1, changed state to up
Sep 19 02:51:47.291: %LINEPROTO-5-UPDOWN: Line protocol on Interface
Vlan99, changed state to up
```

You should also receive link status messages on S2.

```
S2#
Sep 19 02:42:19.424: %LINK-3-UPDOWN: Interface FastEthernet0/1, changed
state to up
Sep 19 02:42:21.454: %LINEPROTO-5-UPDOWN: Line protocol on Interface
Vlan99, changed state to up
Sep 19 02:42:22.419: %LINEPROTO-5-UPDOWN: Line protocol on Interface
FastEthernet0/1, changed state to up
```

b. Issue the **show vlan brief** command on S1 and S2. Interface F0/1 is no longer assigned to VLAN 1. Trunked interfaces are not listed in the VLAN table.

c. Issue the **show interfaces trunk** command to view trunked interfaces. Notice that the mode on S1 is set to desirable, and the mode on S2 is set to auto.

```
S1# show interfaces trunk
S2# show interfaces trunk
```

Note: By default, all VLANs are allowed on a trunk. The **switchport trunk** command allows you to control what VLANs have access to the trunk. For this lab, keep the default settings which allows all VLANs to traverse F0/1.

---

d. Verify that VLAN traffic is traveling over trunk interface F0/1.

Questions:

Can S1 ping S2?

_____

Can PC-A ping PC-B?

_____

Can PC-A ping S1?

_____

Can PC-B ping S2?

_____

If you answered no to any of the above questions, explain below.

_____

Step 3: Manually configure trunk interface F0/1.

The **switchport mode trunk** command is used to manually configure a port as a trunk. This command should be issued on both ends of the link.

a. Change the switchport mode on interface F0/1 to force trunking. Make sure to do this on both switches.

```
S1(config)# interface f0/1
S1(config-if)# switchport mode trunk
```

b. Issue the **show interfaces trunk** command to view the trunk mode. Notice that the mode changed from **desirable** to **on**.

```
S2# show interfaces trunk
```

c. Modify the trunk configuration on both switches by changing the native VLAN from VLAN 1 to VLAN 1000.

```
S1(config)# interface f0/1
S1(config-if)# switchport trunk native vlan 1000
```

d. Issue the show interfaces trunk command to view the trunk. Notice the Native VLAN information is updated.

```
S2# show interfaces trunk
```

Questions:

Why might you want to manually configure an interface to trunk mode instead of using DTP?

_____

Why might you want to change the native VLAN on a trunk?

_____

Part 5: Delete the VLAN Database

In Part 5, you will delete the VLAN Database from the switch. It is necessary to do this when initializing a switch back to its default settings.

Step 1:   Determine if the VLAN database exists.

Issue the **show flash** command to determine if a **vlan.dat** file exists in flash.

```
S1# show flash:
```

Note: If there is a vlan.dat file located in flash, then the VLAN database does not contain its default settings.

Step 2:   Delete the VLAN database.

a. Issue the **delete vlan.dat** command to delete the vlan.dat file from flash and reset the VLAN database back to its default settings. You will be prompted twice to confirm that you want to delete the vlan.dat file. Press Enter both times.

```
S1# delete vlan.dat
Delete filename [vlan.dat]?
Delete flash:/vlan.dat? [confirm]
```

b. Issue the **show flash** command to verify that the vlan.dat file has been deleted.

```
S1# show flash:
```

Question:

To initialize a switch back to its default settings, what other commands are needed?

_____

Reflection Questions

1. What is needed to allow hosts on VLAN 10 to communicate to hosts on VLAN 99?

2. What are some primary benefits that an organization can receive through effective use of VLANs?

3.5.5 Packet Tracer—Configure DTP

Addressing Table

Device	Interface	IP Address	Subnet Mask
PC1	NIC	192.168.10.1	255.255.255.0
PC2	NIC	192.168.20.1	255.255.255.0
PC3	NIC	192.168.30.1	255.255.255.0
PC4	NIC	192.168.30.2	255.255.255.0
PC5	NIC	192.168.20.2	255.255.255.0
PC6	NIC	192.168.10.2	255.255.255.0
S1	VLAN 99	192.168.99.1	255.255.255.0
S2	VLAN 99	192.168.99.2	255.255.255.0
S3	VLAN 99	192.168.99.3	255.255.255.0

Objectives

- Configure static trunking
- Configure and Verify DTP

Background / Scenario

As the number of switches in a network increases, the administration necessary to manage the VLANs and trunks can be challenging. To ease some of the VLAN and trunking configurations, trunk negotiation between network devices is managed by the Dynamic Trunking Protocol (DTP), and is automatically enabled on Catalyst 2960 and Catalyst 3650 switches.

In this activity, you will configure trunk links between the switches. You will assign ports to VLANs and verify end-to-end connectivity between hosts in the same VLAN. You will configure trunk links between the switches, and you will configure VLAN 999 as the native VLAN.

Instructions

Part 1: Verify VLAN configuration.

Verify the configured VLANs on the switches.

a. On S1, go to privileged EXEC mode and enter the **show vlan brief** command to verify the VLANs that are present.

```
S1# show vlan brief


VLAN Name                             Status     Ports
---- ------------------------------   ---------  ---------------------------

1    default                          active     Fa0/1, Fa0/2, Fa0/3, Fa0/4
                                                 Fa0/5, Fa0/6, Fa0/7, Fa0/8
```

```
                                           Fa0/9, Fa0/10, Fa0/11, Fa0/12

                                           Fa0/13, Fa0/14, Fa0/15, Fa0/16

                                           Fa0/17, Fa0/18, Fa0/19, Fa0/20

                                           Fa0/21, Fa0/22, Fa0/23, Fa0/24

                                           Gig0/1, Gig0/2

99    Management            active

999   Native                active

1002  fddi-default          active

1003  token-ring-default    active

1004  fddinet-default       active

1005  et-default            active
```

b. Repeat Step 1a on S2 and S3.

Question:

What VLANs are configured on the switches?

Part 2: Create additional VLANs on S2 and S3.

a. On S2, create VLAN 10 and name it Red.

```
S2(config)# vlan 10

S2(config-vlan)# name Red
```

b. Create VLANs 20 and 30 according to the table below.

VLAN Number	VLAN Name
10	Red
20	Blue
30	Yellow

c. Verify the addition of the new VLANs. Enter **show vlan brief** at the privileged EXEC mode.

Question:

In addition to the default VLANs, which VLANs are configured on S2?

d. Repeat the previous steps to create the additional VLANs on S3.

Part 3: Assign VLANs to Ports

Use the **switchport mode access** command to set access mode for the access links. Use the **switchport access vlan** *vlan-id* command to assign a VLAN to an access port.

Ports	Assignments	Network
S2 F0/1 – 8	VLAN 10 (Red)	192.168.10.0 /24
S3 F0/1 – 8		

Ports	Assignments	Network
S2 F0/9 – 16	VLAN 20 (Blue)	192.168.20.0 /24
S3 F0/9 – 16		
S2 F0/17 – 24	VLAN 30 (Yellow)	192.168.30.0 /24
S3 F0/17 – 24		

   a. Assign VLANs to ports on S2 using assignments from the table above.

```
S2(config-if)# interface range f0/1 - 8
S2(config-if-range)# switchport mode access
S2(config-if-range)# switchport access vlan 10
S2(config-if-range)# interface range f0/9 - 16
S2(config-if-range)# switchport mode access
S2(config-if-range)# switchport access vlan 20
S2(config-if-range)# interface range f0/17 - 24
S2(config-if-range)# switchport mode access
S2(config-if-range)# switchport access vlan 30
```

   b. Assign VLANs to ports on S3 using the assignments from the table above.

   Now that you have the ports assigned to VLANs, try to ping from **PC1** to **PC6**.

   Question:

   Was the ping successful? Explain.

Part 4: Configure Trunks on S1, S2, and S3.

Dynamic trunking protocol (DTP) manages the trunk links between Cisco switches. Currently, all the switchports are in the default trunking mode, which is dynamic auto. In this step, you will change the trunking mode to dynamic desirable for the link between switches S1 and S2. The link between switches S1 and S3 will be set as a static trunk. Use VLAN 999 as the native VLAN in this topology.

   a. On switch S1, configure the trunk link to dynamic desirable on the GigabitEthernet 0/1 interface. The configuration of S1 is shown below.

```
S1(config)# interface g0/1
S1(config-if)# switchport mode dynamic desirable
```

   Question:

   What will be the result of trunk negotiation between S1 and S2?

   b. On switch S2, verify that the trunk has been negotiated by entering the **show interfaces trunk** command. Interface GigabitEthernet 0/1 should appear in the output.

   Question:

   What is the mode and status for this port?

c. For the trunk link between S1 and S3, configure interface GigabitEthernet 0/2 as a static trunk link on S1. In addition, disable DTP negotiation on interface G0/2 on S1.

```
S1(config)# interface g0/2
S1(config-if)# switchport mode trunk
S1(config-if)# switchport nonegotiate
```

d. Use the **show dtp** command to verify the status of DTP.

```
S1# show dtp
Global DTP information
    Sending DTP Hello packets every 30 seconds
    Dynamic Trunk timeout is 300 seconds
    1 interfaces using DTP
```

e. Verify trunking is enabled on all the switches using the **show interfaces trunk** command.

```
S1# show interfaces trunk
Port        Mode          Encapsulation  Status        Native vlan
Gig0/1      desirable     n-802.1q       trunking      1
Gig0/2      on            802.1q         trunking      1


Port        Vlans allowed on trunk
Gig0/1      1-1005
Gig0/2      1-1005


Port        Vlans allowed and active in management domain
Gig0/1      1,99,999
Gig0/2      1,99,999


Port        Vlans in spanning tree forwarding state and not pruned
Gig0/1      1,99,999
Gig0/2      1,99,999
```

Question:

What is the native VLAN for these trunks currently?

_____

f. Configure VLAN 999 as the native VLAN for the trunk links on S1.

```
S1(config)# interface range g0/1 - 2
S1(config-if-range)# switchport trunk native vlan 999
```

Question:

What messages did you receive on S1? How would you correct it?

_____

g. On S2 and S3, configure VLAN 999 as the native VLAN.

h. Verify trunking is successfully configured on all the switches. You should be able ping one switch from another switch in the topology using the IP addresses configured on the SVI.

i. Attempt to ping from PC1 to PC6.

Question:

Why was the ping unsuccessful?

Hint: Look at the 'show vlan brief' output from all three switches. Compare the outputs from the 'show interface trunk' on all switches.

j. Correct the configuration as necessary.

Part 5: Reconfigure trunk on S3.

a. Issue the 'show interface trunk' command on S3.

Question:

What is the mode and encapsulation on G0/2?

b. Configure G0/2 to match G0/2 on S1.

Question:

What is the mode and encapsulation on G0/2 after the change?

c. Issue the command 'show interface G0/2 switchport' on switch S3.

Question:

What is the 'Negotiation of Trunking' state displayed?

Part 6: Verify end to end connectivity.

Step 1: From PC1 ping PC6.

Step 2: From PC2 ping PC5.

Step 3: From PC3 ping PC4.

Packet Tracer
☐ Activity

3.6.1 Packet Tracer—Implement VLANs and Trunking

Addressing Table

Device	Interface	IP Address	Subnet Mask	Switchport	VLAN
PC1	NIC	192.168.10.10	255.255.255.0	SWB F0/1	VLAN 10
PC2	NIC	192.168.20.20	255.255.255.0	SWB F0/2	VLAN 20
PC3	NIC	192.168.30.30	255.255.255.0	SWB F0/3	VLAN 30
PC4	NIC	192.168.10.11	255.255.255.0	SWC F0/1	VLAN 10
PC5	NIC	192.168.20.21	255.255.255.0	SWC F0/2	VLAN 20
PC6	NIC	192.168.30.31	255.255.255.0	SWC F0/3	VLAN 30
PC7	NIC	192.168.10.12	255.255.255.0	SWC F0/4	VLAN 10
					VLAN 40 (Voice)
SWA	SVI	192.168.99.252	255.255.255.0	N/A	VLAN 99
SWB	SVI	192.168.99.253	255.255.255.0	N/A	VLAN 99
SWC	SVI	192.168.99.254	255.255.255.0	N/A	VLAN 99

Objectives

Part 1: Configure VLANs

Part 2: Assign Ports to VLANs

Part 3: Configure Static Trunking

Part 4: Configure Dynamic Trunking

Background

You are working in a company that is getting ready to deploy a set of new 2960 switches in a branch office. You are working in the lab to test out the VLAN and trunking configurations that are planned. Configure and test the VLANs and trunks.

Instructions

Part 1: Configure VLANs

Configure VLANs on all three switches. Refer to the VLAN Table. Note that the VLAN names must match the values in the table exactly.

VLAN Table

VLAN Number	VLAN Name
10	Admin
20	Accounts
30	HR
40	Voice
99	Management
100	Native

Part 2: Assign Ports to VLANs

Step 1:   Assign access ports to VLANs

On SWB and SWC, assign ports to the VLANs. Refer to the Addressing Table.

Step 2:   Configure the Voice VLAN port

Configure the appropriate port on switch SWC for voice VLAN functionality.

Step 3:   Configure the virtual management interfaces

    a.   Create the virtual management interfaces, on all three switches.

    b.   Address the virtual management interfaces according to the Addressing Table.

    c.   The switches should not be able to ping each other.

Part 3: Configure Static Trunking

    a.   Configure the link between SWA and SWB as a static trunk. Disable dynamic trunking on this port.

    b.   Disable DTP on the switch port on both ends of the trunk link.

    c.   Configure the trunk with the native VLAN and eliminate native VLAN conflicts if any.

Part 4: Configure Dynamic Trunking

    a.   Assume that the trunk port on SWC is set to the default DTP mode for 2960 switches. Configure G0/2 on SWA so that it successfully negotiates trunking with SWC.

    b.   Configure the trunk with the native VLAN and eliminate native VLAN conflicts if any.

3.6.2 Lab—Implement VLANs and Trunking

Topology

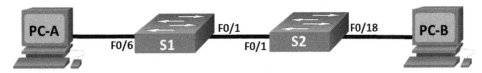

Addressing Table

Device	Interface	IP Address	Subnet Mask
S1	VLAN 10	192.168.10.11	255.255.255.0
	VLAN 20	192.168.20.11	255.255.255.0
	VLAN 30	192.168.30.11	255.255.255.0
S2	VLAN 10	192.168.10.12	255.255.255.0
PC-A	NIC	192.168.20.13	255.255.255.0
PC-B	NIC	192.168.30.13	255.255.255.0

VLAN Table

VLAN	Name	Interface Assigned
10	Management	S1: VLAN 10
		S2: VLAN 10
20	Sales	S1: VLAN 20 and F0/6
30	Operations	S1: VLAN 30
		S2: F0/18
999	ParkingLot	S1: F0/2-5, F0/7-24, G0/1-2
		S2: F0/2-17, F0/19-24, G0/1-2
1000	Native	N/A

Objectives

Part 1: Build the Network and Configure Basic Device Settings

Part 2: Create VLANs and Assign Switch Ports

Part 3: Configure an 802.1Q Trunk between the Switches

Background / Scenario

Modern switches use virtual local-area networks (VLANs) to improve network performance by separating large Layer 2 broadcast domains into smaller ones. VLANs address scalability, security, and network management. In general, VLANs make it easier to design a network to support the goals of an organization. Communication between VLANs requires a device operating at Layer 3 of the OSI model.

VLAN trunks are used to span VLANs across multiple devices. Trunks allow the traffic from multiple VLANs to travel over a single link, while keeping the VLAN identification and segmentation intact.

In this lab, you will create VLANs on both switches in the topology, assign VLANs to switch access ports, verify that VLANs are working as expected and create VLAN trunks between the two switches.

Note: The switches used with CCNA hands-on labs are Cisco Catalyst 2960s with Cisco IOS Release 15.2(2) (lanbasek9 image). Other switches and Cisco IOS versions can be used. Depending on the model and Cisco IOS version, the commands available and the output produced might vary from what is shown in the labs. Refer to the Router Interface Summary Table at the end of the lab for the correct interface identifiers.

Note: Ensure that the switches have been erased and have no startup configurations. If you are unsure contact your instructor.

Required Resources

- 2 Switches (Cisco 2960 with Cisco IOS Release 15.2(2) lanbasek9 image or comparable)
- 2 PCs (Windows with a terminal emulation program, such as Tera Term)
- Console cables to configure the Cisco IOS devices via the console ports
- Ethernet cables as shown in the topology

Instructions

Part 1: Build the Network and Configure Basic Device Settings

In Part 1, you will set up the network topology and configure basic settings on the PC hosts and switches.

Step 1: Cable the network as shown in the topology.

Attach the devices as shown in the topology diagram, and cable as necessary.

Step 2: Configure basic settings for each switch.

a. Console into the switch and enable privileged EXEC mode.

b. Assign a device name to the switch.

c. Disable DNS lookup.

d. Assign **class** as the privileged EXEC encrypted password.

e. Assign **cisco** as the console password and enable login.

f. Assign **cisco** as the VTY password and enable login.

g. Encrypt the plaintext passwords.

h. Create a banner that warns anyone accessing the device that unauthorized access is prohibited.

i. Copy the running configuration to the startup configuration.

Step 3:   Configure PC hosts.

Refer to the Addressing Table for PC host address information.

Part 2: Create VLANs and Assign Switch Ports

In Part 2, you will create VLANs as specified in the table above on both switches. You will then assign the VLANs to the appropriate interface. The **show vlan brief** command is used to verify your configuration settings. Complete the following tasks on each switch.

Step 1:   Create VLANs on both switches.

    a.   Create and name the required VLANs on each switch from the table above.

    b.   Configure the management interface on each switch using the IP address information in the Addressing Table.

    c.   Assign all unused ports on the switch to the ParkingLot VLAN, configure them for static access mode, and administratively deactivate them.

Step 2:   Assign VLANs to the correct switch interfaces.

    a.   Assign used ports to the appropriate VLAN (specified in the VLAN table above) and configure them for static access mode.

    b.   Verify that the VLANs are assigned to the correct interfaces.

Part 3: Configure an 802.1Q Trunk Between the Switches

In Part 3, you will manually configure interface F0/1 as a trunk.

Step 1:   Manually configure trunk interface F0/1.

    a.   Change the switchport mode on interface F0/1 to force trunking. Make sure to do this on both switches.

    b.   Set the native VLAN to 1000 on both switches.

    c.   As another part of trunk configuration, specify that only VLANs 10, 20, 30, and 1000 are allowed to cross the trunk.

    d.   Issue the **show interfaces trunk** command to verify trunking ports, the native VLAN and allowed VLANs across the trunk.

Step 2:   Verify connectivity.

Verify connectivity within a VLAN. For example, PC-A should be able to ping S1 VLAN 20 successfully.

Question:

Were the pings from PC-B to S2 successful? Explain.

CHAPTER 4

Inter-VLAN Routing

The "Study Guide" portion of this chapter uses a variety of exercises to test your knowledge and skills in implementing inter-VLAN routing. The "Labs and Activities" portion of this chapter includes all the online curriculum labs and Packet Tracer activity instructions.

As you work through this chapter, use Chapter 4 in *Switching, Routing, and Wireless Essentials v7 Companion Guide* or use the corresponding Module 4 in the Switching, Routing, and Wireless Essentials online curriculum for assistance.

Study Guide

Inter-VLAN Routing Operation

In this section, you review inter-VLAN operation, including legacy inter-VLAN routing, router-on-a-stick inter-VLAN routing, and inter-VLAN routing on a Layer 3 switch.

What is Inter-VLAN Routing?

There are three inter-VLAN routing options:

- **Legacy inter-VLAN routing:** This is a legacy solution. It does not scale well.
- **Router-on-a-stick:** This is an acceptable solution for a small to medium-sized network.
- **Layer 3 switch using switched virtual interfaces (SVIs):** This is the most scalable solution for medium to large organizations.

Legacy Inter-VLAN Routing

Briefly describe legacy inter-VLAN routing.

_____

_____

_____

_____

Router-on-a-Stick Inter-VLAN Routing

Briefly describe router-on-a-stick inter-VLAN routing.

_____

_____

_____

_____

Inter-VLAN Routing on a Layer 3 Switch

Briefly describe inter-VLAN routing on a Layer 3 switch.

_____

_____

_____

_____

Check Your Understanding—Inter-VLAN Routing Operation

This Check Your Understanding activity uses Figures 4-1, 4-2, and 4-3 for one question.

Figure 4-1   Scenario A

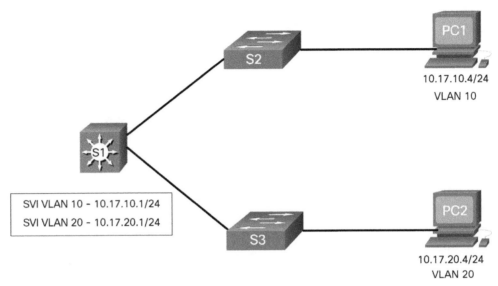

Figure 4-2   Scenario B

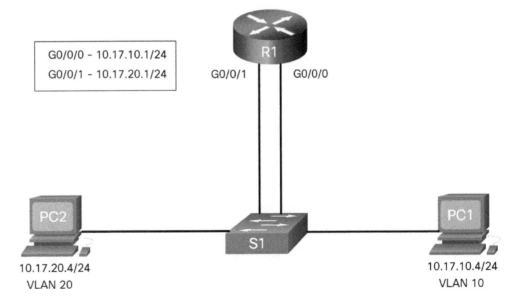

Figure 4-3 Scenario C

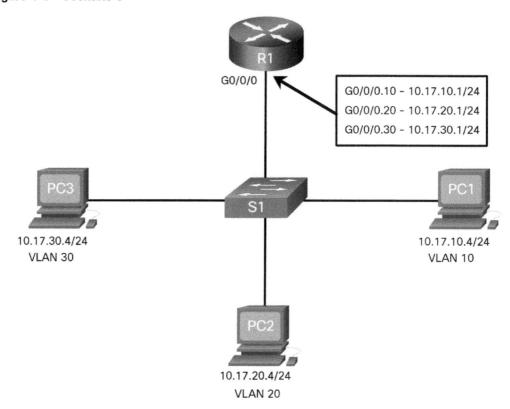

In Figures 4-1, 4-2, and 4-3, which statements best describe each of the inter-VLAN routing solutions? (Choose three.)

- **a.** Scenario A is a legacy inter-VLAN solution.
- **b.** Scenario B is a Layer 3 inter-VLAN solution.
- **c.** Scenario B and C are both router-on-a-stick inter-VLAN solutions.
- **d.** Scenario A is a Layer 3 inter-VLAN solution.
- **e.** Scenario B is a legacy inter-VLAN solution.
- **f.** Scenario C is a router-on-a-stick inter-VLAN solution.

Router-on-a-Stick Inter-VLAN Routing

In this section, you review the skills necessary to implement router-on-a-stick inter-VLAN routing.

Router-on-a-Stick Command Syntax

List the commands, including command syntax and prompt, to configure a router for router-on-a-stick inter-VLAN routing:

_____

_____

_____

_____

List the commands, including syntax and prompt, to configure a switch to support inter-VLAN routing:

_____

_____

_____

_____

Router-on-a-Stick Configuration

Refer to Figure 4-4 and enter the commands for both R1 and S1 to enable inter-VLAN routing.

Figure 4-4   Router-on-a-Stick Inter-VLAN Routing Topology

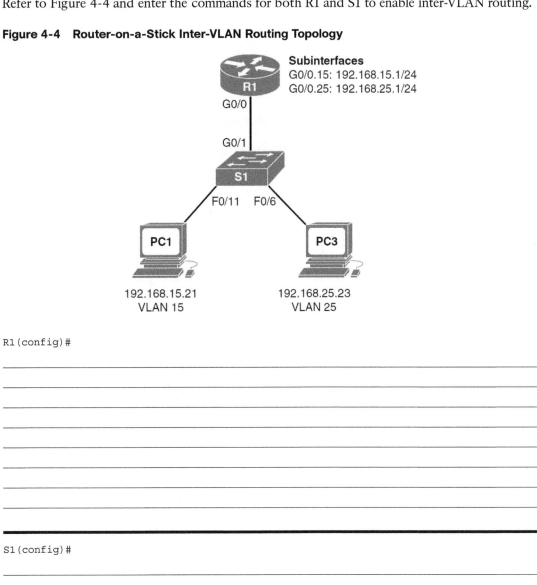

```
R1(config)#
```

_____

_____

_____

_____

_____

_____

_____

_____

```
S1(config)#
```

_____

_____

Packet Tracer Exercise 4-1: Router-on-a-Stick Inter-VLAN Routing Configuration

Now you are ready to use Packet Tracer to apply your knowledge about router-on-a-stick inter-VLAN routing configuration. Download and open the file LSG02-0401.pka from the companion website for this book. Refer to the Introduction of this book for specifics on accessing files.

Note: The following instructions are also contained in the Packet Tracer Exercise.

In this Packet Tracer activity, you will configure and verify router-on-a-stick inter-VLAN routing. Use the commands you documented in the "Router-on-a-Stick Configuration" section to complete the activity.

Requirements

Configure the following:

- Configure R1 for inter-VLAN routing.

- Configure the S1 link to R1 as a trunk.

- Verify that PC1 and PC3 can ping each other.

Your completion percentage should be 100%. If it is not, click Check Results to see which required components are not yet completed.

Inter-VLAN Routing Using Layer 3 Switches

In this section, you review the skills necessary to implement inter-VLAN routing on a Layer 3 switch.

Layer 3 Switch Inter-VLAN Routing

Enterprise campus LANs use Layer 3 switches to provide inter-VLAN routing. Layer 3 switches use hardware-based switching to achieve higher packet processing rates than routers. Layer 3 switches are also commonly implemented in enterprise distribution layer wiring closets.

Capabilities of a Layer 3 switch include the ability to do the following:

- Route from one VLAN to another, using multiple switched virtual interfaces (SVIs).

- Convert a Layer 2 switchport to a Layer 3 interface (that is, a routed port).

To provide inter-VLAN routing, Layer 3 switches use SVIs. SVIs are configured using the same **interface vlan** *vlan-id* command used to create the management SVI on a Layer 2 switch. A Layer 3 SVI must be created for each of the routable VLANs.

Layer 3 Switch Configuration

Refer to Figure 4-5 and enter the commands for Dist-A to enable inter-VLAN routing.

Figure 4-5   Layer 3 Switch Inter-VLAN Routing Topology

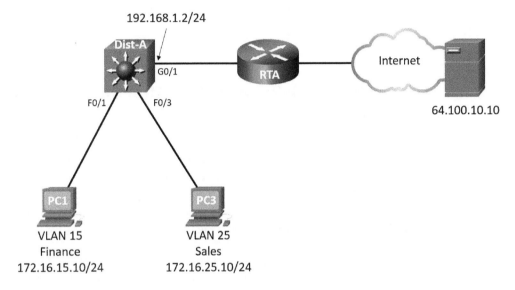

Step 1.   Create the VLANs.

Using the information in the topology shown in Figure 4-5, record the command(s), including switch prompt, for this step.

Step 2.   Create the SVN VLAN interfaces.

Using the information in the topology shown in Figure 4-5, record the command(s), including switch prompt, for this step.

_____

_____

Step 3.   Configure access ports.

Using the information in the topology shown in Figure 4-5, record the command(s), including switch prompt, for this step.

_____

_____

Step 4.   Enable IP routing.

Using the information in the topology shown in Figure 4-5, record the command(s), including switch prompt, for this step.

_____

_____

Step 5.   Configure the routed port.

Using the information in the topology shown in Figure 4-5, record the command(s), including switch prompt, for this step.

_____

_____

Step 6.   Configure routing.

Dist-A and RTA must be configured for routing. This can be accomplished using static routing or any number of dynamic routing protocols. For this activity, you will use Open Shortest Path First (OSPF) dynamic routing. The commands to configure Dist-A are as follows. RTA is already configured.

Packet Tracer 4-2: Layer 3 Switch Inter-VLAN Routing Configuration

Now you are ready to use Packet Tracer to apply your knowledge about Layer 3 switch inter-VLAN routing configuration. Download and open the file LSG02-0402.pka from the companion website for this book. Refer to the Introduction of this book for specifics on accessing files.

Note: The following instructions are also contained in the Packet Tracer Exercise.

In this Packet Tracer activity, you will configure and verify Layer 3 switch inter-VLAN routing. Use the commands you documented in the "Layer 3 Switch Configuration" section to complete the activity.

Requirements

Configure the following:

- Configure Dist-A with the VLANs. Names are case-sensitive.
- Create the SVN VLAN interfaces for each VLAN.
- Configure the access ports for each VLAN.
- Enable IP routing on Dist-A.
- Configure a routed port on Dist-A.
- Configure Dist-A with OSPF routing.

Your completion percentage should be 100%. If it is not, click Check Results to see which required components are not yet completed.

Troubleshoot Inter-VLAN Routing

In this section, you review common inter-VLAN routing implementation issues and how to troubleshoot them.

Common Inter-VLAN Issues

There are a number of reasons an inter-VLAN configuration might not work. Table 4-1 lists some of the reasons inter-VLAN connectivity commonly fails.

Table 4-1   Inter-VLAN Routing Troubleshooting Commands

Issue Type	How to Fix	How to Verify

Missing VLANs	▪ Create (or re-create) the VLAN if it does not exist.
	▪ Ensure that the host port is assigned to the correct VLAN.
		`show vlan [brief]`
		
		`show interfaces switchport`
		
		`ping`

Switch trunk port issues	▪ Ensure that trunks are configured correctly.
	▪ Ensure that the port is a trunk port and enabled.
		`show interfaces trunk`
		
		`show running-config`

Switch access port issues	▪ Assign the correct VLAN to the access port.
	▪ Ensure that the port is an access port and enabled.
	▪ Ensure that the host addressing is configured for the correct subnet.
		`show interfaces switchport`
		
		`show running-config interface`
		
		`ipconfig`

Router configuration issues	▪ Ensure that the correct IP addresses are configured for the subinterfaces.
	▪ Ensure that the correct VLAN IDs are assigned to the subinterfaces.
		`show ip interface brief`
		
		`show interfaces`

Troubleshoot Router-on-a-Stick Inter-VLAN Routing

As you know, **ping** and **tracert/traceroute** can be helpful in isolating the general location of a connectivity problem. But to further isolate an inter-VLAN routing issue, you might need several additional commands.

In Examples 4-1 and 4-2, fill in the command used to generate the output. Highlight relevant parts of the output that would help in isolating inter-VLAN routing issues. Then document the error and possible solution.

Example 4-1   Inter-VLAN Troubleshooting Scenario 1

```
Switch# _____

Name: Gi0/23

Switchport: Enabled

Administrative Mode: dynamic auto

Operational Mode: static access

Administrative Trunking Encapsulation: dot1q

Operational Trunking Encapsulation: native

Negotiation of Trunking: On

Access Mode VLAN: 1 (default)

Trunking Native Mode VLAN: 1 (default)

 (output omitted)
```

What error or errors do you see in Example 4-1?

_____

What solution would you recommend?

_____

Example 4-2 Inter-VLAN Troubleshooting Scenario 2

```
Router#

Interface IP-Address OK? Method Status Protocol

Embedded-Service-Engine0/0 unassigned YES unset administratively down down

GigabitEthernet0/0 unassigned YES unset administratively down down

GigabitEthernet0/0.10 172.17.10.1 YES manual up up

GigabitEthernet0/0.30 172.17.30.1 YES manual up up

GigabitEthernet0/1 unassigned YES unset administratively down down

Serial0/0/0 unassigned YES unset administratively down down

Serial0/0/1 unassigned YES unset administratively down down
```

What error or errors do you see in Example 4-2?

_____

What solution would you recommend?

_____

Refer to the topology in Figure 4-6.

_____

Figure 4-6   Inter-VLAN Troubleshooting Scenario 3

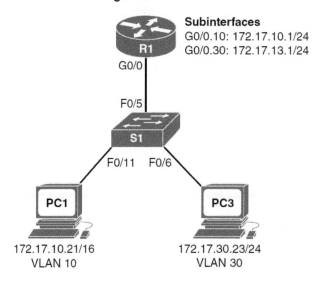

Subinterfaces
G0/0.10: 172.17.10.1/24
G0/0.30: 172.17.13.1/24

R1

G0/0

F0/5

S1

F0/11   F0/6

PC1

PC3

172.17.10.21/16
VLAN 10

172.17.30.23/24
VLAN 30

What error or errors do you see in Figure 4-6?

_____

What solution would you recommend?

_____

Troubleshoot Layer 3 Switch Inter-VLAN Routing

Use Figure 4-7 for each of the following Layer 3 switch inter-VLAN routing troubleshooting scenarios.

Figure 4-7 Layer 3 Switching Troubleshooting Topology

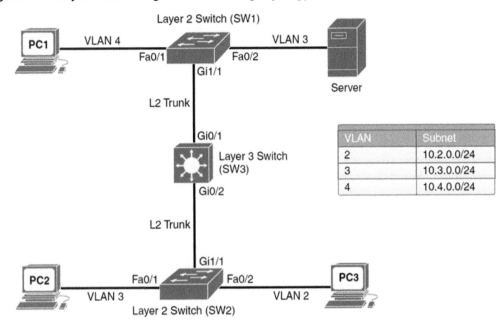

Scenario 1

PC2 is unable to communicate with PC3 but can communicate with all other devices. Refer to the command output in Example 4-3 and select the most likely causes for this issue. More than one answer choice may be selected.

Example 4-3 Layer 3 Switching Troubleshooting Scenario 1

```
SW3# show ip route
<output omitted>
Gateway of last resort is not set

     10.0.0.0/8 is variably subnetted, 3 subnets, 3 masks
C       10.2.0.0/24 is directly connected, Vlan5
C       10.3.0.0/24 is directly connected, Vlan3
C       10.4.0.0/24 is directly connected, Vlan4
```

VLAN 5 does not exist.

VLAN 4 has no IP address.

VLAN 3 IP address is not correct.

VLAN 2 is not configured.

VLANs 3 and 4 are shut down.

Scenario 2

PC3 is unable to communicate with any of the other devices, including its own gateway. Refer to the command output in Example 4-4. Then select the most likely causes for this issue. More than one answer choice may be selected.

Example 4-4 Layer 3 Switching Troubleshooting Scenario 2

```
SW3# show ip route
<output omitted>
Gateway of last resort is not set
     10.0.0.0/8 is variably subnetted, 3 subnets, 3 masks
C       10.2.0.0/30 is directly connected, Vlan2
C       10.3.0.0/24 is directly connected, Vlan3
C       10.4.0.0/24 is directly connected, Vlan4
```

The VLAN 4 subnet mask is not correct.

The VLAN 4 IP address is not correct.

The VLAN 2 subnet mask is not correct.

VLAN 2 is not configured.

The VLAN 3 IP address is not correct.

Scenario 3

PC1 is unable to communicate with PC2 or PC3 but can communicate with the server. Refer to the command output in Example 4-5. Then select the most likely causes for this issue. More than one answer choice may be selected.

Example 4-5 Layer 3 Switching Troubleshooting Scenario 3

```
SW3# show interface trunk

Port          Mode          Encapsulation     Status        Native vlan
Gig0/1        auto          n-802.1q          trunking      1
```

VLANs 2 and 3 are being pruned from the trunk links.

SW2 is shut down.

The trunk encapsulation is not correct.

The Gigabit 0/2 port is not configured as a trunk.

The Gigabit 0/1 port is not configured as a trunk.

VLAN 2 is not configured.

Check Your Understanding—Troubleshoot Inter-VLAN Routing

Check your understanding of inter-VLAN routing methods by choosing the BEST answer to each of the following questions.

1. You are troubleshooting an inter-VLAN issue on a router and need to verify that the sub-interfaces are in the routing table. Which inter-VLAN routing troubleshooting command would you use to do this?

    a. show interfaces

    b. show interfaces *interface-id* switchport

    c. show ip interface brief

    d. show ip route

    e. show vlan

2. You are troubleshooting an inter-VLAN issue on a switch and need to check the list of VLANs and their assigned ports. Which inter-VLAN routing troubleshooting command would you use to do this?

    a. show interfaces

    b. show interfaces *interface-id* switchport

    c. show ip interface brief

    d. show ip route

    e. show vlan

3. You are troubleshooting an inter-VLAN issue on a router and need to verify the status of an access port and its access mode VLAN. Which troubleshooting command would you use to do this?

    a. show interfaces

    b. show interfaces *interface-id* switchport

    c. show ip interface brief

    d. show ip route

    e. show vlan

4. You are troubleshooting an inter-VLAN issue on a router and need to verify the status and IP address of all interfaces in a condensed format. Which inter-VLAN routing troubleshooting command would you use to do this?

    a. show interfaces

    b. show interfaces *interface-id* switchport

    c. show ip interface brief

    d. show ip route

    e. show vlan

Labs and Activities

Command Reference

In Table 4-2, record the command, including the correct router or switch prompt, that fits each description.

Table 4-2   Commands for Chapter 4, "Inter-VLAN Routing"

Command	Description
	Display the status of all trunk ports.
	Create subinterface 100 on a router G0/1 interface.
	Configure a subinterface to use 801.Q encapsulation for VLAN 75.
	Enable routing on a switch.
	Convert a Layer 2 switchport to Layer 3 routing.

4.2.7 Packet Tracer—Configure Router-on-a-Stick Inter-VLAN Routing

Addressing Table

Device	Interface	IPv4 Address	Subnet Mask	Default Gateway
R1	G0/0.10	172.17.10.1	255.255.255.0	N/A
	G0/0.30	172.17.30.1	255.255.255.0	
PC1	NIC	172.17.10.10	255.255.255.0	172.17.10.1
PC2	NIC	172.17.30.10	255.255.255.0	172.17.30.1

Objectives

Part 1: Add VLANs to a Switch

Part 2: Configure Subinterfaces

Part 3: Test Connectivity with Inter-VLAN Routing

Scenario

In this activity, you will configure VLANs and inter-VLAN routing. You will then enable trunk interfaces and verify connectivity between VLANs.

Instructions

Part 1: Add VLANs to a Switch

Step 1:   Create VLANs on S1.

Create VLAN 10 and VLAN 30 on S1.

Step 2:   Assign VLANs to ports.

    a. Configure interfaces F0/6 and F0/11 as access ports and assign VLANs.

       ■ Assign the port connected to **PC1** to VLAN 10.

       ■ Assign the port connected to **PC3** to VLAN 30.

    b. Issue the **show vlan brief** command to verify VLAN configuration.

```
S1# show vlan brief

VLAN Name                        Status    Ports

---- ------------------------ --------- ------------------------
1    default                  active    Fa0/1,  Fa0/2,  Fa0/3,  Fa0/4
                                        Fa0/5,  Fa0/7,  Fa0/8,  Fa0/9
                                        Fa0/10, Fa0/12, Fa0/13, Fa0/14
                                        Fa0/15, Fa0/16, Fa0/17, Fa0/18
                                        Fa0/19, Fa0/20, Fa0/21, Fa0/22
                                        Fa0/23, Fa0/24, Gig0/1, Gig0/2
10   VLAN0010                 active    Fa0/11
30   VLAN0030                 active    Fa0/6
1002 fddi-default             active
1003 token-ring-default       active
1004 fddinet-default          active
1005 trnet-default            active
```

Step 3:   Test connectivity between PC1 and PC3.

From **PC1**, ping **PC3**.

Question:

Were the pings successful? Why did you get this result?

_____

Part 2: Configure Subinterfaces

Step 1:   Configure subinterfaces on R1 using the 802.1Q encapsulation.

    a. Create the subinterface G0/0.10.

       ■ Set the encapsulation type to 802.1Q and assign VLAN 10 to the subinterface.

       ■ Refer to the **Address Table** and assign the correct IP address to the subinterface.

```
R1(config)# int g0/0.10
R1(config-subif)# encapsulation dot1Q 10
R1(config-subif)# ip address 172.17.10.1 255.255.255.0
```

b. Repeat for the G0/0.30 subinterface.

Step 2: Verify Configuration.

    a. Use the **show ip interface brief** command to verify subinterface configuration. Both subinterfaces are down. Subinterfaces are virtual interfaces that are associated with a physical interface. Therefore, in order to enable subinterfaces, you must enable the physical interface that they are associated with.

    b. Enable the G0/0 interface. Verify that the subinterfaces are now active.

Part 3: Test Connectivity with Inter-VLAN Routing

Step 1: Ping between PC1 and PC3.

Question:

From **PC1**, ping **PC3**. The pings should still fail. Explain.

_____

Step 2: Enable trunking.

    a. On **S1**, issue the **show vlan** command.

    Question:

    What VLAN is G0/1 assigned to?

    _____

    b. Because the router was configured with multiple subinterfaces assigned to different VLANs, the switch port connecting to the router must be configured as a trunk. Enable trunking on interface G0/1.

    Question:

    How can you determine that the interface is a trunk port using the **show vlan** command?

    _____

    c. Issue the **show interface trunk** command to verify that the interface is configured as a trunk.

Step 3: Test Connectivity

If the configurations are correct, PC1 and PC3 should be able to ping their default gateways and each other.

Question:

What addresses do PC1 and PC3 use as their default gateway addresses?

_____

4.2.8 Lab—Configure Router-on-a-Stick Inter-VLAN Routing

Topology

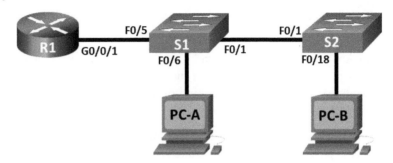

Addressing Table

Device	Interface	IP Address	Subnet Mask	Default Gateway
R1	G0/0/1.3	192.168.3.1	255.255.255.0	N/A
	G0/0/1.4	192.168.4.1	255.255.255.0	
	G0/0/1.8	N/A	N/A	
S1	VLAN 3	192.168.3.11	255.255.255.0	192.168.3.1
S2	VLAN 3	192.168.3.12	255.255.255.0	192.168.3.1
PC-A	NIC	192.168.3.3	255.255.255.0	192.168.3.1
PC-B	NIC	192.168.4.3	255.255.255.0	192.168.4.1

VLAN Table

VLAN	Name	Interface Assigned
3	Management	S1: VLAN 3
		S2: VLAN 3
		S1: F0/6
4	Operations	S2: F0/18
7	ParkingLot	S1: F0/2–4, F0/7–24, G0/1–2
		S2: F0/2–17, F0/19–24, G0/1–2
8	Native	N/A

Objectives

Part 1: Build the Network and Configure Basic Device Settings

Part 2: Create VLANs and Assign Switch Ports

Part 3: Configure an 802.1Q Trunk between the Switches

Part 4: Configure Inter-VLAN Routing on the Router

Part 5: Verify Inter-VLAN Routing is Working

Background / Scenario

Modern switches use virtual local-area networks (VLANs) to provide segmentation services traditionally provided by routers in LAN configurations. VLANs address scalability, security, and network management. In general, VLANs make it easier to design a network to support the goals of an organization. Communication between VLANs requires a device operating at Layer 3 of the OSI model. Routers in VLAN topologies provide additional security and traffic flow management.

VLAN trunks are used to span VLANs across multiple devices. Trunks allow the traffic from multiple VLANS to travel over a single link, while keeping the VLAN identification and segmentation intact. A particular kind of inter-VLAN routing, called "Router-on-a-Stick," uses a trunk from the router to the switch to enable all VLANs to pass to the router.

In this lab, you will create VLANs on both switches in the topology, assign VLANs to switch access ports, verify that VLANs are working as expected, create VLAN trunks between the two switches and between S1 and R1, and configure Inter-VLAN routing on R1 to allow hosts in different VLANs to communicate, regardless of which subnet the host resides.

Note: The routers used with CCNA hands-on labs are Cisco 4221 with Cisco IOS XE Release 16.9.4 (universalk9 image). The switches used in the labs are Cisco Catalyst 2960s with Cisco IOS Release 15.2(2) (lanbasek9 image). Other routers, switches, and Cisco IOS versions can be used. Depending on the model and Cisco IOS version, the commands available and the output produced might vary from what is shown in the labs. Refer to the Router Interface Summary Table at the end of the lab for the correct interface identifiers.

Note: Ensure that the routers and switches have been erased and have no startup configurations. If you are unsure, contact your instructor.

Required Resources

- 1 Router (Cisco 4221 with Cisco IOS XE Release 16.9.4 universal image or comparable)
- 2 Switches (Cisco 2960 with Cisco IOS Release 15.2(2) lanbasek9 image or comparable)
- 2 PCs (Windows with a terminal emulation program, such as Tera Term)
- Console cables to configure the Cisco IOS devices via the console ports
- Ethernet cables as shown in the topology

Instructions

Part 1: Build the Network and Configure Basic Device Settings

In Part 1, you will set up the network topology and configure basic settings on the PC hosts and switches.

Step 1:   Cable the network as shown in the topology.

Attach the devices as shown in the topology diagram, and cable as necessary.

Step 2: Configure basic settings for the router.

    a. Console into the router and enable privileged EXEC mode.

    b. Enter configuration mode.

    c. Assign a device name to the router.

    d. Disable DNS lookup to prevent the router from attempting to translate incorrectly entered commands as though they were host names.

    e. Assign **class** as the privileged EXEC encrypted password.

    f. Assign **cisco** as the console password and enable login.

    g. Assign **cisco** as the VTY password and enable login.

    h. Encrypt the plaintext passwords.

    i. Create a banner that warns anyone accessing the device that unauthorized access is prohibited.

    j. Save the running configuration to the startup configuration file.

    k. Set the clock on the router.

> **Note:** Use the question mark (**?**) to help with the correct sequence of parameters needed to execute this command.

Step 3: Configure basic settings for each switch.

    a. Console into the switch and enable privileged EXEC mode.

    b. Enter configuration mode.

    c. Assign a device name to the switch.

    d. Disable DNS lookup to prevent the router from attempting to translate incorrectly entered commands as though they were host names.

    e. Assign **class** as the privileged EXEC encrypted password.

    f. Assign **cisco** as the console password and enable login.

    g. Assign **cisco** as the VTY password and enable login.

    h. Encrypt the plaintext passwords.

    i. Create a banner that warns anyone accessing the device that unauthorized access is prohibited.

    j. Set the clock on the switch.

> **Note:** Use the question mark (**?**) to help with the correct sequence of parameters needed to execute this command.

    k. Copy the running configuration to the startup configuration.

Step 4: Configure PC hosts.

Refer to the Addressing Table for PC host address information.

Part 2: Create VLANs and Assign Switch Ports

In Part 2, you will create VLANs, as specified in the table above, on both switches. You will then assign the VLANs to the appropriate interface. The **show vlan** command is used to verify your configuration settings. Complete the following tasks on each switch.

Step 1:   Create VLANs on both switches.

    a.   Create and name the required VLANs on each switch from the table above.

    b.   Configure the management interface and default gateway on each switch using the IP address information in the Addressing Table.

    c.   Assign all unused ports on both switches to the ParkingLot VLAN, configure them for static access mode, and administratively deactivate them.

    Note: The interface range command is helpful to accomplish this task with as few commands as necessary.

Step 2:   Assign VLANs to the correct switch interfaces.

    a.   Assign used ports to the appropriate VLAN (specified in the VLAN table above) and configure them for static access mode. Be sure to do this on both switches.

    b.   Issue the **show vlan brief** command and verify that the VLANs are assigned to the correct interfaces.

Part 3: Configure an 802.1Q Trunk Between the Switches

In Part 3, you will manually configure interface F0/1 as a trunk.

Step 1:   Manually configure trunk interface F0/1.

    a.   Change the switchport mode on interface F0/1 to force trunking. Make sure to do this on both switches.

    b.   As a part of the trunk configuration, set the native VLAN to 8 on both switches. You may see error messages temporarily while the two interfaces are configured for different native VLANs.

    c.   As another part of trunk configuration, specify that VLANs 3, 4, and 8 are only allowed to cross the trunk.

    d.   Issue the **show interfaces trunk** command to verify trunking ports, the Native VLAN and allowed VLANs across the trunk.

Step 2:   Manually configure S1's trunk interface F0/5.

    a.   Configure F0/5 on S1 with the same trunk parameters as F0/1. This is the trunk to the router.

    b.   Save the running configuration to the startup configuration file on S1 and S2.

c. Issue the **show interfaces trunk** command to verify trunking.

Question:

Why does F0/5 not appear in the list of trunks?

Part 4: Configure Inter-VLAN Routing on the Router

a. Activate interface G0/0/1 on the router.

b. Configure sub-interfaces for each VLAN as specified in the IP addressing table. All sub-interfaces use 802.1Q encapsulation. Ensure the sub-interface for the native VLAN does not have an IP address assigned. Include a description for each sub-interface.

c. Use the **show ip interface brief** command to verify the sub-interfaces are operational.

Part 5: Verify Inter-VLAN Routing is Working

Step 1: Complete the following tests from PC-A. All should be successful.

Note: You may have to disable the PC firewall for pings to be successful.

a. Ping from PC-A to its default gateway

b. Ping from PC-A to PC-B

c. Ping from PC-A to S2

Step 2: Complete the following test from PC-B.

From the command prompt on PC-B, issue the **tracert** command to the address of PC-A.

Question:

What intermediate IP addresses are shown in the results?

Router Interface Summary Table

Router Model	Ethernet Interface #1	Ethernet Interface #2	Serial Interface #1	Serial Interface #2
1800	Fast Ethernet 0/0 (F0/0)	Fast Ethernet 0/1 (F0/1)	Serial 0/0/0 (S0/0/0)	Serial 0/0/1 (S0/0/1)
1900	Gigabit Ethernet 0/0 (G0/0)	Gigabit Ethernet 0/1 (G0/1)	Serial 0/0/0 (S0/0/0)	Serial 0/0/1 (S0/0/1)
2801	Fast Ethernet 0/0 (F0/0)	Fast Ethernet 0/1 (F0/1)	Serial 0/1/0 (S0/1/0)	Serial 0/1/1 (S0/1/1)
2811	Fast Ethernet 0/0 (F0/0)	Fast Ethernet 0/1 (F0/1)	Serial 0/0/0 (S0/0/0)	Serial 0/0/1 (S0/0/1)
2900	Gigabit Ethernet 0/0 (G0/0)	Gigabit Ethernet 0/1 (G0/1)	Serial 0/0/0 (S0/0/0)	Serial 0/0/1 (S0/0/1)

Router Model	Ethernet Interface #1	Ethernet Interface #2	Serial Interface #1	Serial Interface #2
4221	Gigabit Ethernet 0/0/0 (G0/0/0)	Gigabit Ethernet 0/0/1 (G0/0/1)	Serial 0/1/0 (S0/1/0)	Serial 0/1/1 (S0/1/1)
4300	Gigabit Ethernet 0/0/0 (G0/0/0)	Gigabit Ethernet 0/0/1 (G0/0/1)	Serial 0/1/0 (S0/1/0)	Serial 0/1/1 (S0/1/1)

Note: To find out how the router is configured, look at the interfaces to identify the type of router and how many interfaces the router has. There is no way to effectively list all the combinations of configurations for each router class. This table includes identifiers for the possible combinations of Ethernet and Serial interfaces in the device. The table does not include any other type of interface, even though a specific router may contain one. An example of this might be an ISDN BRI interface. The string in parenthesis is the legal abbreviation that can be used in Cisco IOS commands to represent the interface.

Packet Tracer
☐ Activity

4.3.8 Packet Tracer—Configure Layer 3 Switching and Inter-VLAN Routing

Addressing Table

Device	Interface	IP Address / Prefix
MLS	VLAN 10	192.168.10.254/24
		2001:db8:acad:10::1/64
	VLAN 20	192.168.20.254/24
		2001:db8:acad:20::1/64
	VLAN 30	192.168.30.254/24
		2001:db8:acad:30::1/64
	VLAN 99	192.168.99.254/24
	G0/2	209.165.200.225
		2001:db8:acad:a::1/64
PC0	NIC	192.168.10.1
PC1	NIC	192.168.20.1
PC2	NIC	192.168.30.1
PC3	NIC	192.168.10.2/24
		2001:db8:acad:10::2/64
PC4	NIC	192.168.20.2/24
		2001:db8:acad:20::2/64
PC5	NIC	192.168.30.2
		2001:db8:acad:10::2/64
S1	VLAN 99	192.168.99.1
S2	VLAN 99	192.168.99.2
S3	VLAN 99	192.168.99.3

Objectives

Part 1: Configure Layer 3 Switching

Part 2: Configure Inter-VLAN Routing

Part 3: Configure IPv6 Inter-VLAN Routing

Background / Scenario

A multilayer switch like the Cisco Catalyst 3650 is capable of both Layer 2 switching and Layer 3 routing. One of the advantages of using a multilayer switch is this dual functionality. A benefit for a small to medium-sized company would be the ability to purchase a single multilayer switch instead of separate switching and routing network devices. Capabilities of a multilayer switch include the ability to route from one VLAN to another using multiple switched virtual interfaces (SVIs), as well as the ability to convert a Layer 2 switch port to a Layer 3 interface.

Instructions

Part 1: Configure Layer 3 Switching

In Part 1, you will configure the GigabitEthernet 0/2 port on switch MLS as a routed port and verify that you can ping another Layer 3 address.

- **a.** On MLS, configure G0/2 as a routed port and assign an IP address according to the Addressing Table.

  ```
  MLS(config)# interface g0/2
  MLS(config-if)# no switchport
  MLS(config-if)# ip address 209.165.200.225 255.255.255.252
  ```

- **b.** Verify connectivity to **Cloud** by pinging 209.165.200.226.

  ```
  MLS# ping 209.165.200.226

  Type escape sequence to abort.
  Sending 5, 100-byte ICMP Echos to 209.165.200.226, timeout is 2 seconds:
  !!!!!
  Success rate is 100 percent (5/5), round-trip min/avg/max = 0/0/0 ms
  ```

Part 2: Configure Inter-VLAN Routing

Step 1:   Add VLANs.

Add VLANs to MLS according to the table below. Packet Tracer scoring is case-sensitive, so type the names exactly as shown.

VLAN Number	VLAN Name
10	Staff
20	Student
30	Faculty

Step 2:   Configure SVI on MLS.

Configure and activate the SVI interfaces for VLANs 10, 20, 30, and 99 according to the Addressing Table. The configuration for VLAN 10 is shown below as an example.

```
MLS(config)# interface vlan 10
MLS(config-if)# ip address 192.168.10.254 255.255.255.0
```

Step 3:   Configure Trunking on MLS.

Trunk configuration differs slightly on a Layer 3 switch. On the Layer 3 switch, the trunking interface needs to be encapsulated with the dot1q protocol, however it is not necessary to specify VLAN numbers as it is when working with a router and subinterfaces.

- **a.** On MLS, configure interface **g0/1**.

- **b.** Make the interface a static trunk port.

  ```
  MLS(config-if)# switchport mode trunk
  ```

c. Specify the native VLAN as 99.

```
MLS(config-if)# switchport trunk native vlan 99
```

d. Encapsulate the link with the dot1q protocol.

```
MLS(config-if)# switchport trunk encapsulation dot1q
```

Note: Packet Tracer may not score the trunk encapsulation.

Step 4: Configure trunking on S1.

a. Configure interface **g0/1** of S1 as a static trunk.

b. Configure the native VLAN on the trunk.

Step 5: Enable routing.

Question:

a. Use the **show ip route** command. Are there any active routes?

b. Enter the **ip routing** command to enable routing in global configuration mode.

```
MLS(config)# ip routing
```

c. Use the **show ip route** command to verify routing is enabled.

```
MLS# show ip route
Codes: C - connected, S - static, I - IGRP, R - RIP, M - mobile,
       B - BGP
       D - EIGRP, EX - EIGRP external, O - OSPF, IA - OSPF inter area
       N1 - OSPF NSSA external type 1, N2 - OSPF NSSA external type 2
       E1 - OSPF external type 1, E2 - OSPF external type 2, E - EGP
       i - IS-IS, L1 - IS-IS level-1, L2 - IS-IS level-2, ia - IS-IS
       inter area
       * - candidate default, U - per-user static route, o - ODR
       P - periodic downloaded static route

Gateway of last resort is not set

C    192.168.10.0/24 is directly connected, Vlan10
C    192.168.20.0/24 is directly connected, Vlan20
C    192.168.30.0/24 is directly connected, Vlan30
C    192.168.99.0/24 is directly connected, Vlan99
     209.165.200.0/30 is subnetted, 1 subnets
C    209.165.200.224 is directly connected, GigabitEthernet0/2
```

Step 6: Verify end-to-end connectivity.

a. From PC0, ping PC3 or MLS to verify connectivity within VLAN 10.

b. From PC1, ping PC4 or MLS to verify connectivity within VLAN 20.

c. From PC2, ping PC5 or MLS to verify connectivity within VLAN 30.

d. From S1, ping S2, S3, or MLS to verify connectivity with VLAN 99.

e. To verify inter-VLAN routing, ping devices outside the sender's VLAN.

f. From any device, ping this address inside **Cloud**, 209.165.200.226.

The Layer 3 switch is now routing between VLANs and providing routed connectivity to the cloud.

Part 3: Configure IPv6 Inter-VLAN Routing

Layer 3 switches also route between IPv6 networks.

Step 1:   Enable IPv6 routing.

Enter the **ipv6 unicast-routing** command to enable IPv6 routing in global configuration mode.

```
MLS(config)# ipv6 unicast-routing
```

Step 2:   Configure SVI for IPv6 on MLS.

Configure IPv6 addressing on SVI for VLANs 10, 20, and 30 according to the Addressing Table. The configuration for VLAN 10 is shown below.

```
MLS(config)# interface vlan 10
MLS(config-if)# ipv6 address 2001:db8:acad:10::1/64
```

Step 3:   Configure G0/2 with IPv6 on MLS.

   a.   Configure IPv6 addressing on G0/2.

```
MLS(config)# interface G0/2
MLS(config-if)# ipv6 address 2001:db8:acad:a::1/64
```

   b.   Use the **show ipv6 route** command to verify IPv6 connected networks.

```
MLS# show ipv6 route
IPv6 Routing Table - 10 entries
Codes: C - Connected, L - Local, S - Static, R - RIP, B - BGP
       U - Per-user Static route, M - MIPv6
       I1 - ISIS L1, I2 - ISIS L2, IA - ISIS interarea, IS - ISIS
       summary
       O - OSPF intra, OI - OSPF inter, OE1 - OSPF ext 1, OE2 - OSPF
       ext 2
       ON1 - OSPF NSSA ext 1, ON2 - OSPF NSSA ext 2
       D - EIGRP, EX - EIGRP external
S    ::/0 [1/0]
       via 2001:DB8:ACAD:A::2, GigabitEthernet0/2
C    2001:DB8:ACAD:A::/64 [0/0]
       via ::, GigabitEthernet0/2
L    2001:DB8:ACAD:A::1/128 [0/0]
       via ::, GigabitEthernet0/2
C    2001:DB8:ACAD:10::/64 [0/0]
       via ::, Vlan10
L    2001:DB8:ACAD:10::1/128 [0/0]
       via ::, Vlan10
C    2001:DB8:ACAD:20::/64 [0/0]
       via ::, Vlan20
L    2001:DB8:ACAD:20::1/128 [0/0]
       via ::, Vlan20
C    2001:DB8:ACAD:30::/64 [0/0]
       via ::, Vlan30
```

```
L    2001:DB8:ACAD:30::1/128 [0/0]
        via ::, Vlan30
L    FF00::/8 [0/0]
        via ::, Null0
```

Step 4: Verify IPv6 connectivity.

Devices PC3, PC4, and PC5 have been configured with IPv6 addresses. Verify IPv6 inter-VLAN routing and connectivity to **Cloud**.

a. From PC3, ping MLS to verify connectivity within VLAN 10.

b. From PC4, ping MLS to verify connectivity within VLAN 20.

c. From PC5, ping MLS to verify connectivity within VLAN 30.

d. To verify inter-VLAN routing, ping between devices PC3, PC4, and PC5.

e. From PC3, ping the address inside **Cloud**, 2001:db8:acad:a::2.

4.4.8 Packet Tracer—Troubleshoot Inter-VLAN Routing

Addressing Table

Device	Interface	IP Address	Subnet Mask	Default Gateway	VLAN
R1	G0/1.10	172.17.10.1	255.255.255.0	N/A	VLAN 10
	G0/1.30	172.17.30.1	255.255.255.0	N/A	VLAN 30
PC1	NIC	172.17.10.10	255.255.255.0	172.17.10.1	VLAN 10
PC3	NIC	172.17.30.10	255.255.255.0	172.17.30.1	VLAN 30

Objectives

Part 1: Locate Network Problems

Part 2: Implement the Solution

Part 3: Verify Network Connectivity

Scenario

In this activity, you will troubleshoot connectivity problems caused by improper configurations related to VLANs and inter-VLAN routing.

Instructions

Part 1: Locate the Network Problems

Examine the network and locate the source of any connectivity issues.

Commands you may find useful include:

```
R1# show ip interface brief
R1# show interface g0/1.10
R1# show interface g0/1.30
S1# show interface trunk
```

- Test connectivity and use the necessary **show** commands to verify configurations.

- Verify that all configured settings match the requirements shown in the Addressing Table.

- List all of the problems and possible solutions in the Documentation Table.

Documentation Table

Problems	Solutions

Part 2: Implement the Solutions

Implement your recommended solutions.

Part 3: Verify Network Connectivity

Verify the PCs can ping each other and R1. If not, continue to troubleshoot until the pings are successful.

4.4.9 Lab—Troubleshoot Inter-VLAN Routing

Topology

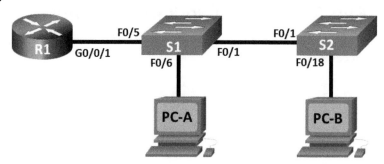

Addressing Table

Device	Interface	IP Address	Subnet Mask	Default Gateway
R1	G0/0/1.3	10.3.0.1	255.255.255.0	N/A
	G0/0/1.4	10.4.0.1	255.255.255.0	
	G0/0/1.13	10.13.0.1	255.255.255.0	
S1	VLAN 3	10.3.0.11	255.255.255.0	10.3.0.1
S2	VLAN 3	10.3.0.12	255.255.255.0	10.3.0.1
PC-A	NIC	10.4.0.50	255.255.255.0	10.4.0.1
PC-B	NIC	10.13.0.50	255.255.255.0	10.13.0.1

VLAN Table

VLAN	Name	Interface Assigned
3	Management	S1: VLAN 3
		S2: VLAN 3
4	Operations	S1: F0/6
7	ParkingLot	S1: F0/2-4, F0/7-24, G0/1-2
		S2: F0/2-17, F0/19-24, G0/1-2
8	Native	N/A
13	Maintenance	S2: F0/18

Objectives

Part 1: Evaluate Network Operation

Part 2: Gather information, create an action plan, and implement corrections

Background / Scenario

Your instructor has preconfigured all the network equipment and has included intentional errors that are keeping the inter-VLAN routing from working. Your task is to evaluate the network and identify and correct the configuration errors to restore full connectivity. You may find errors with the configurations which are not directly related to inter-VLAN routing that impact the ability of the network devices to perform this function.

Note: The design approach used in this lab is to assess your ability to configure and troubleshoot inter-VLAN routing only. This design may not reflect networking best practices.

Note: The router used with CCNA hands-on labs it the Cisco 4221 with Cisco IOS XE Release 16.9.4 (universalk9 image). The switches used in the labs are Cisco Catalyst 2960s with Cisco IOS Release 15.2(2) (lanbasek9 image). Other routers, switches, and Cisco IOS versions can be used. Depending on the model and Cisco IOS version, the commands available and the output produced might vary from what is shown in the labs. Refer to the Router Interface Summary Table at the end of the lab for the correct interface identifiers.

Note: Ensure that the routers and switches have been erased and have no startup configurations. If you are unsure contact your instructor.

Required Resources

- 1 Router (Cisco 4221 with Cisco IOS XE Release 16.9.4 universal image or comparable)
- 2 Switches (Cisco 2960 with Cisco IOS Release 15.2(2) lanbasek9 image or comparable)
- 2 PCs (Windows with a terminal emulation program, such as Tera Term)
- Console cables to configure the Cisco IOS devices via the console ports
- Ethernet cables as shown in the topology

Instructions

Part 1: Evaluate Network Operation.

Note: You may need to disable the Windows Firewall on PC-A and PC-B.

Requirement:

- No VLAN 7 trunk traffic because there are no devices in VLAN 7.
- VLAN 8 is the native VLAN.
- All trunks are static.
- End-to-end connectivity.

Use Ping to test the following criteria and record the results in the table below.

From	To	Ping Results
R1	S1 VLAN 3 (10.3.0.11)	
	S2 VLAN 3 (10.3.0.12)	
	PC-A (10.4.0.50)	
	PC-B (10.13.0.50)	

From	To	Ping Results
S1	S2 VLAN 3 (10.3.0.12)	
	PC-A (10.4.0.50)	
	PC-B (10.13.0.50)	
S2	PC-A (10.4.0.50)	
	PC-B (10.13.0.50)	

Part 2: Gather information, create an action plan, and implement corrections.

a. For each criterion that is not met, gather information by examining the running configuration and routing tables and develop a hypothesis for what is causing the malfunction.

b. Create an action plan that you think will fix the issue. Develop a list of all the commands you intend to issue to fix the issue, and a list of all the commands you need to revert the configuration, should your action plan fail to correct the issue.

Hint: If you need to reset a switch port to default configuration, use the command **default interface** *interface name*.

As an example for F0/10:

```
S1(config)# default interface f0/10
```

c. Execute your action plans one at a time for each criterion that fails and record the fix actions.

Packet Tracer
☐ Activity

4.5.1 Packet Tracer—Inter-VLAN Routing Challenge

Addressing Table

Device	Interface	IP Address	Subnet Mask	Default Gateway
R1	G0/0	172.17.25.2	255.255.255.252	N/A
	G0/1.10	172.17.10.1	255.255.255.0	
	G0/1.20	172.17.20.1	255.255.255.0	
	G0/1.30	172.17.30.1	255.255.255.0	
	G0/1.88	172.17.88.1	255.255.255.0	
	G0/1.99	172.17.99.1	255.255.255.0	
S1	VLAN 99	172.17.99.10	255.255.255.0	172.17.99.1
PC1	NIC	172.17.10.21	255.255.255.0	172.17.10.1
PC2	NIC	172.17.20.22	255.255.255.0	172.17.20.1
PC3	NIC	172.17.30.23	255.255.255.0	172.17.30.1
Server	NIC	172.17.50.254	255.255.255.0	172.17.50.1

VLAN and Port Assignments Table

VLAN	Name	Interface
10	Faculty/Staff	F0/11-17
20	Students	F0/18-24
30	Guest(Default)	F0/6-10
88	Native	G0/1
99	Management	VLAN 99

Scenario

In this activity, you will demonstrate and reinforce your ability to implement inter-VLAN routing, including configuring IP addresses, VLANs, trunking, and subinterfaces.

Instructions

Configure the devices to meet the following requirements.

- Assign IP addressing to R1 and S1 based on the Addressing Table.

- Configure the default gateway on S1.

- Create, name, and assign VLANs on S1 based on the VLAN and Port Assignments Table. Ports should be in access mode. Your VLAN names should match the names in the table exactly.

- Configure G0/1 of S1 as a static trunk and assign the native VLAN.

- All ports that are not assigned to a VLAN should be disabled.

- Configure inter-VLAN routing on R1 based on the Addressing Table.

- Verify connectivity. R1, S1, and all PCs should be able to ping each other and the server.

4.5.2 Lab—Implement Inter-VLAN Routing

Topology

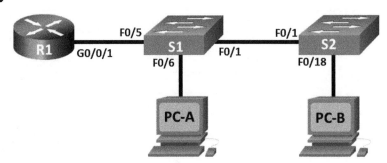

Addressing Table

Device	Interface	IP Address	Subnet Mask	Default Gateway
R1	G0/0/1.10	192.168.10.1	255.255.255.0	N/A
	G0/0/1.20	192.168.20.1	255.255.255.0	
	G0/0/1.30	192.168.30.1	255.255.255.0	
	G0/0/1.1000	N/A	N/A	
S1	VLAN 10	192.168.10.11	255.255.255.0	192.168.10.1
S2	VLAN 10	192.168.10.12	255.255.255.0	192.168.10.1
PC-A	NIC	192.168.20.3	255.255.255.0	192.168.20.1
PC-B	NIC	192.168.30.3	255.255.255.0	192.168.30.1

VLAN Table

VLAN	Name	Interface Assigned
10	Management	S1: VLAN 10
		S2: VLAN 10
20	Sales	S1: F0/6
30	Operations	S2: F0/18
999	Parking_Lot	S1: F0/2-4, F0/7-24, G0/1-2
		S2: F0/2-17, F0/19-24, G0/1-2
1000	Native	N/A

Objectives

Part 1: Build the Network and Configure Basic Device Settings

Part 2: Create VLANs and Assign Switch Ports

Part 3: Configure an 802.1Q Trunk between the Switches

Part 4: Configure Inter-VLAN Routing on the Router

Part 5: Verify Inter-VLAN Routing is Working

Background / Scenario

Modern switches use virtual local-area networks (VLANs) to improve network performance by separating large Layer 2 broadcast domains into smaller ones. VLANs can also be used as a security measure by separating sensitive data traffic from the rest of the network. In general, VLANs make it easier to design a network to support the goals of an organization. Communication between VLANs requires a device operating at Layer 3 of the OSI model. Adding an inter-VLAN router allows the organization to segregate and separate broadcast domains while simultaneously allowing them to communicate with each other.

VLAN trunks are used to span VLANs across multiple devices. Trunks allow the traffic from multiple VLANs to travel over a single link, while keeping the VLAN identification and segmentation intact. A particular kind of inter-VLAN routing, called "Router-on-a-Stick", uses a trunk from the router to the switch to enable all VLANs to pass to the router.

In this lab, you will create VLANs on both switches in the topology, assign VLANs to switch access ports, verify that VLANs are working as expected, create VLAN trunks between the two switches and between S1 and R1, and configure inter-VLAN routing on R1 to allow hosts in different VLANs to communicate, regardless of which subnet the host resides.

Note: The routers used with CCNA hands-on labs are Cisco 4221 with Cisco IOS XE Release 16.9.4 (universalk9 image). The switches used in the labs are Cisco Catalyst 2960s with Cisco IOS Release 15.2(2) (lanbasek9 image). Other routers, switches, and Cisco IOS versions can be used. Depending on the model and Cisco IOS version, the commands available and the output produced might vary from what is shown in the labs. Refer to the Router Interface Summary Table at the end of the lab for the correct interface identifiers.

Note: Ensure that the routers and switches have been erased and have no startup configurations. If you are unsure contact your instructor.

Required Resources

- 1 Router (Cisco 4221 with Cisco IOS XE Release 16.9.4 universal image or comparable)
- 2 Switches (Cisco 2960 with Cisco IOS Release 15.2(2) lanbasek9 image or comparable)
- 2 PCs (Windows with a terminal emulation program, such as Tera Term)
- Console cables to configure the Cisco IOS devices via the console ports
- Ethernet cables as shown in the topology

Instructions

Part 1: Build the Network and Configure Basic Device Settings

In Part 1, you will set up the network topology and configure basic settings on the PC hosts and switches.

Step 1:   Cable the network as shown in the topology.

Attach the devices as shown in the topology diagram, and cable as necessary.

Step 2:   Configure basic settings for the router.

    a.   Console into the router and enable privileged EXEC mode.

    b.   Enter configuration mode.

    c.   Assign a device name to the router.

    d.   Disable DNS lookup to prevent the router from attempting to translate incorrectly entered commands as though they were host names.

    e.   Assign **class** as the privileged EXEC encrypted password.

    f.   Assign **cisco** as the console password and enable login.

    g.   Assign **cisco** as the VTY password and enable login.

    h.   Encrypt the plaintext passwords.

    i.   Create a banner that warns anyone accessing the device that unauthorized access is prohibited.

    j.   Save the running configuration to the startup configuration file.

    k.   Set the clock on the router.

Step 3:   Configure basic settings for each switch.

    a.   Assign a device name to the switch.

    b.   Disable DNS lookup to prevent the router from attempting to translate incorrectly entered commands as though they were host names.

    c.   Assign **class** as the privileged EXEC encrypted password.

    d.   Assign **cisco** as the console password and enable login.

    e.   Assign **cisco** as the VTY password and enable login.

    f.   Encrypt the plaintext passwords.

    g.   Create a banner that warns anyone accessing the device that unauthorized access is prohibited.

    h.   Set the clock on the switch.

    i.   Save the running configuration to the startup configuration.

Step 4:   Configure PC hosts.

Refer to the Addressing Table for PC host address information.

Part 2: Create VLANs and Assign Switch Ports

In Part 2, you will create VLANs as specified in the table above on both switches. You will then assign the VLANs to the appropriate interface and verify your configuration settings. Complete the following tasks on each switch.

Step 1:   Create VLANs on both switches.

    a.   Create and name the required VLANs on each switch from the table above.

    b.   Configure the management interface and default gateway on each switch using the IP address information in the Addressing Table.

c.   Assign all unused ports on the switch to the Parking_Lot VLAN, configure them for static access mode, and administratively deactivate them.

Note: The interface range command is helpful to accomplish this task with as few commands as necessary.

Step 2:   Assign VLANs to the correct switch interfaces.

a.   Assign used ports to the appropriate VLAN (specified in the VLAN table above) and configure them for static access mode.

b.   Verify that the VLANs are assigned to the correct interfaces.

Part 3: Configure an 802.1Q Trunk Between the Switches

In Part 3, you will manually configure interface F0/1 as a trunk.

Step 1:   Manually configure trunk interface F0/1 on switch S1 and S2.

a.   Configure static trunking on interface F0/1 for both switches.

b.   Set the native VLAN to 1000 on both switches.

c.   Specify that VLANs 10, 20, 30, and 1000 are allowed to cross the trunk.

d.   Verify trunking ports, the Native VLAN and allowed VLANs across the trunk.

Step 2:   Manually configure S1's trunk interface F0/5

a.   Configure S1's interface F0/5 with the same trunk parameters as F0/1. This is the trunk to the router.

b.   Save the running configuration to the startup configuration file.

c.   Verify trunking.

Question:

What happens if G0/0/1 on R1 is down?

Part 4: Configure Inter-VLAN Routing on the Router

Step 1:   Configure the router.

a.   Activate interface G0/0/1 as necessary on the router.

b.   Configure sub-interfaces for each VLAN as specified in the IP addressing table. All sub-interfaces use 802.1Q encapsulation. Ensure the sub-interface for the native VLAN does not have an IP address assigned. Include a description for each sub-interface.

c.   Verify the sub-interfaces are operational.

Part 5: Verify Inter-VLAN Routing is Working

Step 1:   Complete the following tests from PC-A. All should be successful.

Note: You may have to disable the PC firewall for pings to work

---

a.   Ping from PC-A to its default gateway

b.   Ping from PC-A to PC-B

c.   Ping from PC-A to S2

Step 2:   Complete the following test from PC-B.

From the Command Prompt window on PC-B, issue the **tracert** command to the address of PC-A.

Question:

What intermediate IP addresses are shown in the results?

Router Interface Summary Table

Router Model	Ethernet Interface #1	Ethernet Interface #2	Serial Interface #1	Serial Interface #2
1800	Fast Ethernet 0/0 (F0/0)	Fast Ethernet 0/1 (F0/1)	Serial 0/0/0 (S0/0/0)	Serial 0/0/1 (S0/0/1)
1900	Gigabit Ethernet 0/0 (G0/0)	Gigabit Ethernet 0/1 (G0/1)	Serial 0/0/0 (S0/0/0)	Serial 0/0/1 (S0/0/1)
2801	Fast Ethernet 0/0 (F0/0)	Fast Ethernet 0/1 (F0/1)	Serial 0/1/0 (S0/1/0)	Serial 0/1/1 (S0/1/1)
2811	Fast Ethernet 0/0 (F0/0)	Fast Ethernet 0/1 (F0/1)	Serial 0/0/0 (S0/0/0)	Serial 0/0/1 (S0/0/1)
2900	Gigabit Ethernet 0/0 (G0/0)	Gigabit Ethernet 0/1 (G0/1)	Serial 0/0/0 (S0/0/0)	Serial 0/0/1 (S0/0/1)
4221	Gigabit Ethernet 0/0/0 (G0/0/0)	Gigabit Ethernet 0/0/1 (G0/0/1)	Serial 0/1/0 (S0/1/0)	Serial 0/1/1 (S0/1/1)
4300	Gigabit Ethernet 0/0/0 (G0/0/0)	Gigabit Ethernet 0/0/1 (G0/0/1)	Serial 0/1/0 (S0/1/0)	Serial 0/1/1 (S0/1/1)

Note: To find out how the router is configured, look at the interfaces to identify the type of router and how many interfaces the router has. There is no way to effectively list all the combinations of configurations for each router class. This table includes identifiers for the possible combinations of Ethernet and Serial interfaces in the device. The table does not include any other type of interface, even though a specific router may contain one. An example of this might be an ISDN BRI interface. The string in parenthesis is the legal abbreviation that can be used in Cisco IOS commands to represent the interface.

CHAPTER 5

STP Concepts

The "Study Guide" portion of this chapter uses a variety of exercises to test your knowledge of how Spanning Tree Protocol (STP) enables redundancy in a Layer 2 network. The "Labs and Activities" portion of this chapter includes the online curriculum Packet Tracer activity instructions. There are no labs for this chapter.

As you work through this chapter, use Chapter 5 in *Switching, Routing, and Wireless Essentials v7 Companion Guide* or use the corresponding Chapter 5 in the Switching, Routing, and Wireless Essentials online curriculum for assistance.

Study Guide

Purpose of STP

In this section, you review common problems in a redundant Layer 2 switched network.

Issues with Redundant Switch Links

When multiple paths exist between two devices on an Ethernet network, and there is no spanning-tree implementation on the switches, a Layer 2 loop occurs. A Layer 2 loop can result in Media Access Control (MAC) address table instability, link saturation, and high CPU utilization on switches and end devices; these factors contribute to the network becoming unusable.

Layer 2 Loops

Briefly explain why a broadcast frame would cause a loop in a redundant switched network without STP.

_____

_____

_____

_____

Briefly explain how a unicast frame could cause a loop in a redundant switched network without STP.

_____

_____

_____

_____

Broadcast Storm

Briefly describe a broadcast storm and how these storms are caused.

_____

_____

_____

_____

The Spanning-Tree Algorithm

Briefly describe how STP uses the spanning-tree algorithm (STA) to create a loop-free topology and adjusts when there is a link failure.

_____

_____

_____

_____

_____

_____

Check Your Understanding—Purpose of STP

Check your understanding of the purpose of STP by choosing the BEST answer to each of the following questions.

1. Which statement best describes STP?

   a. STP is a Layer 2 routing protocol.

   b. STP is a Layer 3 routing protocol for Ethernet LANs.

   c. STP is a Layer 2 loop-prevention protocol for Ethernet LANs.

   d. STP is a Layer 3 loop-prevention protocol for IP networks.

2. Without STP on an Ethernet LAN, which three types of frames could cause catastrophic loops in the network? (Choose three.)

   a. unicast

   b. unknown unicast

   c. multicast

   d. broadcast

3. Which of the following is the device the spanning-tree algorithm elects as the device to which all other switches determine a single least-cost path?

   a. root bridge

   b. dedicated bridge

   c. default gateway

   d. core switch

STP Operation

In this section, you review the steps STP uses to create a loop-free topology.

Steps to a Loop-Free Topology

STP builds a loop-free topology in a four-step process:

Step 1.   Elect the root bridge.

Step 2.   Elect the root ports.

Step 3.   Elect designated ports.

Step 4.   Elect alternate (blocked) ports.

During STA and STP functions, switches use bridge protocol data units (BPDUs) to share information about themselves and their connections. The BPDU includes a field that identifies the switch's bridge identification (BID). The structure of the BID is shown in Figure 5-1.

Figure 5-1   BID Structure

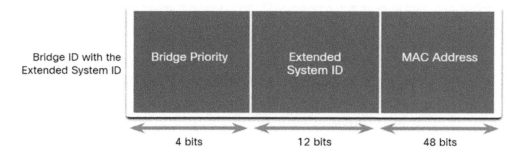

Briefly describe the purpose of each field in the BID.

Bridge Priority

_____

_____

Extended System ID

_____

_____

MAC Address

_____

_____

_____

Note: The curriculum does not show the structure of the full BPDU. However, important fields that you should know about, including the BID, are shown in Table 5-1.

Table 5-1   Fields in the BPDU

Field	Description
Root ID	The BID of the switch that currently believes it is root.
Sender BID	The BID of the sending switch.
Sender root cost	The cost between this switch and the root switch.
Timers	The root switch hello, MaxAge, and forwarding delay timers.

1. Elect the Root Bridge

An election process determines which switch becomes the root bridge. All switches in the broadcast domain participate in the election process.

How often does a switch send out BPDUs?

_____

These BPDU frames contain the BID of the sending switch and the BID of the root bridge, known as the root ID.

What will be the root ID for the BPDU that the switch sends out when it first boots?

_____

In an election, which switch becomes the root bridge?

_____

Which switch becomes root if two switches have the same priority or the default priority 32,768?

_____

How can an administrator ensure that the desired switch becomes root?

_____

When the root bridge has been elected for a given spanning-tree instance, the STA starts the process of determining the best paths to the root bridge from all destinations in the broadcast domain. The path information, known as the internal root path cost, is determined by the sum of all the individual port costs along the path from the switch to the root bridge.

In Table 5-2, fill in the default port costs suggested by IEEE for both STP and RSTP.

Table 5-2   IEEE Recommended Path Costs

Link Speed	STP Cost: IEEE 802.1D-1998	RSTP Cost: IEEE 802.1w-2004
10 Gbps		
1 Gbps		
100 Mbps		
10 Mbps		

2. Elect the Root Ports

After the root bridge has been determined, the STA is used to select the root port.

Which switches select root ports?

_____

How is the root port determined?

_____

How is the internal root path cost calculated?

_____

3. Elect Designated Ports

After each switch selects a root port, the switches select designated ports. Every segment between two switches has one designated port.

Briefly describe a designated port.

_____

A port that is not a root port or a designated port becomes an alternate or blocked port. The end result is a single path from every switch to the root bridge.

- All ports on the root bridge are designated ports because the root bridge has the lowest cost to itself.

- If one end of a segment is a root port, the other end is a designated port.

- If neither end of a segment is a root port, then the port on the switch with the least-cost path to the root bridge is the designated port for the segment.

4. Elect Alternate (Blocked) Ports

If a port is not a root port or a designated port, then it becomes an alternate (or backup) port. Alternate ports and backup ports are in discarding or blocking state to prevent loops.

Elect a Root Port from Multiple Equal-Cost Paths

Briefly describe how a switch designates a root port when there are multiple equal-cost paths to the root bridge.

_____

_____

_____

_____

STP Timers and Port States

Briefly describe each timer used for STP convergence:

- Hello timer: _____

_____

_____

- Forward delay timer: _____

_____

_____

- Max age timer: _____

_____

_____

Figure 5-2 shows the port states and timers that STP uses to reach convergence.

Figure 5-2   STP Port States

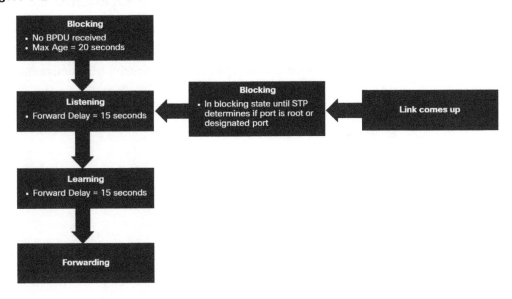

In Table 5-3, fill in a brief description for each port state.

Table 5-3   Port State Details

Port State	Description
Blocking	
Listening	
Learning	
Forwarding	
Disabled	

Operational Details of Each Port State

In Table 5-4, fill in the missing operational details of each port state.

Table 5-4   Operational Details of Each Port State

Port State	BPDU	MAC Address Table	Forwarding Data Frames
Blocking			
Listening			
Learning		Updating table	
Forwarding	Receive and send		Yes
Disabled		No update	

Check Your Understanding—STP Operations

Check your understanding of STP operations by choosing the BEST answer to each of the following questions.

1. By default (without any configuration on a switch), what determines which switch is the root bridge?

    a. the bridge priority

    b. the extended system ID

    c. the MAC address of the switch

    d. the bridge ID

2. The root bridge is the switch with the _____.

    a. lowest bridge ID

    b. highest bridge ID

    c. lowest port priority

    d. highest port priority

3. The port closest to the root bridge in terms of least overall cost (best path) to the root bridge is the _____.

    a. designated port

    b. blocked port or non-dedicated port

    c. root port

    d. routed port

4. The port on the segment (with two switches) that has the lowest path cost to the root bridge is the _____.

    a. designated port

    b. blocked port or non-dedicated port

    c. root port

    d. routed port

5. Which of the following ports forward Ethernet frames? (Choose two.)

    a. designated port

    b. blocked port or non-dedicated port

    c. root port

6. The sum of individual port costs along the path from the switch to the root bridge is known as the _____.

    a. least-cost path

    b. shortest-path cost

    c. best-path cost

    d. root-path cost

7. How often does a switch send a BPDU?

  a. every 2 seconds

  b. every 15 seconds

  c. every 20 seconds

  d. only when there is a change in the topology

Evolution of STP

In this section, you review the various versions of STP, focusing on how Rapid Per VLAN Spanning Tree Plus (Rapid PVST+) operates.

Different Versions of STP

Several varieties of spanning-tree protocols have emerged since the original IEEE 802.1D specification. In Table 5-5, fill in the missing information for each STP variety.

Table 5-5   Varieties of STP

Full Name	Abbreviation	Description
Spanning Tree Protocol	STP	The original IEEE 802.1D version (802.1D-1998 and earlier). Also called Common Spanning Tree (CST), it assumes one spanning tree instance for the entire bridged network, regardless of the number of VLANs.
		A Cisco enhancement of STP that provides a separate 802.1D spanning-tree instance for each VLAN configured in the network.
802.1D-2004	N/A	An updated version of the STP standard that incorporates IEEE 802.1w.
		IEEE 802.1w, an evolution of STP that provides faster convergence than STP.
		A Cisco enhancement of RSTP that uses PVST+ and provides a separate instance of 802.1w per VLAN.
		An IEEE standard that maps multiple VLANs to the same spanning-tree instance.
		The Cisco implementation of MSTP, which provides up to 16 instances of RSTP and combines many VLANs with the same physical and logical topology into a common RSTP instance.

What version of STP does Cisco IOS use by default?

RSTP Port States and Port Roles

RSTP increases the speed of the recalculation of the spanning tree when the Layer 2 network topology changes. If a port is configured to be an alternate port, it can immediately change to a forwarding state without waiting for the network to converge.

The STP and RSTP port states and port roles are similar. In Table 5-6, list the corresponding RSTP port states.

Table 5-6   STP and RSTP Port States

STP	RSTP
Disabled	
Blocking	
Listening	
Learning	
Forwarding	

In Table 5-7, list the corresponding RSTP port roles.

Table 5-7   STP and RSTP Port Roles

STP	RSTP
Root Port	
Designated Port	
Blocked Port	

PortFast and BPDU Guard

The default STP delay timers total 30 seconds and can present problems for Dynamic Host Configuration Protocol (DHCP) clients trying to discover a DHCP server. When a switch port is configured with PortFast, that port transitions from blocking to forwarding state immediately, bypassing the 30-second delay. You can use PortFast on access ports to allow devices connected to these ports to access the network immediately.

In a valid PortFast configuration, BPDUs should never be received on PortFast-enabled switch ports because that would indicate that another bridge or switch is connected to the port. To prevent this type of scenario, BPDU Guard can be configured to immediately put the switch port in an errdisabled (error-disabled) state on receipt of any BPDU. This protects against potential loops by effectively shutting down the port.

Check Your Understanding—Evolution of STP

Check your understanding of the evolution of STP by choosing the BEST answer to each of the following questions.

1. Which three STP port states are merged into the RSTP discarding port state? (Choose three.)

   a. multiple

   b. disabled

   c. blocking

   d. listening

   e. learning

   f. forwarding

2. Which protocol was designed to bring faster convergence to STP?

   a. PortFast

   b. RSTP

   c. PVST

   d. MSTP

3. Which technology solves the problem of a device being unable to get an IPv4 address from a DHCP server due to STP forwarding delay timers?

   a. PortFast

   b. BPDU Guard

   c. PVST

   d. MSTP

Labs and Activities

Command Reference

There are no commands for this chapter.

5.1.9 Packet Tracer—Investigate STP Loop Prevention

Objectives

In this lab, you will observe spanning-tree port states and watch the spanning-tree convergence process.

- Describe the operation of Spanning Tree Protocol.
- Explain how Spanning Tree Protocol prevents switching loops while allowing redundancy in switched networks.

Background / Scenario

In this activity you will use Packet Tracer to observe the operation of Spanning Tree Protocol in a simple switched network that has redundant paths.

Instructions

Part 1: Observe a Converged Spanning-Tree Instance

Step 1:   Verify Connectivity.

Ping from PC1 to PC2 to verify connectivity between the hosts. Your ping should be successful.

Step 2:   View spanning-tree status on each switch.

Use the **show spanning-tree vlan 1** command to gather information about the spanning tree status of each switch. Complete the table. For the purposes of the activity, only consider information about the Gigabit trunk ports. The Fast Ethernet ports are access ports that have end devices connected and are not part of the inter-switch trunk-based spanning tree.

Switch	Port	Status (FWD, BLK...)	Root Bridge?
S1	G0/1		
	G0/2		
S2	G0/1		
	G0/2		
S3	G0/1		
	G0/2		

Packet Tracer uses a different link light on one of the connections between the switches.

Questions:

What do you think this this link light means?

_____

What path will frames take from PC1 to PC2?

_____

Why do the frames not travel through S3?

_____

Why has spanning tree placed a port in blocking state?

_____

Part 2: Observe spanning-tree convergence

Step 1:   Remove the connection between S1 and S2.

   a.   Open a CLI window on switch S3 and issue the command **show spanning-tree vlan 1**. Leave the CLI window open.

   b.   Select the delete tool from the menu bar and click the cable that connects S1 and S2.

Step 2:   Observe spanning-tree convergence.

   a.   Quickly return to the CLI prompt on switch S3 and issue the **show spanning-tree vlan 1** command.

   b.   Use the up-arrow key to recall the **show spanning-tree vlan 1** command and issue it repeatedly until the orange link light on the cable turns green. Observe the status of port G0/2.

   Question:

   What do you see happen to the status of the G0/2 port during this process?

   _____

   You have observed the transition in port status that occurs as a spanning-tree port moves from blocking to forwarding state.

   c.   Verify Connectivity by pinging from PC1 to PC2. Your ping should be successful.

   Are any ports showing an orange link light that indicates that the port is in a spanning-tree state other than forwarding? Why or why not?

   _____

CHAPTER 6

EtherChannel

The "Study Guide" portion of this chapter uses a variety of exercises to test your knowledge of and skills in implementing EtherChannel on switched links. The "Labs and Activities" portion of this chapter includes all the online curriculum labs and Packet Tracer activity instructions.

As you work through this chapter, use Chapter 6 in *Switching, Routing, and Wireless Essentials v7 Companion Guide* or use the corresponding Chapter 6 in the Switching, Routing, and Wireless Essentials online curriculum for assistance.

Study Guide

EtherChannel Operation

One of the best ways to reduce the time required for Spanning Tree Protocol (STP) convergence is to simply avoid using STP. EtherChannel is a form of link aggregation used in switched networks.

EtherChannel Advantages

Cisco originally developed EtherChannel as a technique for grouping several FastEthernet or Gigabit Ethernet switch ports into one logical channel.

List at least three advantages to using EtherChannel:

_____

_____

_____

_____

_____

Implementation Restrictions

Briefly describe five EtherChannel implementation restrictions:

_____

_____

_____

_____

_____

PAgP and LACP Autonegotiation Protocols

You can configure EtherChannel as static or unconditional. However, there are also two protocols that can be used to configure the negotiation process: Port Aggregation Protocol (PAgP), which is Cisco proprietary, and Link Aggregation Control Protocol (LACP), which is specified as IEEE 802.3ad. These two protocols ensure that the two sides of the link have compatible configurations: the same speed, duplex setting, and VLAN information. The modes for the two protocols differ slightly.

For PAgP, briefly describe each of the following modes:

- On: _____

- Desirable: _____

- Auto: _____

For LACP, briefly describe each of the following modes:

- On: _____

- Active: _____

- Passive: _____

In Table 6-1, indicate what mode is described in each row.

Table 6-1   PAgP and LACP Modes

Mode	PAgP and/or LACP Mode Description
	Initiates LACP negotiations with other interfaces.
	Forces EtherChannel state without PAgP- or LACP-initiated negotiations.
	Places an interface in a passive, responding state. Does not initiate PAgP negotiations.
	Actively initiates PAgP negotiations with other interfaces.
	Places an interface in a passive, responding state. Does not initiate LACP negotiations.

The mode that is configured on each side of the EtherChannel link determines whether EtherChannel will be operational.

In Table 6-2, two switches are using PAgP. Use "yes" or "no" to indicate for each situation whether EtherChannel is established.

Table 6-2   EtherChannel Negotiation Using PAgP

Switch 1 Mode	Switch 2 Mode	EtherChannel Established?
Auto	Auto	
Auto	Desirable	
On	Desirable	
On	Off	
Desirable	Desirable	

In Table 6-3, two switches are using LACP. Use "yes" or "no" to indicate for each situation whether EtherChannel is established.

Table 6-3   EtherChannel Negotiation Using LACP

Switch 1 Mode	Switch 2 Mode	EtherChannel Established?
Passive	On	
Passive	Active	
On	On	
Passive	Passive	
On	Active	

Check Your Understanding—EtherChannel Operation

Check your understanding of EtherChannel operation by choosing the BEST answer to each of the following questions.

1. Which are benefits of EtherChannel technology? (Choose all that apply.)

   a. fault tolerance

   b. load sharing

   c. increased bandwidth

   d. link redundancy

2. True or false: FastEthernet and GigabitEthernet links can be combined into a single EtherChannel.

   a. true

   b. false

3. True or false: PAgP and LACP are both Cisco-proprietary link aggregation protocols.

   a. true

   b. false

4. Which three are PAgP interface modes? (Choose three.)

   a. on

   b. auto

   c. active

   d. passive

   e. desirable

5. Which PAgP interface mode initiates negotiation with other interfaces?

   a. on

   b. desirable

   c. auto

6. Which combinations of PAgP modes form an EtherChannel? (Choose all that apply.)

   a. auto > desirable

   b. desirable > on

   c. auto > on

   d. on > on

   e. on > active

   f. active > passive

Configure EtherChannel

EtherChannel configuration is straightforward once you decide which protocol you will use. In fact, the easiest method is to just force both sides to be on.

Configuration Guidelines

The following guidelines and restrictions are useful for configuring EtherChannel:

- **EtherChannel support:** All Ethernet interfaces must support EtherChannel; there is no requirement that interfaces be physically contiguous.

- **Speed and duplex:** All interfaces in an EtherChannel should be configured to operate at the same speed and in the same duplex mode.

- **VLAN match:** All interfaces in the EtherChannel bundle must be assigned to the same VLAN or must be configured as a trunk.

- **Range of VLANs:** An EtherChannel supports the same allowed range of VLANs on all the interfaces in a trunking EtherChannel.

EtherChannel Configuration Steps

To configure EtherChannel, complete the following steps:

Step 1. Specify the interfaces that participate in the EtherChannel group by using the **interface range** *interface* command.

What are the requirements for each interface before they can form an EtherChannel?

Step 2. Create the port channel interface with the **channel-group** *identifier* **mode {on | auto | desirable | active | passive}** command in interface range configuration mode. The keyword _____ forces the port to channel without PAgP or LACP. The keywords _____ and _____ enable PAgP. The keywords _____ and _____ enable LACP.

Step 3. The **channel-group** *identifier* command automatically creates a port channel interface using the *identifier* as the number. Use the **interface port-channel** *identifier* command to configure channel-wide settings like trunking, native VLANs, or allowed VLANs.

As you can see from the configuration steps, the way you specify whether to use PAgP, LACP, or no negotiations is by configuring one keyword in the **channel-group** command.

EtherChannel Configuration Scenarios

With the EtherChannel configuration steps in mind, consider Figure 6-1 in each of the following configuration scenarios.

Figure 6-1   EtherChannel Topology

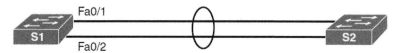

Fa0/1
S1
Fa0/2
S2

EtherChannel Configuration Scenario 1

Record the commands, including the switch prompt, to configure S1 Fa0/1 and Fa0/2 into an EtherChannel without negotiations. Then force the channel to trunk, using native VLAN 99.

_____

EtherChannel Configuration Scenario 2

Record the commands, including the switch prompt, to configure the S1 Fa0/1 and Fa0/2 into an EtherChannel using PAgP. S1 should initiate the negotiations. The channel should trunk, allowing only VLANs 1, 10, and 20.

_____

EtherChannel Configuration Scenario 3

Record the commands, including the switch prompt, to configure the S1 Fa0/1 and Fa0/2 into an EtherChannel using LACP. S1 should not initiate the negotiations. The channel should trunk, allowing all VLANs.

_____

Verify and Troubleshoot EtherChannel

An EtherChannel configuration can be verified with several commands. These same commands also help you troubleshoot common issues.

Verify EtherChannel

Record the commands used to display the output in Example 6-1.

Example 6-1   EtherChannel Verification Commands

```
S1# _____

Port-channel1 is up, line protocol is up (connected)
  Hardware is EtherChannel, address is 0cd9.96e8.8a01 (bia 0cd9.96e8.8a01)
  MTU 1500 bytes, BW 200000 Kbit/sec, DLY 100 usec,
     reliability 255/255, txload 1/255, rxload 1/255
<output omitted>


S1# _____

Flags:  D - down        P - bundled in port-channel
        I - stand-alone s - suspended
        H - Hot-standby (LACP only)
```

```
            R - Layer3        S - Layer2

            U - in use        f - failed to allocate aggregator

            M - not in use, minimum links not met

            u - unsuitable for bundling

            w - waiting to be aggregated

            d - default port




Number of channel-groups in use: 1

Number of aggregators:            1


Group  Port-channel  Protocol     Ports
------+-------------+-----------+--------------------------------------------------
1      Po1(SU)       LACP         Fa0/1(P)     Fa0/2(P)


S1# _____
                 Channel-group listing:

                 ----------------------


Group: 1

----------

                 Port-channels in the group:

                 --------------------------

Port-channel: Po1     (Primary Aggregator)

------------


Age of the Port-channel   = 0d:00h:25m:17s

Logical slot/port    = 2/1            Number of ports = 2

HotStandBy port = null

Port state             = Port-channel Ag-Inuse

Protocol               =    LACP

Port security          = Disabled


Ports in the Port-channel:


Index   Load   Port    EC state          No of bits
------+------+------+-----------------+-----------
  0      00     Fa0/1    Active               0
  0      00     Fa0/2    Active               0


Time since last port bundled:    0d:00h:05m:41s     Fa0/2

Time since last port Un-bundled: 0d:00h:05m:48s     Fa0/2
```

```
S1# _____

Port state      = Up Mstr Assoc In-Bndl

Channel group = 1              Mode = Active          Gcchange = -

Port-channel  = Po1            GC   =  -              Pseudo port-channel = Po1

Port index    = 0              Load = 0x00            Protocol =   LACP


Flags:  S - Device is sending Slow LACPDUs   F - Device is sending fast LACPDUs.
        A - Device is in active mode.        P - Device is in passive mode.


Local information:

LACP port Admin   Oper      Port          Port
Port      Flags   State     Priority      Key        Key      Number       State
Fa0/1     SA      bndl      32768         0x1        0x1      0x102        0x3D


Partner's information:


LACP port Admin   Oper      Port          Port
Port      Flags   Priority  Dev ID        Age     key    Key      Number   State
Fa0/1     SA      32768     0cd9.96d2.4000  4s    0x0    0x1      0x102    0x3D


Age of the port in the current state: 0d:00h:24m:59s
S1#
```

When troubleshooting an EtherChannel issue, keep in mind the configuration restrictions for interfaces that participate in the channel. List at least four of these restrictions.

_____

_____

_____

_____

_____

Troubleshoot EtherChannel

Refer to the output for S1 and S2 in Example 6-2. Record the command that generated each part of the output.

Example 6-2   Troubleshooting an EtherChannel Issue

```
S1# _____
Flags:  D - down         P - bundled in port-channel
        I - stand-alone  s - suspended
        H - Hot-standby (LACP only)
        R - Layer3       S - Layer2
        U - in use       f - failed to allocate aggregator
        M - not in use, minimum links not met
        u - unsuitable for bundling
        w - waiting to be aggregated
        d - default port
Number of channel-groups in use: 1
Number of aggregators:           1
Group  Port-channel  Protocol    Ports
------+-------------+-----------+-------------------------------------------
1      Po1(SD)         -         Fa0/1(D)    Fa0/2(D)
S1# _____
interface Port-channel1
 switchport mode trunk
!
interface FastEthernet0/1
 switchport mode trunk
 channel-group 1 mode auto
!
interface FastEthernet0/2
 switchport mode trunk
 channel-group 1 mode auto
!
<output omitted>
S 1#
S2# _____
interface Port-channel1
 switchport mode trunk
!
interface FastEthernet0/1
 switchport mode trunk
 channel-group 1 mode auto
!
interface FastEthernet0/2
 switchport mode trunk
 channel-group 1 mode auto
!
<output omitted>
S2#
```

Refer to Example 6-2 and explain why the EtherChannel between S1 and S2 is down.

_____

_____

EtherChannel and spanning tree must interoperate. For this reason, the order in which EtherChannel-related commands are entered is important. To correct this issue, you must first remove the port channel. Otherwise, spanning-tree errors cause the associated ports to go into blocking or errdisabled state. With that in mind, what would you suggest to correct the issue shown in Example 6-2 if the requirement is to use PAgP? What commands would be required?

_____

_____

_____

_____

_____

_____

_____

_____

_____

Labs and Activities

Command Reference

In Table 6-4, record the command, including the correct router or switch prompt, that fits each description.

Table 6-4   Commands for Chapter 6, "EtherChannel"

Command	Description
	Enter interface configuration mode on S1 for both Fa0/1 and Fa0/2.
	Configure EtherChannel group 1 without LACP or PAgP negotiations.
	Enter port channel configuration mode.
	Configure the port channel to trunk.
	Verify that the EtherChannel is up and in use.

6.2.4 Packet Tracer—Configure EtherChannel

Objectives

Part 1: Configure Basic Switch Settings

Part 2: Configure an EtherChannel with Cisco PAgP

Part 3: Configure an 802.3ad LACP EtherChannel

Part 4: Configure a Redundant EtherChannel Link

Background

Three switches have just been installed. There are redundant uplinks between the switches. As configured, only one of these links can be used; otherwise, a bridging loop might occur. However, using only one link utilizes only half of the available bandwidth. EtherChannel allows up to eight redundant links to be bundled together into one logical link. In this lab, you will configure Port Aggregation Protocol (PAgP), a Cisco EtherChannel protocol, and Link Aggregation Control Protocol (LACP), an IEEE 802.3ad open standard version of EtherChannel.

Before beginning the configuration, review the EtherChannel Configuration Guidelines and Restrictions listed at the end of this activity.

Port Channel Table

Channel Group	Ports	Protocol
1	S1 F0/21, F0/22	PAgP
	S3 F0/21, F0/22	
2	S1 G0/1, G0/2	LACP
	S2 G0/1, G0/2	
3	S2 F0/23, F0/24	Negotiated LACP
	S3 F0/23, F0/24	

Instructions

Part 1: Configure Basic Switch Settings

a. Assign each switch a hostname according to the topology diagram.

b. Before beginning the link aggregation between switches, verify the existing configuration of the ports that connect the switches to ensure that the ports will successfully join the EtherChannels. Commands that provide information about the state of the switch ports include:

```
S1# show interfaces | include Ethernet
S1# show interface status
S1# show interfaces trunk
```

c. Configure all ports that are required for the EtherChannels as static trunk ports.

Note: If the ports are configured with DTP dynamic auto mode, and you do not set the mode of the ports to trunk, the links do not form trunks and remain access ports. The default mode on a 2960 switch is for DTP to be enabled and set to dynamic auto. DTP can be disabled on interfaces with the **switchport nonegotiate** command.

Part 2: Configure an EtherChannel with Cisco PAgP

Note: When configuring EtherChannels, it is recommended to shut down the physical ports being grouped on both devices before configuring them into channel groups. Otherwise, EtherChannel Misconfig Guard may place these ports into err-disabled state. The ports and port channels can be re-enabled after EtherChannel is configured.

Step 1:   Configure Port Channel 1.

a. The first EtherChannel that is created for this activity aggregates ports F0/21 and F0/22 between **S1** and **S3**. Configure the ports on both switches as static trunk ports.

b. Use the **show interfaces trunk** command to ensure that you have an active trunk link for those two links, and the native VLAN on both links is the same.

```
S1# show interfaces trunk
Port        Mode          Encapsulation    Status        Native vlan
F0/21       on            802.1q           trunking      1
F0/22       on            802.1q           trunking      1
G0/1        on            802.1q           trunking      1
G0/2        on            802.1q           trunking      1

<output omitted>
```

c. On S1 and S3, add ports F0/21 and F0/22 to Port Channel 1 with the **channel-group 1 mode desirable** command. The **mode desirable** option enables the switch to actively negotiate to form a PAgP link.

Note: Interfaces must be **shutdown** before adding them to the channel group.

```
S1(config)# interface range f0/21 - 22
S1(config-if-range)# shutdown
S1(config-if-range)# channel-group 1 mode desirable
S1(config-if-range)# no shutdown
S3(config)# interface range f0/21 - 22

S3(config-if-range)# shutdown
S3(config-if-range)# channel-group 1 mode desirable
S3(config-if-range)# no shutdown
```

The message "Creating a port-channel interface Port-channel 1" should appear on both switches when the channel-group is configured. This interface designation will appear as Po1 in command output.

d. Configure the logical interface to become a trunk by first entering the **interface port-channel** *number* command and then the **switchport mode trunk** command. Add this configuration to both switches.

```
S1(config)# interface port-channel 1
S1(config-if)# switchport mode trunk
S3(config)# interface port-channel 1
S3(config-if)# switchport mode trunk
```

Step 2:   Verify Port Channel 1 status.

a. Issue the **show etherchannel summary** command on S1 and S3 to verify that EtherChannel is working on both switches. This command displays the type of EtherChannel, the ports utilized, and the port states. Command output is shown for S1.

```
S1# show etherchannel summary
Flags:  D - down         P - in port-channel
        I - stand-alone  s - suspended
        H - Hot-standby  (LACP only)
        R - Layer3       S - Layer2
        U - in use       f - failed to allocate aggregator
        u - unsuitable for bundling
        w - waiting to be aggregated
        d - default port
```

```
Number of channel-groups in use: 1
Number of aggregators:            1

Group  Port-channel  Protocol     Ports
------+-------------+-----------+------------------------------------------
1      Po1(SU)         PAgP       F0/21(P)   F0/22(P)
```

    b. If the EtherChannel does not come up, shut down the physical interfaces on both ends of the EtherChannel and then bring them back up again. The **show interfaces trunk** and **show spanning-tree** commands should show the port channel as one logical link.

Part 3: Configure an 802.3ad LACP EtherChannel

Step 1:   Configure Port Channel 2.

    a. In 2000, the IEEE released 802.3ad, which is an open standard version of EtherChannel. It is commonly referred to as LACP. Using the previous commands, configure the link between **S1** and **S2**, using ports G0/1 and G0/2, as an LACP EtherChannel. You must use a different port channel number on S1 than 1, because you already used that in the previous step. To configure port channel 2 as LACP, use the interface configuration mode **channel-group 2 mode active** command. Active mode indicates that the switch actively tries to negotiate that link as LACP, as opposed to PAgP. The configuration of S1 is shown below.

```
S1(config)# interface range g0/1 - 2
S1(config-if-range)# shutdown
S1(config-if-range)# channel-group 2 mode active
S1(config-if-range)# no shutdown
S1(config-if-range)# interface port-channel 2
S1(config-if)# switchport mode trunk
```

Step 2:   Verify Port Channel 2 status.

    Use the **show** commands from Part 1 Step 2 to verify the status of Port Channel 2. Look for the protocol used by each port.

Part 4: Configure a Redundant EtherChannel Link

Step 1:   Configure Port Channel 3.

    There are various options for the **channel-group** *number* **mode** command:

```
S2(config)# interface range f0/23 - 24
S2(config-if-range)# channel-group 3 mode ?
  active      Enable LACP unconditionally
  auto        Enable PAgP only if a PAgP device is detected
  desirable   Enable PAgP unconditionally
  on          Enable Etherchannel only
  passive     Enable LACP only if a LACP device is detected
```

    a. On switch **S2**, add ports F0/23 and F0/24 to Port Channel 3 with the **channel-group 3 mode passive** command. The **passive** option indicates that you want the switch to use LACP only if another LACP device is detected. Statically configure Port Channel 3 as a trunk interface.

```
S2(config)# interface range f0/23 - 24
S2(config-if-range)# shutdown
S2(config-if-range)# channel-group 3 mode passive
S2(config-if-range)# no shutdown
S2(config-if-range)# interface port-channel 3
S2(config-if)# switchport mode trunk
```

b. On **S3**, add ports F0/23 and F0/24 to Port Channel 3 with the **channel-group 3 mode active** command. The **active** option indicates that you want the switch to use LACP unconditionally. Statically configure Port Channel 3 as a trunk interface.

Step 2: Verify Port Channel 3 status.

a. Use the **show** commands from Part 1 Step 2 to verify the status of Port Channel 3. Look for the protocol used by each port.

b. Creating EtherChannel links does not prevent Spanning Tree from detecting switching loops. View the spanning tree status of the active ports on **S1**.

```
S1# show spanning-tree active
VLAN0001
  Spanning tree enabled protocol ieee
  Root ID    Priority    32769
             Address     0001.436E.8494
             Cost        9
             Port        27(Port-channel1)
             Hello Time  2 sec  Max Age 20 sec  Forward Delay 15 sec

  Bridge ID  Priority    32769   (priority 32768 sys-id-ext 1)
             Address     000A.F313.2395
             Hello Time  2 sec  Max Age 20 sec  Forward Delay 15 sec
             Aging Time  20
Interface        Role Sts Cost      Prio.Nbr Type
---------------- ---- --- --------- -------- --------------------------
Po1              Root FWD 9         128.27   Shr
Po2              Altn BLK 3         128.28   Shr
```

Port Channel 2 is not operative because Spanning Tree Protocol placed some ports into blocking mode. Unfortunately, those ports were the Gigabit ports. In this topology, you can restore these ports by configuring **S1** to be **primary** root for VLAN 1. You could also set the priority to **24576**.

```
S1(config)# spanning-tree vlan 1 root primary
```

or

```
S1(config)# spanning-tree vlan 1 priority 24576
```

You may have to wait for STP to recalculate the tree topology. Press fast-forward if necessary. Use the **show spanning-tree active** command to verify that the Gigabit ports are now in the forwarding state.

EtherChannel Configuration Guidelines and Restrictions

EtherChannel has some specific guidelines that must be followed in order to avoid configuration problems.

1) All Ethernet interfaces support EtherChannel up to a maximum of eight interfaces with no requirement that the interfaces be on the same interface module.

2) All interfaces within an EtherChannel must operate at the same speed and duplex.

3) EtherChannel links can function as either single VLAN access ports or as trunk links between switches.

4) All interfaces in a Layer 2 EtherChannel must be members of the same VLAN or be configured as trunks.

5) If configured as trunk links, Layer 2 EtherChannel must have the same native VLAN and have the same VLANs allowed on both switches connected to the trunk.

6) When configuring EtherChannel links, all interfaces should be shutdown prior to beginning the EtherChannel configuration. When configuration is complete, the links can be re-enabled.

7) After configuring the EtherChannel, verify that all interfaces are in the up/up state.

8) It is possible to configure an EtherChannel as static, or for it to use either PAgP or LACP to negotiate the EtherChannel connection. The determination of how an EtherChannel is set up is the value of the **channel-group** *number* **mode** command. Valid values are:

active	LACP is enabled unconditionally
passive	LACP is enabled only if another LACP-capable device is connected.
desirable	PAgP is enabled unconditionally.
auto	PAgP is enabled only if another PAgP-capable device is connected.
on	EtherChannel is enabled, but without either LACP or PAgP.

9) LAN ports can form an EtherChannel using PAgP if the modes are compatible. Compatible PAgP modes are:

desirable => desirable

desirable => auto

If both interfaces are in **auto** mode, an Etherchannel cannot form.

10) LAN ports can form an EtherChannel using LACP if the modes are compatible. Compatible LACP modes are:

active => active

active => passive

If both interfaces are in **passive** mode, an EtherChannel cannot form using LACP.

11) Channel-group numbers are local to the individual switch. Although this activity uses the same Channel-group number on either end of the EtherChannel connection, it is not a requirement. Channel-group 1 (interface po1) on one switch can form an EtherChannel with Channel-group 5 (interface po5) on another switch.

6.3.4 Packet Tracer—Troubleshoot EtherChannel

Objectives

Part 1: Examine the Physical Layer and Correct Switch Port Mode Issues

Part 2: Identify and Correct Port Channel Assignment Issues

Part 3: Identify and Correct Port Channel Protocol Issues

Background

A junior technician recently configured four switches. Users are complaining that the network is running slowly, and they would like you to investigate.

Port Channel Table

Channel Group	Ports	Protocol
1	S1: G0/1, G0/2	LACP active
	S2: G0/1, G0/2	
2	S2: G0/1, G0/2	LACP active
	S4: G0/1, G0/2	
3	S1: F0/23, F0/24	LACP active
	S2: F0/23, F0/24	
4	S3: F0/23, F0/24	LACP active
	S4: F0/23, F0/24	
5	S1: F0/21, F0/22	LACP active
	S4: F0/21, F0/22	
6	S2: F0/21, F0/22	LACP active
	S3: F0/21, F0/22	

Device Table

Device	Group	Ports
S1	1	G0/1, G0/2
	3	F0/23, F0/24
	5	F0/21, F0/22
S2	2	G0/1, G0/2
	3	F0/23, F0/24
	6	F0/21, F0/22
S3	1	G0/1, G0/2
	4	F0/23, F0/24
	6	F0/21, F0/22
S4	2	G0/1, G0/2
	4	F0/23, F0/24
	5	F0/21, F0/22

Instructions

Part 1: Examine the Physical Layer and Correct Switch Port Mode Issues

Step 1:   Look for access ports.

Examine the switches. When two or more redundant links connect the same switches, Spanning Tree protocol will only put one port in forwarding mode to prevent switching loops. You can see this in Packet Tracer. When physical ports are assigned to an EtherChannel port, they behave as one logical port. Each pair will either be operational or down.

Step 2:   Verify ports are in trunk mode.

a.   Verify that all physical ports in the topology are configured as trunks. Correct any ports that are in access mode.

b.   Correct any EtherChannel ports that are not configured as trunks.

Part 2: Identify and Correct Port Channel Assignment Issues

Step 1:   Examine port channel assignments.

The Packet Tracer topology and the Port Channel and Device tables provide details about the physical ports and their EtherChannel assignments. Use the **show etherchannel summary** command to learn how the EtherChannel links are configured. Verify that the switches are configured as shown in the documentation.

Step 2:   Correct port channel assignments.

Correct any switch ports that are not assigned to the correct EtherChannel port.

Part 3: Identify and Correct Port Channel Protocol Issues

Step 1:   Identify protocol issues.

In 2000, the IEEE released 802.3ad (LACP), which is an open standard version of EtherChannel. For compatibility reasons, the network design team chose to use LACP across the network. The design team has made it a requirement that all ports that participate in EtherChannel need to actively negotiate the link as LACP. Verify that the physical ports are configured as indicated in the topology and Port Channel Table.

Step 2:   Correct protocol issues.

a.   Correct any switch ports that are not negotiating using LACP.

b.   Reissue the **show etherchannel summary** command to verify that all EtherChannel links are now correctly configured.

6.4.1 Packet Tracer—Implement EtherChannel

Objectives

Part 1: Build the network

Part 2: Configure EtherChannel

Background

You have been assigned the task of designing an EtherChannel implementation for a company that wants to improve the performance of their switch trunk links. You will try several different ways of implementing the EtherChannel links in order to evaluate which is the best for the company. You will build the topology, configure trunk ports, and implement LACP and PAgP EtherChannels.

Instructions

Part 1: Build the Network.

Use the table below to build the switch topology.

Step 1:   Obtain the devices that are required.

  a.   Click the **Network Devices** icon in the bottom tool bar.

  b.   Click the **Switches** entry in the submenu.

  c.   Locate the **2960** switch icon. Click and drag the icon for the 2960 switch into the topology area.

  d.   Repeat the step above so that there are **three** 2960 switches in the topology area.

  e.   Arrange the devices into a layout that you can work with by clicking and dragging.

Step 2:   Name the devices.

  The devices have default names that you will need to change. You will name the devices **SWA**, **SWB**, and **SWC**. You are changing the display names of the devices. This is the text label that appears below each device. It is **not** the host name. Your display names must match the names that are given in this step **exactly**. If a display name does not match, you will not be scored for your device configuration.

  a.   Click the device display name that is below the device icon. A text field should appear with a flashing insertion point. If the configuration window for the device appears, close it and try again by clicking a little further away from the device icon.

  b.   Replace the current display name with the appropriate display name.

  c.   Repeat until all devices are named.

Step 3:   Connect the devices.

a.   Click the orange lightning bolt Connections icon in the bottom toolbar.

b.   Locate the Ethernet straight-through cable icon. It looks like a solid black diagonal line.

c.   To connect the device, click the Ethernet straight-through cable icon and then click the first device that you want to connect. Select the correct port and then click the second device. Select the correct port and the devices will be connected.

d.   Connect the devices as specified in the table below.

Port Channel	Devices	Port Connections	Type
1	SWA to SWB	G0/1 to G0/1	PAgP
		G0/2 to G0/2	
2	SWA to SWC	F0/21 to F0/21	LACP
		F0/22 to F0/22	
3	SWB to SWC	F0/23 to F0/23	LACP
		F0/24 to F0/24	

Part 2: Configure EtherChannel

On each switch, configure the ports that will be used in the Port Channels as static trunk ports.

Step 1:   Configure a PAgP EtherChannel.

Follow the procedure that was used in previous activities to configure Port Channel 1 as a PAgP EtherChannel between SWA and SWB. Both sides should negotiate the EtherChannel.

Step 2:   Configure a LACP EtherChannel.

Configure Port Channel 2 as an LACP channel between SWA and SWC. Both sides should negotiate the EtherChannel.

Step 3:   Configure a Backup LACP EtherChannel

Configure Port Channel 3 channel as an LACP channel between SWB and SWC. In this case, SWC initiates negotiation with SWB. SWB does not initiate negotiation of the channel.

6.4.2 Lab—Implement EtherChannel

Topology

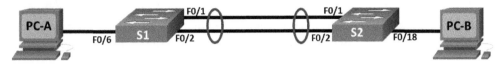

Addressing Table

Device	Interface	IP Address	Subnet Mask
S1	VLAN 10	192.168.10.11	255.255.255.0
S2	VLAN 10	192.168.10.12	255.255.255.0
PC-A	NIC	192.168.20.3	255.255.255.0
PC-B	NIC	192.168.20.4	255.255.255.0

VLAN Table

VLAN	Name	Interface Assigned
10	Management	VLAN 10
20	Clients	S1: F0/6
		S2: F0/18
999	Parking_Lot	S1: F0/3–5, F0/7–24, G0/1–2
		S2: F0/3–17, F0/19–24, G0/1–2
1000	Native	N/A

Objectives

Part 1: Build the Network and Configure Basic Device Settings

Part 2: Create VLANs and Assign Switch Ports

Part 3: Configure 802.1Q Trunks between the Switches

Part 4: Implement and Verify an EtherChannel between the switches

Background / Scenario

Link aggregation allows the creation of logical links that are comprised of two or more physical links. This provides increased throughput beyond using only one physical link. Link aggregation also provides redundancy if one of the links fails.

In this lab, you will configure EtherChannel, a form of link aggregation used in switched networks. You will configure EtherChannel using Link Aggregation Control Protocol (LACP).

Note: LACP is a link aggregation protocol that is defined by IEEE 802.3ad, and it is not associated with any specific vendor.

LACP allows Cisco switches to manage Ethernet channels between switches that conform to the 802.3ad protocol. You can configure up to 16 ports to form a channel. Eight of the ports are in active mode and the other eight are in standby mode. When any of the active ports fail, a standby port becomes active. Standby mode works only for LACP, not for PAgP.

Note: The switches used with CCNA hands-on labs are Cisco Catalyst 2960s with Cisco IOS Release 15.2(2) (lanbasek9 image). Other switches and Cisco IOS versions can be used. Depending on the model and Cisco IOS version, the commands available and output produced might vary from what is shown in the labs.

Note: Make sure that the switches have been erased and have no startup configurations. If you are unsure, contact your instructor.

Required Resources

- 2 Switches (Cisco 2960 with Cisco IOS Release 15.2(2) lanbasek9 image or comparable)
- 2 PCs (Windows with a terminal emulation program, such as Tera Term)
- Console cables to configure the Cisco IOS devices via the console ports
- Ethernet cables as shown in the topology

Instructions

Part 1: Build the Network and Configure Basic Device Settings

In Part 1, you will set up the network topology and configure basic settings on the PC hosts and switches.

Step 1: Cable the network as shown in the topology.

Attach the devices as shown in the topology diagram, and cable as necessary.

Step 2: Configure basic settings for each switch.

   a. Assign a device name to the switch.

   b. Disable DNS lookup to prevent the router from attempting to translate incorrectly entered commands as though they were host names.

   c. Assign class as the privileged EXEC encrypted password.

   d. Assign cisco as the console password and enable login.

   e. Assign cisco as the VTY password and enable login.

   f. Encrypt the plaintext passwords.

   g. Create a banner that warns anyone accessing the device that unauthorized access is prohibited.

   h. Save the running configuration to the startup configuration file.

   i. Set the clock on the switch to today's time and date.

Note: Use the question mark (?) to help with the correct sequence of parameters needed to execute this command.

     j. Copy the running configuration to the startup configuration.

Step 3: Configure PC hosts.

Refer to the Addressing Table for PC host address information.

Part 2: Create VLANs and Assign Switch Ports

In Part 2, you will create VLANs as specified in the table above on both switches. You will then assign the VLANs to the appropriate interface and verify your configuration settings. Complete the following tasks on each switch.

Step 1: Create VLANs on the switches.

     a. On both switches create and name the required VLANs from the VLAN Table above.

     b. Configure and activate the management interface on each switch using the IP address information in the Addressing Table.

     c. Assign all unused ports on the switch to the Parking_Lot VLAN, configure them for static access mode, and administratively deactivate them.

Step 2: Assign VLANs to the correct switch interfaces.

     a. Assign used ports to the appropriate VLAN (specified in the VLAN table above) and configure them for static access mode.

     b. Issue the **show vlan brief** command and verify that the VLANs are assigned to the correct ports.

Part 3: Configure 802.1Q trunks between the switches.

In Part 3, you will manually configure interfaces F0/1 and F0/2 as 802.1Q trunks.

     a. Change the switchport mode on the interfaces to force trunking. Use the **interface range** command to reduce the number of commands required. Make sure to do this on both switches.

     b. As a part of the trunk configuration, set the native VLAN to 1000 on both switches. You may see error messages temporarily while the two interfaces are configured for different native VLANs.

     c. As another part of trunk configuration, specify that VLANs 10, 20, and 1000 are allowed to cross the trunk.

     d. Issue the **show interfaces trunk** command to verify the trunking ports, Native VLAN and allowed VLANs across the trunk.

     Question:

     Why is the "Vlans in spanning tree forwarding state and not pruned" entry different for F0/1 and F0/2?

Part 4: Implement and Verify an EtherChannel between the switches.

a. Create a LACP-based EtherChannel using F0/1 and F0/2 using group number 1, with both switches actively negotiating the EtherChannel protocol. Use the **interface range** command to reduce the number of commands required.

b. After the EtherChannel is configured, a virtual Port-Channel interface is automatically created. Now interface Port-Channel 1 represents the logical interface of the bundled physical ports F0/1 and F0/2. Additionally, the Port-Channel will inherit the configuration of the first physical port added to the EtherChannel.

c. Issue the **show interfaces trunk** command to verify trunking is still in place.

Question:

What does the port 'Po1' represent?

_____

d. Use the **show etherchannel summary** command to verify the EtherChannel configuration.

The "Study Guide" portion of this chapter uses a variety of exercises to test your knowledge and skills related to implementing Dynamic Host Configuration Protocol version 4 (DHCPv4) to operate across multiple LANs. The "Labs and Activities" portion of this chapter includes all the online curriculum labs and Packet Tracer activity instructions.

As you work through this chapter, use Chapter 7 in *Switching, Routing, and Wireless Essentials v7 Companion Guide* or use the corresponding Module 7 in the Switching, Routing, and Wireless Essentials online curriculum for assistance.

Study Guide

DHCPv4 Concepts

DHCPv4 assigns IPv4 addresses and other network configuration information dynamically. Because desktop clients usually make up the bulk of network nodes, DHCPv4 is an extremely useful and time-saving tool for network administrators.

DHCPv4 Operation

When a DHCPv4 client boots, it begins a four-step process to obtain a DHCPv4 lease. In Figure 7-1, label each DHCP message type sent between the server and client when originating a lease.

Figure 7-1   DHCPv4 Lease-Origination Operation

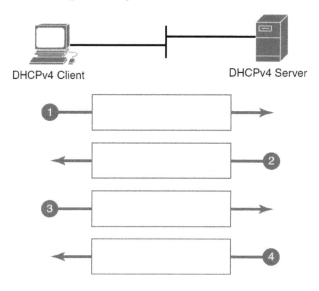

Prior to lease expiration, the client begins a two-step process to renew the lease with the DHCPv4 server. Briefly describe these two steps.

Step 1. _____

_____

Step 2. _____

_____

Check Your Understanding—DHCPv4 Concepts

Check your understanding of DHCPv4 concepts by choosing the BEST answer to each of the following questions.

1. Which message does a DHCPv4 client send to initiate the process of obtaining a lease?

    a. DHCPDISCOVER

    b. DHCPOFFER

    c. DHCPREQUEST

    d. DHCPACK

2. Which two DHCPv4 messages does a server send in the process of obtaining a lease? (Choose two.)

   a. DHCPDISCOVER

   b. DHCPOFFER

   c. DHCPREQUEST

   d. DHCPACK

3. Which two DHCPv4 messages are used in the lease renewal process? (Choose two.)

   a. DHCPDISCOVER

   b. DHCPOFFER

   c. DHCPREQUEST

   d. DHCPACK

Configure a Cisco IOS DHCPv4 Server

The Cisco IOS supports DHCPv4 server and DHCPv4 relay configuration.

Steps to Configure a Cisco IOS DHCPv4 Server

Use the following steps to configure a Cisco router or switch to act as a DHCPv4 server:

Step 1. Exclude statically assigned IPv4 addresses.

Typically, some IPv4 addresses in a pool are assigned to network devices that require static address assignments. To exclude these addresses, use the **ip dhcp excluded-address** *low-address* [*high-address*] global configuration command.

Step 2. Configure a DHCPv4 pool name.

Use the **ip dhcp pool** *pool-name* global configuration command to create a pool with the specified name. The router will then be in DHCPv4 configuration mode, as indicated by the prompt changing to Router(dhcp-config)#.

Step 3. Configure the DHCPv4 pool settings.

Some settings are required, and others are optional. In Table 7-1, record the command syntax for the two required DHCPv4 settings and four optional DHCPv4 settings.

Table 7-1   DHCPv4 Pool Settings

Required Tasks	Command Syntax
Define the address pool.	
Define the default router or gateway.	
Optional Tasks	**Command Syntax**
Define a DNS server.	
Define a domain name.	
Define the duration of the DHCP lease.	
Define the NetBIOS WINS server.	

Refer to Figure 7-2. Record the commands to configure R1 as the DHCP server for the 172.16.1.0/24 LAN. Exclude the first 10 IP addresses. Use an appropriate name. Include a setting for the DNS server and the domain R1.com.

Figure 7-2   DHCPv4 Configuration Topology

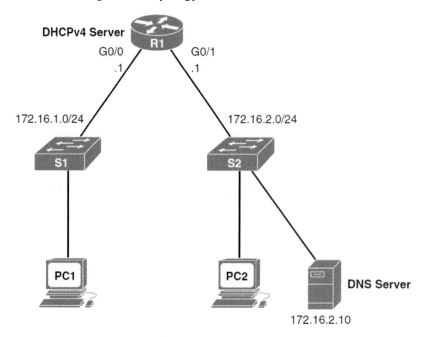

R1(config)# _____

_____

_____

_____

_____

_____

To verify DHCPv4 settings, use the **show run** command to see the configuration. There are also two other DHCPv4 **show** commands you can use. In Example 7-1, record the commands that display the information shown.

Example 7-1   DHCPv4 Verification Commands

```
R1# _____
Bindings from all pools not associated with VRF:
IP address          Client-ID/                Lease expiration       Type
                    Hardware address/
                    User name
172.16.1.11         0100.5056.be8e.bb         Jul 05 2020 12:35 AM   Automatic
R1# _____
Memory usage        49491
Address pools       1
Database agents     0
```

```
Automatic bindings    3
Manual bindings       0
Expired bindings      0
Malformed messages    0
Secure arp entries    0
Message               Received
BOOTREQUEST           0
DHCPDISCOVER          3
DHCPREQUEST           3
DHCPDECLINE           0
DHCPRELEASE           0
DHCPINFORM            6

Message               Sent
BOOTREPLY             0
DHCPOFFER             3
DHCPACK               9
DHCPNAK               0
R1#
```

DHCPv4 Relay

Refer to Figure 7-3. It is just like Figure 7-2 except that now there is a DHCP server on the 172.16.2.0/24 LAN that provides addressing services to both 172.16.1.0/24 and 172.16.2.0/24.

Figure 7-3   DHCPv4 Topology with a Dedicated DHCPv4 Server

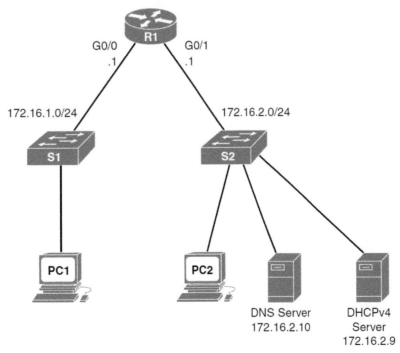

Assume that the DHCP pool for 172.16.1.0/24 has been removed from R1. Record the commands to configure R1 to send DHCP requests to the new DHCP server.

`R1(config)#` _____

Other Service Broadcasts Relayed

By default, what eight UDP services are forwarded by a router when it is configured for DHCPv4 relay?

Configure a DHCPv4 Client

Routers commonly receive IP addressing from a DHCP server. This is particularly true in small office/home office (SOHO) networks. Refer to Figure 7-4. Record the commands to configure a SOHO network to request IPv4 addressing for its G0/1 interface.

Figure 7-4   Configuring a Router as a DHCPv4 Client

`SOHO(config)#` _____

Labs and Activities

Command Reference

In Table 7-2, record the command, including the correct router or switch prompt, that fits each description.

Table 7-2   Commands for Chapter 7, "DHCPv4"

Command	Description
	Exclude the IP address range 10.1.1.1 to 10.1.1.10 from the DHCP pool.
	Create a DHCPv4 pool named MYPOOL.
	Define the network 10.1.1.0/24 as the address pool.
	Set 10.1.1.1 as the gateway for a host that belongs to the 10.1.1.0/24 network.
	Set the domain to mydomain.com.
	Set the DNS server to 10.1.1.10.
	Set the lease to never expire.
	Display the current IPv4 addresses that are assigned from the pool.
	Display DHCPv4 server statistics.
	Configure the interface to relay DHCP requests to 10.1.1.5.
	Configure the interface to request IPv4 addressing information from a DHCPv4 server.

7.2.10 Packet Tracer—Configure DHCPv4

Addressing Table

Device	Interface	IPv4 Address	Subnet Mask	Default Gateway
R1	G0/0	192.168.10.1	255.255.255.0	N/A
	S0/0/0	10.1.1.1	255.255.255.252	N/A
R2	G0/0	192.168.20.1	255.255.255.0	N/A
	G0/1	DHCP Assigned	DHCP Assigned	N/A
	S0/0/0	10.1.1.2	255.255.255.252	N/A
	S0/0/1	10.2.2.2	255.255.255.252	N/A
R3	G0/0	192.168.30.1	255.255.255.0	N/A
	S0/0/1	10.2.2.1	255.255.255.0	N/A
PC1	NIC	DHCP Assigned	DHCP Assigned	DHCP Assigned

Device	Interface	IPv4 Address	Subnet Mask	Default Gateway
PC2	NIC	DHCP Assigned	DHCP Assigned	DHCP Assigned
DNS Server	NIC	192.168.20.254	255.255.255.0	192.168.20.1

Objectives

Part 1: Configure a Router as a DHCP Server

Part 2: Configure DHCP Relay

Part 3: Configure a Router as a DHCP Client

Part 4: Verify DHCP and Connectivity

Scenario

A dedicated DHCP server is scalable and relatively easy to manage but it can be costly to have one at every location in a network. However, a Cisco router can be configured to provide DHCP services without the need for a dedicated server. As the network technician for your company, you have been assigned the task of configuring a Cisco router as a DHCP server. You are also required to configure the edge router as a DHCP client so that it receives an IP address from the ISP network.

Instructions

Part 1: Configure a Router as a DHCP Server

Step 1:   Configure the excluded IPv4 addresses.

Addresses that have been statically assigned to devices in the networks that will use DHCP must be excluded from the DHCP pools. This avoids errors associated with duplicate IP addresses. In this case the IP addresses of the R1 and R3 LAN interfaces must be excluded from DHCP. In addition, nine other addresses are excluded for static assignment to other devices such servers and device management interfaces.

a. Configure **R2** to exclude the first 10 addresses from the R1 LAN.

```
R2(config)# ip dhcp excluded-address 192.168.10.1 192.168.10.10
```

b. Configure **R2** to exclude the first 10 addresses from R3 LAN.

Step 2:   Create a DHCP pool on R2 for the R1 LAN.

a. Create a DHCP pool named **R1-LAN** (case-sensitive).

```
R2(config)# ip dhcp pool R1-LAN
```

b. Configure the DHCP pool to include the network address, the default gateway, and the IP address of the DNS server.

```
R2(dhcp-config)# network 192.168.10.0 255.255.255.0
R2(dhcp-config)# default-router 192.168.10.1
R2(dhcp-config)# dns-server 192.168.20.254
```

Step 3:   Create a DHCP pool on R2 for the R3 LAN.

a. Create a DHCP pool named **R3-LAN** (case-sensitive).

b. Configure the DHCP pool to include the network address, the default gateway, and the IP address of the DNS server. Refer to the Addressing Table.

Part 2: Configure DHCP Relay

Step 1: Configure R1 and R3 as a DHCP relay agent.

For DHCP clients to obtain an address from a server on a different LAN segment, the interface that the clients are attached to must include a helper address pointing to the DHCP server. In this case, the hosts on the LANs that are attached to R1 and R3 will access the DHCP server that is configured on R2. The IP addresses of the R2 serial interfaces that are attached to R1 and R3 are used as the helper addresses. DHCP traffic from the hosts on the R1 and R3 LANs will be forwarded to these addresses and processed by the DHCP server that is configured on R2.

a. Configure the helper address for the LAN interface on R1.

```
R1(config)# interface g0/0
R1(config-if)# ip helper-address 10.1.1.2
```

b. Configure the helper address for the LAN interface on R3.

Step 2: Configure hosts to receive IP addressing information from DHCP.

a. Configure hosts PC1 and PC2 to receive their IP addresses from a DHCP server.

b. Verify that the hosts have received their addresses from the correct DHCP pools.

Part 3: Configure a Router as a DHCP Client

Just as a PC is able to receive an IPv4 address from a server, a router interface has the ability to do the same. Router **R2** needs to be configured to receive addressing from the ISP.

a. Configure the Gigabit Ethernet 0/1 interface on **R2** to receive IP addressing from DHCP and activate the interface.

```
R2(config)# interface g0/1
R2(config-if)# ip address dhcp
R2(config-if)# no shutdown
```

Note: Use Packet Tracer's **Fast Forward Time** feature to speed up the process.

---

b. Use the **show ip interface brief** command to verify that R2 received an IP address from DHCP.

Part 4: Verify DHCP and Connectivity

Step 1: Verify DHCP bindings.

```
R2# show ip dhcp binding
```

IP address	Client-ID/ Hardware address	Lease expiration	Type
192.168.10.11	0002.4AA5.1470	--	Automatic
192.168.30.11	0004.9A97.2535	--	Automatic

Step 2: Verify configurations.

Verify that **PC1** and **PC2** can now ping each other and all other devices.

7.4.1 Packet Tracer—Implement DHCPv4

Addressing Table

Device	Interface	IPv4 Address	Subnet Mask	Default Gateway
R1	G0/0	192.168.10.1	255.255.255.0	N/A
	S0/0/0	10.1.1.1	255.255.255.252	
R2	G0/0	192.168.20.1	255.255.255.0	N/A
	G0/1	DHCP Assigned	DHCP Assigned	
	S0/0/0	10.1.1.2	255.255.255.252	
	S0/0/1	10.2.2.2	255.255.255.252	
R3	G0/0	192.168.30.1	255.255.255.0	N/A
	S0/0/1	10.2.2.1	255.255.255.0	
PC1	NIC	DHCP Assigned	DHCP Assigned	DHCP Assigned
PC2	NIC	DHCP Assigned	DHCP Assigned	DHCP Assigned
DNS Server	NIC	192.168.20.254	255.255.255.0	192.168.20.1

Objectives

Part 1: Configure a Router as a DHCP Server

Part 2: Configure DHCP Relay

Part 3: Configure a Router as a DHCP Client

Scenario

As the network technician for your company, you are tasked with configuring a Cisco router as a DHCP server to provide dynamic allocation of addresses to clients on the network. You are also required to configure the edge router as a DHCP client so that it receives an IP address from the ISP network. Since the server is centralized, you will need to configure the two LAN routers to relay DHCP traffic between the LANs and the router that is serving as the DHCP server.

Instructions

Part 1: Configure a Router as a DHCP Server

Step 1: Configure the excluded IPv4 addresses.

Configure R2 to exclude the first 10 addresses from the R1 and R3 LANs. All other addresses should be available in the DHCP address pool.

Step 2: Create a DHCP pool on **R2** for the R1 LAN.

a. Create a DHCP pool named **R1-LAN**. The pool name must match this value in order for you to get credit for your configuration.

    b. Configure the DHCP pool to include the network address, the default gateway, and the IP address of the DNS server.

Step 3:   Create a DHCP pool on **R2** for the R3 LAN.

    a. Create a DHCP pool named **R3-LAN** (case-sensitive).

    b. Configure the DHCP pool to include the network address, the default gateway, and the IP address of the DNS server.

Part 2: Configure DHCP Relay

Step 1:   Configure R1 and R3 as a DHCP relay agent.

Step 2:   Set PC1 and PC2 to receive IP addressing information from DHCP.

Part 3: Configure R2 as a DHCP Client

Step 1:   Configure the Gigabit Ethernet 0/1 interface on **R2** to receive IP addressing from DHCP.

Step 2:   Activate the interface.

7.4.2 Lab—Implement DHCPv4

Topology

Addressing Table

Device	Interface	IP Address	Subnet Mask	Default Gateway
R1	G0/0/0	10.0.0.1	255.255.255.252	N/A
	G0/0/1	N/A	N/A	
	G0/0/1.100			
	G0/0/1.200			
	G0/0/1.1000	N/A	N/A	
R2	G0/0/0	10.0.0.2	255.255.255.252	N/A
	G0/0/1			
S1	VLAN 200			
S2	VLAN 1			
PC-A	NIC	DHCP	DHCP	DHCP
PC-B	NIC	DHCP	DHCP	DHCP

VLAN Table

VLAN	Name	Interface Assigned
1	N/A	S2: F0/18
100	Clients	S1: F0/6
200	Management	S1: VLAN 200
999	Parking_Lot	S1: F0/1–4, F0/7–24, G0/1–2
1000	Native	N/A

Objectives

Part 1: Build the Network and Configure Basic Device Settings

Part 2: Configure and verify two DHCPv4 Servers on R1

Part 3: Configure and verify a DHCP Relay on R2

Background / Scenario

The Dynamic Host Configuration Protocol (DHCP) is a network protocol that lets network administrators manage and automate the assignment of IP addresses. Without DHCP for IPv4, the administrator must manually assign and configure IP addresses, preferred DNS servers, and default gateways. As the network grows in size, this becomes an administrative problem when devices are moved from one internal network to another.

In this scenario, the company has grown in size, and the network administrators can no longer assign IP addresses to devices manually. Your job is to configure the R1 router to assign IPv4 addresses on two different subnets.

Note: The routers used with CCNA hands-on labs are Cisco 4221 with Cisco IOS XE Release 16.9.4 (universalk9 image). The switches used in the labs are Cisco Catalyst 2960s with Cisco IOS Release 15.2(2) (lanbasek9 image). Other routers, switches, and Cisco IOS versions can be used. Depending on the model and Cisco IOS version, the commands available and the output produced might vary from what is shown in the labs. Refer to the Router Interface Summary Table at the end of the lab for the correct interface identifiers.

Note: Ensure that the routers and switches have been erased and have no startup configurations. If you are unsure contact your instructor.

Required Resources

- 2 Routers (Cisco 4221 with Cisco IOS XE Release 16.9.4 universal image or comparable)
- 2 Switches (Cisco 2960 with Cisco IOS Release 15.2(2) lanbasek9 image or comparable)
- 2 PCs (Windows with a terminal emulation program, such as Tera Term)
- Console cables to configure the Cisco IOS devices via the console ports
- Ethernet cables as shown in the topology

Instructions

Part 1: Build the Network and Configure Basic Device Settings

In Part 1, you will set up the network topology and configure basic settings on the PC hosts and switches.

Step 1:   Establish an addressing scheme.

Subnet the network 192.168.1.0/24 to meet the following requirements:

a.   One subnet, "Subnet A", supporting 58 hosts (the client VLAN at R1).

Subnet A:

Record the first IP address in the Addressing Table for R1 G0/0/1.100. Record the second IP address in the Address Table for S1 VLAN 200 and enter the associated default gateway.

b. One subnet, "Subnet B", supporting 28 hosts (the management VLAN at R1).

Subnet B: _____

Record the first IP address in the Addressing Table for R1 G0/0/1.200. Record the second IP address in the Address Table for S1 VLAN 1 and enter the associated default gateway.

c. One subnet, "Subnet C", supporting 12 hosts (the client network at **R2**).

Subnet C: _____

Record the first IP address in the Addressing Table for R2 G0/0/1.

Step 2: Cable the network as shown in the topology.

Attach the devices as shown in the topology diagram, and cable as necessary.

Step 3: Configure basic settings for each router.

a. Assign a device name to the router.

b. Disable DNS lookup to prevent the router from attempting to translate incorrectly entered commands as though they were host names.

c. Assign **class** as the privileged EXEC encrypted password.

d. Assign **cisco** as the console password and enable login.

e. Assign **cisco** as the VTY password and enable login.

f. Encrypt the plaintext passwords.

g. Create a banner that warns anyone accessing the device that unauthorized access is prohibited.

h. Save the running configuration to the startup configuration file.

i. Set the clock on the router to today's time and date.

Note: Use the question mark (**?**) to help with the correct sequence of parameters needed to execute this command.

Step 4: Configure Inter-VLAN Routing on R1.

a. Activate interface G0/0/1 on the router.

b. Configure sub-interfaces for each VLAN as required by the IP addressing table. All sub-interfaces use 802.1Q encapsulation and are assigned the first usable address from the IP address pool you have calculated. Ensure the sub-interface for the native VLAN does not have an IP address assigned. Include a description for each sub-interface.

c. Verify the sub-interfaces are operational.

Step 5: Configure G0/0/1 on R2, then G0/0/0 and static routing for both routers.

a. Configure G0/0/1 on R2 with the first IP address of Subnet C you calculated earlier.

b. Configure interface G0/0/0 for each router based on the IP addressing table above.

c. Configure a default route on each router pointed to the IP address of G0/0/0 on the other router.

d. Verify static routing is working by pinging R2's G0/0/1 address from R1.

e. Save the running configuration to the startup configuration file.

Step 6: Configure basic settings for each switch.

a. Assign a device name to the switch.

b. Disable DNS lookup to prevent the router from attempting to translate incorrectly entered commands as though they were host names.

c. Assign **class** as the privileged EXEC encrypted password.

d. Assign **cisco** as the console password and enable login.

e. Assign **cisco** as the VTY password and enable login.

f. Encrypt the plaintext passwords.

g. Create a banner that warns anyone accessing the device that unauthorized access is prohibited.

h. Save the running configuration to the startup configuration file.

i. Set the clock on the switch to today's time and date.

Note: Use the question mark (**?**) to help with the correct sequence of parameters needed to execute this command.

j. Copy the running configuration to the startup configuration.

Step 7: Create VLANs on S1.

Note: S2 is only configured with basic settings.

a. Create and name the required VLANs on switch 1 from the table above.

b. Configure and activate the management interface on S1 (VLAN 200) using the second IP address from the subnet calculated earlier. Additionally, set the default gateway on S1.

c. Configure and activate the management interface on S2 (VLAN 1) using the second IP address from the subnet calculated earlier. Additionally, set the default gateway on S2

d. Assign all unused ports on S1 to the Parking_Lot VLAN, configure them for static access mode, and administratively deactivate them. On S2, administratively deactivate all the unused ports.

Note: The interface range command is helpful to accomplish this task with as few commands as necessary.

Step 8:   Assign VLANs to the correct switch interfaces.

   a.   Assign used ports to the appropriate VLAN (specified in the VLAN table above) and configure them for static access mode.

   b.   Verify that the VLANs are assigned to the correct interfaces.

   Question:

   Why is interface F0/5 listed under VLAN 1?

   _____

Step 9:   Manually configure S1's interface F0/5 as an 802.1Q trunk.

   a.   Change the switchport mode on the interface to force trunking.

   b.   As a part of the trunk configuration, set the native VLAN to 1000.

   c.   As another part of trunk configuration, specify that VLANs 100, 200, and 1000 are allowed to cross the trunk.

   d.   Save the running configuration to the startup configuration file.

   e.   Verify trunking status.

   Question:

   At this point, what IP address would the PCs have if they were connected to the network using DHCP?

   _____

Part 2: Configure and verify two DHCPv4 Servers on R1

In Part 2, you will configure and verify a DHCPv4 Server on R1. The DHCPv4 server will service two subnets, Subnet A and Subnet C.

Step 1:   Configure R1 with DHCPv4 pools for the two supported subnets. Only the DHCP Pool for subnet A is given below.

   a.   Exclude the first five useable addresses from each address pool.

   b.   Create the DHCP pool (Use a unique name for each pool).

   c.   Specify the network that this DHCP server is supporting.

   d.   Configure the domain name as ccna-lab.com

   e.   Configure the appropriate default gateway for each DHCP pool.

   f.   Configure the lease time for 2 days 12 hours and 30 minutes.

   g.   Next, configure the second DHCPv4 Pool using the pool name R2_Client_LAN and the calculated network, default-router and use the same domain name and lease time from the previous DHCP pool.

Step 2:   Save your configuration.

   Save the running configuration to the startup configuration file.

Step 3:   Verify the DHCPv4 Server configuration.

    a.   Issue the command **show ip dhcp pool** to examine the pool details.

    b.   Issue the command **show ip dhcp bindings** to examine established DHCP address assignments.

    c.   Issue the command **show ip dhcp server statistics** to examine DHCP messages.

Step 4:   Attempt to acquire an IP address from DHCP on PC-A.

    a.   Open a command prompt on PC-A and issue the command **ipconfig /renew**.

    b.   Once the renewal process is complete, issue the command **ipconfig** to view the new IP information.

    c.   Test connectivity by pinging R1's G0/0/1 interface IP address.

Part 3: Configure and verify a DHCP Relay on R2

In Part 3, you will configure R2 to relay DHCP requests from the local area network on interface G0/0/1 to the DHCP server (R1).

Step 1:   Configure R2 as a DHCP relay agent for the LAN on G0/0/1.

    a.   Configure the **ip helper-address** command on G0/0/1 specifying R1's G0/0/0 IP address.

    b.   Save your configuration.

Step 2:   Attempt to acquire an IP address from DHCP on PC-B.

    a.   Open a command prompt on PC-B and issue the command **ipconfig /renew**.

    b.   Once the renewal process is complete, issue the command **ipconfig** to view the new IP information.

    c.   Test connectivity by pinging R1's G0/0/1 interface IP address.

    d.   Issue the **show ip dhcp binding** on R1 to verify DHCP bindings.

    e.   Issue the **show ip dhcp server statistics** on R1 and R2 to verify DHCP messages.

CHAPTER 8

SLAAC and DHCPv6

The "Study Guide" portion of this chapter uses a variety of exercises to test your knowledge of and skills related to stateless address autoconfiguration (SLAAC) and Dynamic Host Configuration Protocol version 6 (DHCPv6) implementations. The "Labs and Activities" portion of this chapter includes all the online curriculum labs and Packet Tracer activity instructions.

As you work through this chapter, use Chapter 8 in *Switching, Routing, and Wireless Essentials v7 Companion Guide* or use the corresponding Module 8 in the Switching, Routing, and Wireless Essentials online curriculum for assistance.

Study Guide

IPv6 GUA Assignment

This section reviews how a device can receive its global unicast address (GUA) and link-local address (LLA).

IPv6 Host Configuration

On a router, an IPv6 GUA is manually configured using the **ipv6 address** *ipv6-address/prefix-length* interface configuration command. On end devices, the IPv6 address can be manually configured or set to dynamically acquire an IPv6 GUA.

IPv6 Host Link-Local Address

When automatic IPv6 addressing is selected, the host attempts to automatically obtain and configure IPv6 address information on the interface. The host uses one of three methods to configure its IPv6 address. An IPv6 router that is on the same link as the host sends out Router Advertisement (RA) messages, which suggest to the hosts how to obtain their IPv6 addressing information.

IPv6 GUA Assignment

An IPv6 GUA can be assigned dynamically using the following stateless and stateful services (see Figure 8-1):

- Stateless address autoconfiguration (SLAAC)

- Stateless DHCPv6

- Stateful DHCPv6

Figure 8-1   Dynamic GUA Assignment Methods

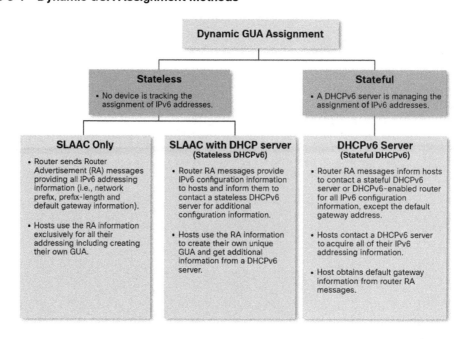

Three RA Message Flags

An Internet Control Message Protocol version 6 (ICMPv6) RA message includes three flags that identify the dynamic options available to a host:

- **A flag:** This is the Address Autoconfiguration flag. Use SLAAC to create an IPv6 GUA.

- **O flag:** This is the Other Configuration flag. Other information is available from a stateless DHCPv6 server.

- **M flag:** This is the Managed Address Configuration flag. Use a stateful DHCPv6 server to obtain an IPv6 GUA.

Check Your Understanding—IPv6 GUA Assignment

Check your understanding of IPv6 global unicast address assignment methods by choosing the BEST answer to each of the following questions.

1. Which address type is automatically created by default on a host interface when no RAs are received?

    a. global unicast address

    b. link-local address

    c. MAC address

2. Which method best describes stateless DHCP?

    a. SLAAC only

    b. SLAAC with stateless DHCPv6 server

    c. Stateful DHCPv6 server

SLAAC

The SLAAC method enables hosts to create their own unique IPv6 global unicast addresses, without the services of a DHCPv6 server.

Enabling SLAAC

A router interface must be activated with an IPv6 address for SLAAC to operate. What other command, including router prompt, is required before the router will send out RA messages informing hosts to use SLAAC?

SLAAC-Only Method

When SLAAC only is enabled on the router, what are the values of the three flags in the RA message?

Host Process to Generate an Interface ID

Briefly describe the two methods a host can use to generate its own interface ID.

_____

_____

_____

_____

Duplicate Address Detection

Briefly describe the operation of Duplicate Address Detection (DAD).

_____

_____

_____

_____

Check Your Understanding—SLAAC

Check your understanding of SLAAC by choosing the BEST answer to each of the following questions.

1. Which two ICMPv6 messages are used in the SLAAC process? (Choose two.)

   a. Neighbor Advertisement (NA)

   b. Neighbor Solicitation (NS)

   c. Router Solicitation (RS)

   d. Router Advertisement (RA)

2. Which command must be configured on a router to enable it to join the IPv6 all-routers multicast address ff02::2?

   a. ip routing

   b. ipv6 unicast-routing

   c. ipv6 address *ipv6-address/prefix-length*

   d. ipv6 address *ipv6-address* link-local

3. What are the flag settings when a host should use the SLAAC-only option?

   a. A = 1, M = 0, O = 0

   b. A = 1, M = 1, O = 0

   c. A = 1, M = 0, O = 1

   d. A = 0, M = 1, O = 1

4. Which ICMPv6 message is sent by a host in an attempt to locate an online IPv6-enabled router to obtain IPv6 addressing information?

   a. Neighbor Advertisement (NA)

   b. Neighbor Solicitation (NS)

   c. Router Solicitation (RS)

   d. Router Advertisement (RA)

5. Which of the following does a host use to verify that an IPv6 address is unique on the local network before assigning that address to an interface?

   a. Address Resolution Protocol (ARP)

   b. DAD

   c. ping

   d. SLAAC

DHCPv6

Stateless DHCPv6 uses parts of SLAAC to ensure that all the necessary information is supplied to the host. Stateful DHCPv6 does not require SLAAC.

DHCPv6 Operation Steps

The host begins the DHCPv6 client/server communications after stateless DHCPv6 or stateful DHCPv6 is indicated in the RA.

What User Datagram Protocol (UDP) ports does DHCPv6 use?

In Figure 8-2, label the steps for DHCPv6 operations.

Figure 8-2   Steps in DHCPv6 Operations

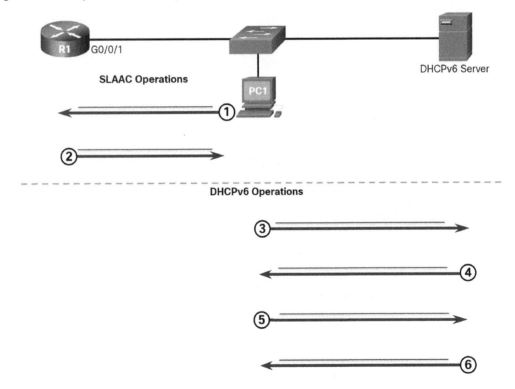

Stateless DHCPv6 Operation

In a stateless DHCPv6 implementation, what are the value of the three flags in the RA message sent by the router to IPv6 clients looking for addressing information?

What command, including router prompt, configures a router to inform IPv6 clients to use stateless DHCPv6 processes?

Stateful DHCPv6 Operation

In a stateful DHCPv6 implementation, what are the values of the three flags in the RA message that the router sends to IPv6 clients who are looking for addressing information?

_____

_____

What command, including router prompt, configures a router to inform IPv6 clients to use stateful DHCPv6 processes?

_____

Check Your Understanding—DHCPv6

Check your understanding of DHCPv6 by choosing the BEST answer to each of the following questions.

1. What UDP port do DHCPv6 clients use to send DHCPv6 messages?

   a. 67

   b. 68

   c. 546

   d. 547

2. What DHCPv6 message does a host send to look for a DHCPv6 server?

   a. ADVERTISE

   b. SOLICIT

   c. INFORMATION-REQUEST

   d. REQUEST

3. What DHCPv6 message does a host send to the DHCPv6 server if it is using stateful DHCPv6?

   a. ADVERTISE

   b. SOLICIT

   c. INFORMATION-REQUEST

   d. REQUEST

4. What flag settings combination is used for stateless DHCP?

   a. A = 1, M = 0, O = 0

   b. A = 0, M = 1, O = 0

   c. A = 1, M = 0, O = 1

   d. A = 0, M = 1, O = 1

5. What M flag setting indicates that stateful DHCPv6 is used?

   a. M = 0

   b. M = 1

Configure DHCPv6 Server

A Cisco IOS router must be configured to be one of the following:

- **DHCPv6 server:** The router provides stateless or stateful DHCPv6 services.

- **DHCPv6 client:** The router interface acquires an IPv6 configuration from a DHCPv6 server.

- **DHCPv6 relay agent:** The router provides DHCPv6 forwarding services when the client and the server are located on different networks.

Configure Stateless DHCPv6

To configure a router as a DHCPv6 server, you must complete four steps:

Step 1. Enable IPv6 routing.

The **ipv6 unicast-routing** command is required before the router will send ICMPv6 RA messages.

Step 2. Define a DHCPv6 pool name.

Use the **ipv6 dhcp pool** *pool-name* global configuration command to create a pool and enter DHCPv6 configuration mode, which is identified by the Router(config-dhcpv6)# prompt.

Step 3. Configure the DHCPv6 pool.

The stateless DHCPv6 server can be configured to provide other information that might not have been included in the RA message, such as the DNS server address (**dns-server** *dns-server*) and the domain name (**domain-name** *domain-name*).

Step 4. Bind the DHCPv6 pool to an interface.

Bind the pool to the interface with the **ipv6 dhcp server** *pool-name* command. For stateless DHCPv6, change the O flag from 0 to 1 with the **ipv6 nd other-config-flag** command.

Refer to Figure 8-3. Record the commands to configure R1 as the DHCPv6 server for the 2001:db8:1:1::/64 LAN. Use an appropriate name. Include a setting for the DNS server and the domain R1.com.

Figure 8-3   DHCPv6 Configuration Topology

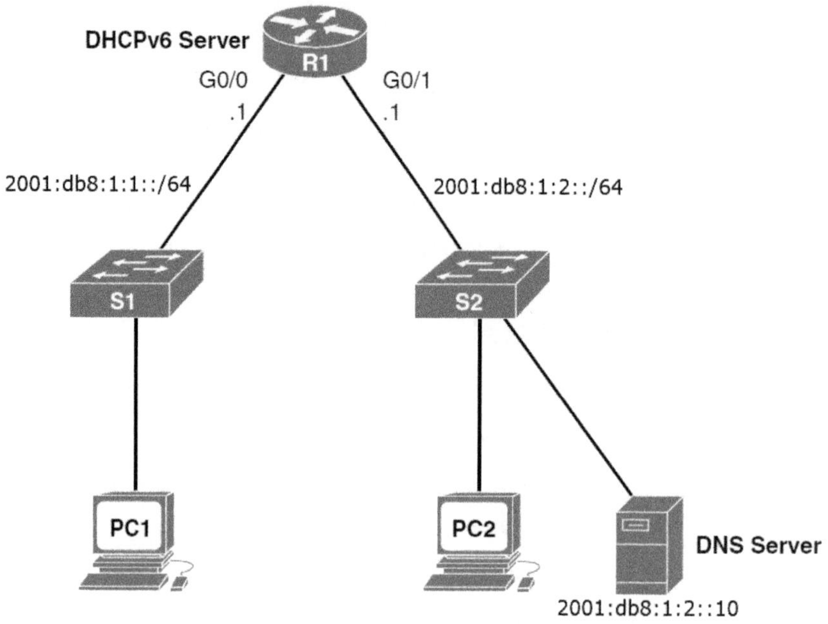

R1(config)# _____

_____

_____

_____

_____

_____

_____

_____

_____

_____

What are the commands to configure a router interface as a DHCPv6 client?

_____

_____

Configure Stateful DHCPv6

Configuring a router as a stateful DHCPv6 server is similar to configuring a stateless server. The most significant difference is that a stateful server also includes IPv6 addressing information, much like a DHCPv4 server, and you set the M flag instead of the O flag.

What is the command to define the DHCPv6 pool with IPv6 addressing information?

_____

For the previous configuration, add the commands to configure the IPv6 addressing information for infinite lifetime, set the O flag back to 0, and set the M flag to 1.

R1(config)# _____

_____

_____

_____

_____

If the DHCPv6 server is located on a different network from the client, you can configure the IPv6 router as a DHCPv6 relay agent. What is the command to configure a router as a DHCPv6 relay agent?

Check Your Understanding—Configure DHCPv6 Server

Check your understanding of DHCPv6 server configuration by choosing the BEST answer to each of the following questions.

1. Which DHCPv6 roles can a router perform? (Choose all that apply.)

   a. DHCPv6 client

   b. DHCPv6 relay agent

   c. DHCPv6 server

2. Which command is not configured in stateless DHCPv6?

   a. address prefix *ipv6-address/prefix*

   b. domain-name *name*

   c. dns-server *server-address*

   d. ipv6 dhcp server *pool-name*

3. An IPv6-enabled router is to acquire its IPv6 GUA from another IPv6 router using SLAAC. Which interface configuration command should be configured on the client router?

   a. ipv6 address autoconfig

   b. ipv6 address auto config

   c. ipv6 address dhcp

   d. ipv6 address dhcpv6

4. A router is to provide DHCPv6 server services. Which command should be configured on the client-facing interface?

   a. ipv6 enable

   b. ipv6 dhcp pool *POOL-NAME*

   c. ipv6 dhcp server *POOL-NAME*

   d. ipv6 nd other-config-flag

5. An IPv6-enabled router is to acquire its IPv6 GUA from a DHCPv6 server. Which interface configuration command should be configured on the client router?

   a. ipv6 address autoconfig

   b. ipv6 address auto config

   c. ipv6 address dhcp

   d. ipv6 address dhcpv6

6. Which DHCPv6 verification command would display the link-local address and global unicast assigned address for each active client?

   a. show ip dhcp pool

   b. show ipv6 dhcp binding

   c. show ipv6 dhcp interface

   d. show ipv6 dhcp pool

7. Which command is configured on the client LAN interface of the DHCPv6 relay agent?

   a. ip helper-address

   b. ipv6 dhcp relay destination

   c. ipv6 enable

   d. ipv6 helper-address

Labs and Activities

Command Reference

In Table 8-1, record the command, including the correct router or switch prompt, that fits each description.

Table 8-1   Commands for Chapter 8, "SLAAC and DHCPv6"

Command	Description
	Create a DHCPv6 pool named STATELESS.
	Configure the interface to use STATELESS as the DHCPv6 pool.
	Configure the interface for stateless DHCPv6.
	Create a DHCPv6 pool named STATEFUL.
	Define the network 2001:db8:10:10::/64 as the address pool with an infinite lifetime.
	Configure the interface for stateful DHCPv6.
	Display the current IPv6 addresses that are assigned from the pool.
	Configure the interface to relay DHCPv6 requests to 2001:db8:10:10::5.

8.5.1 Lab—Configure DHCPv6

Topology

Addressing Table

Device	Interface	IPv6 Address
R1	G0/0/0	2001:db8:acad:2::1 /64
		fe80::1
	G0/0/1	2001:db8:acad:1::1/64
		fe80::1

Device	Interface	IPv6 Address
R2	G0/0/0	2001:db8:acad:2::2/64
		fe80::2
	G0/0/1	2001:db8:acad:3::1 /64
		fe80::1
PC-A	NIC	DHCP
PC-B	NIC	DHCP

Objectives

Part 1: Build the Network and Configure Basic Device Settings

Part 2: Verify SLAAC address assignment from R1

Part 3: Configure and verify a Stateless DHCPv6 Server on R1

Part 4: Configure and verify a Stateful DHCPv6 Server on R1

Part 5: Configure and verify a DHCPv6 Relay on R2

Background / Scenario

The dynamic assignment of IPv6 global unicast addresses (GUA) can be configured the following three ways:

- Stateless Address Auoconfiguration (SLAAC)

- Stateless Dynamic Host Configuration Protocol for IPv6 (DHCPv6)

- Stateful DHCPv6

When using SLAAC to assign IPv6 addresses to hosts, a DHCPv6 server is not used. Because a DHCPv6 server is not used when implementing SLAAC, hosts are unable to receive additional critical network information, including a domain name server (DNS) address as well as a domain name.

When using Stateless DHCPv6 to assign IPv6 addresses to host, a DHCPv6 server is used to assign the additional critical network information, however the IPv6 address is assigned using SLAAC.

When implementing Stateful DHCPv6, a DHCPv6 server assigns all network information, including the IPv6 address.

The determination of how hosts obtain their dynamic IPv6 addressing is dependent on the flag setting contained within the router advertisement (RA) messages.

In this scenario, the company has grown in size, and the network administrators can no longer assign IP addresses to devices manually. Your job is to configure the R2 router to assign IPv6 addresses on two different subnets connected to router R1.

Note: The routers used with CCNA hands-on labs are Cisco 4221 with Cisco IOS XE Release 16.9.4 (universalk9 image). The switches used in the labs are Cisco Catalyst 2960s with Cisco IOS Release 15.2(2) (lanbasek9 image). Other routers, switches, and Cisco IOS versions can be used. Depending on the model and Cisco IOS version, the commands available and the output produced might vary from what is shown in the labs. Refer to the Router Interface Summary Table at the end of the lab for the correct interface identifiers.

Note: Ensure that the routers and switches have been erased and have no startup configurations. If you are unsure contact your instructor.

Required Resources

- 2 Routers (Cisco 4221 with Cisco IOS XE Release 16.9.4 universal image or comparable)

- 2 Switches (Cisco 2960 with Cisco IOS Release 15.2(2) lanbasek9 image or comparable) - **Optional**

- 2 PCs (Windows with a terminal emulation program, such as Tera Term)

- Console cables to configure the Cisco IOS devices via the console ports

- Ethernet cables as shown in the topology

Instructions

Part 1: Build the Network and Configure Basic Device Settings

In Part 1, you will set up the network topology and configure basic settings on the PC hosts and switches.

Step 1:   Cable the network as shown in the topology.

Attach the devices as shown in the topology diagram, and cable as necessary.

Step 2:   Configure basic settings for each switch. (Optional)

   a.   Assign a device name to the switch.

   b.   Disable DNS lookup to prevent the router from attempting to translate incorrectly entered commands as though they were host names.

   c.   Assign **class** as the privileged EXEC encrypted password.

   d.   Assign **cisco** as the console password and enable login.

   e.   Assign **cisco** as the VTY password and enable login.

   f.   Encrypt the plaintext passwords.

   g.   Create a banner that warns anyone accessing the device that unauthorized access is prohibited.

   h.   Shutdown all unused ports

   i.   Save the running configuration to the startup configuration file.

Step 3:   Configure basic settings for each router.

   a.   Assign a device name to the router.

   b.   Disable DNS lookup to prevent the router from attempting to translate incorrectly entered commands as though they were host names.

   c.   Assign **class** as the privileged EXEC encrypted password.

   d.   Assign **cisco** as the console password and enable login.

   e.   Assign **cisco** as the VTY password and enable login.

f. Encrypt the plaintext passwords.

g. Create a banner that warns anyone accessing the device that unauthorized access is prohibited.

h. Enable IPv6 Routing

i. Save the running configuration to the startup configuration file.

Step 4:   Configure interfaces and routing for both routers.

a. Configure the G0/0/0 and G0/0/1 interfaces on R1 and R2 with the IPv6 addresses specified in the table above.

b. Configure a default route on each router pointed to the IP address of G0/0/0 on the other router.

c. Verify routing is working by pinging R2's G0/0/1 address from R1.

d. Save the running configuration to the startup configuration file.

Part 2: Verify SLAAC Address Assignment from R1

In Part 2, you will verify that Host PC-A receives an IPv6 address using the SLAAC method.

Power PC-A up and ensure that the NIC is configured for IPv6 automatic configuration.

After a few moments, the results of the command **ipconfig** should show that PC-A has assigned itself an address from the 2001:db8:1::/64 network.

```
C:\Users\Student> ipconfig

Windows IP Configuration


Ethernet adapter Ethernet 2:

   Connection-specific DNS Suffix   . :
   IPv6 Address. . . . . . . . . . . : 2001:db8:acad:1:5c43:ee7c:2959:da68
   Temporary IPv6 Address. . . . . . : 2001:db8:acad:1:3c64:e4f9:46e1:1f23
   Link-local IPv6 Address . . . . . : fe80::5c43:ee7c:2959:da68%6
   IPv4 Address. . . . . . . . . . . : 169.254.218.104
   Subnet Mask . . . . . . . . . . . : 255.255.0.0
   Default Gateway . . . . . . . . . : fe80::1%6
```

Question:

Where did the host-id portion of the address come from?

Part 3: Configure and Verify a DHCPv6 Server on R1

In Part 3, you will configure and verify a stateless DHCP server on R1. The objective is to provide PC-A with DNS server and Domain information.

Step 1: Examine the configuration of PC-A in more detail.

a. Issue the command **ipconfig /all** on PC-A and take a look at the output.

```
C:\Users\Student> ipconfig /all
Windows IP Configuration

        Host Name . . . . . . . . . . . . : DESKTOP-3FR7RKA
        Primary Dns Suffix  . . . . . . . :
        Node Type . . . . . . . . . . . . : Hybrid
        IP Routing Enabled. . . . . . . . : No
        WINS Proxy Enabled. . . . . . . . : No


Ethernet adapter Ethernet0:

        Connection-specific DNS Suffix  . :
        Description . . . . . . . . . . . : Intel(R) 852574L Gigabit
                                            Network Connection
        Physical Address. . . . . . . . . : 00-50-56-83-63-6D
        IPv6 Address. . . . . . . . . . . : 2001:db8:acad:1:5c43:ee7c:2959:d
                                            a68(Preferred)
        Temporary IPv6 Address. . . . . . : 2001:db8:acad:1:3c64:e4f9:46e1:1
                                            f23(Preferred)
        Link-local IPv6 Address . . . . . : fe80::5c43:ee7c:2959:da68%6(
                                            Preferred)
        IPv4 Address. . . . . . . . . . . : 169.254.218.104(Preferred)
        Subnet Mask . . . . . . . . . . . : 255.255.0.0
        Default Gateway . . . . . . . . . : fe80::1%6
        DHCPv6 IAID . . . . . . . . . . . : 50334761
        DHCPv6 Client DUID. . . . . . . . : 00-01-00-01-24-F5-CE-A2-00-50-
                                            56-B3-63-6D
        DNS Servers . . . . . . . . . . . : fec0:0:0:ffff::1%1
                                            fec0:0:0:ffff::2%1
                                            fec0:0:0:ffff::3%1
        NetBIOS over Tcpip. . . . . . . . : Enabled
```

b. Notice that there is no Primary DNS suffix. Also note that the DNS server addresses provided are "site local anycast" addresses, and not unicast addresses, as would be expected.

Step 2: Configure R1 to provide stateless DHCPv6 for PC-A.

a. Create an IPv6 DHCP pool on R1 named R1-STATELESS. As a part of that pool, assign the DNS server address as 2001:db8:acad::1 and the domain name as stateless.com.

```
R1(config)# ipv6 dhcp pool R1-STATELESS
R1(config-dhcp)# dns-server 2001:db8:acad::254
R1(config-dhcp)# domain-name STATELESS.com
```

b. Configure the G0/0/1 interface on R1 to provide the OTHER config flag to the R1 LAN, and specify the DHCP pool you just created as the DHCP resource for this interface.

```
R1(config)# interface g0/0/1
R1(config-if)# ipv6 nd other-config-flag
R1(config-if)# ipv6 dhcp server R1-STATELESS
```

c. Save the running configuration to the startup configuration file.

d. Restart PC-A.

e. Examine the output of **ipconfig /all** and notice the changes.

```
C:\Users\Student> ipconfig /all
Windows IP Configuration
        Host Name . . . . . . . . . . . . : DESKTOP-3FR7RKA
        Primary Dns Suffix  . . . . . . . :
        Node Type . . . . . . . . . . . . : Hybrid
        IP Routing Enabled. . . . . . . . : No
        WINS Proxy Enabled. . . . . . . . : No
        DNS Suffix Search List. . . . . . : STATELESS.com


Ethernet adapter Ethernet0:

        Connection-specific DNS Suffix  . : STATELESS.com
        Description . . . . . . . . . . . : Intel(R) 82574L Gigabit Network
                                            Connection
        Physical Address. . . . . . . . . : 00-50-56-83-63-6D
        DHCP Enabled. . . . . . . . . . . : Yes
        Autoconfiguration Enabled . . . . : Yes
        IPv6 Address. . . . . . . . . . . : 2001:db8:acad:1:5c43:ee7c:2959:
                                            da68(Preferred)
        Temporary IPv6 Address. . . . . . : 2001:db8:acad:1:3c64:e4f9:46e1:
                                            1f23(Preferred)
        Link-local IPv6 Address . . . . . : fe80::5c43:ee7c:2959:da68%6
                                            (Preferred)
        IPv4 Address. . . . . . . . . . . : 169.254.218.104(Preferred)
        Subnet Mask . . . . . . . . . . . : 255.255.0.0
        Default Gateway . . . . . . . . . : fe80::1%6
        DHCPv6 IAID . . . . . . . . . . . : 50334761
        DHCPv6 Client DUID. . . . . . . . : 00-01-00-01-24-F5-CE-A2-00-50-
                                            56-B3-63-6D
        DNS Servers . . . . . . . . . . . : 2001:db8:acad::254
        NetBIOS over Tcpip. . . . . . . . : Enabled
        Connection-specific DNS Suffix Search List :   STATELESS.com
```

f. Test connectivity by pinging R2's G0/0/1 interface IP address.

Part 4: Configure a Stateful DHCPv6 Server on R1

In Part 4, you will configure R1 to respond to DHCPv6 requests from the LAN on R2.

a. Create a DHCPv6 pool on R1 for the 2001:db8:acad:3:aaaa::/80 network. This will provide addresses to the LAN connected to interface G0/0/1 on R2. As a part of the pool, set the DNS server to 2001:db8:acad::254, and set the domain name to STATEFUL.com.

```
R1(config)# ipv6 dhcp pool R2-STATEFUL
R1(config-dhcp)# address prefix 2001:db8:acad:3:aaa::/80
R1(config-dhcp)# dns-server 2001:db8:acad::254
R1(config-dhcp)# domain-name STATEFUL.com
```

b. Assign the DHCPv6 pool you just created to interface g0/0/0 on R1.

```
R1(config)# interface g0/0/0
R1(config-if)# ipv6 dhcp server R2-STATEFUL
```

Part 5: Configure and Verify DHCPv6 Relay on R2.

In Part 5, you will configure and verify DHCPv6 relay on R2, allowing PC-B to receive an IPv6 Address.

Step 1: Power on PC-B and examine the SLAAC address that it generates.

```
C:\Users\Student> ipconfig /all
Windows IP Configuration

  Host Name . . . . . . . . . . . . : DESKTOP-3FR7RKA
    Primary Dns Suffix  . . . . . . . :
    Node Type . . . . . . . . . . . . : Hybrid
    IP Routing Enabled. . . . . . . . : No
    WINS Proxy Enabled. . . . . . . . : No

Ethernet adapter Ethernet0:

    Connection-specific DNS Suffix  . :
    Description . . . . . . . . . . . : Intel(R) 82574L Gigabit Network
                                        Connection
    Physical Address. . . . . . . . . : 00-50-56-B3-7B-06
    DHCP Enabled. . . . . . . . . . . : Yes
    Autoconfiguration Enabled . . . . : Yes
    IPv6 Address. . . . . . . . . . . : 2001:db8:acad:3:a0f3:3d39:f9fb:a020
                                        (Preferred)
    Temporary IPv6 Address. . . . . . : 2001:db8:acad:3:d4f3:7b16:eeee
                                        :b2b5(Preferred)
    Link-local IPv6 Address . . . . . : fe80::a0f3:3d39:f9fb:a020%6
                                        (Preferred)
    IPv4 Address. . . . . . . . . . . : 169.254.160.32(Preferred)
    Subnet Mask . . . . . . . . . . . : 255.255.0.0
    Default Gateway . . . . . . . . . : fe80::1%6
    DHCPv6 IAID . . . . . . . . . . . : 50334761
    DHCPv6 Client DUID. . . . . . . . : 00-01-00-01-24-F2-08-38-00-50-
                                        56-B3-7B-06
    DNS Servers . . . . . . . . . . . : fec0:0:0:ffff::1%1
                                        fec0:0:0:ffff::2%1
                                        fec0:0:0:ffff::3%1
    NetBIOS over Tcpip. . . . . . . . : Enabled
```

Notice in the output that the prefix used is 2001:db8:acad:3::

Step 2:   Configure R2 as a DHCP relay agent for the LAN on G0/0/1.

    a.   Configure the **ipv6 dhcp relay** command on R2 interface G0/0/1, specifying the destination address of the G0/0/0 interface on R1. Also configure the **managed-config-flag** command.

```
R2(config)# interface g0/0/1
R2(config-if)# ipv6 nd managed-config-flag
R2(config-if)# ipv6 dhcp relay destination 2001:db8:acad:2::1 g0/0/0
```

    b.   Save your configuration.

Step 3:   Attempt to acquire an IPv6 address from DHCPv6 on PC-B.

    a.   Restart PC-B.

    b.   Open a command prompt on PC-B and issue the command **ipconfig /all** and examine the output to see the results of the DHCPv6 relay operation.

```
C:\Users\Student> ipconfig /all
Windows IP Configuration

    Host Name . . . . . . . . . . . . : DESKTOP-3FR7RKA
      Primary Dns Suffix  . . . . . . . :
      Node Type . . . . . . . . . . . . : Hybrid
      IP Routing Enabled. . . . . . . . : No
      WINS Proxy Enabled. . . . . . . . : No
      DNS Suffix Search List. . . . . . : STATEFUL.com

Ethernet adapter Ethernet0:

      Connection-specific DNS Suffix  . : STATEFUL.com
      Description . . . . . . . . . . . : Intel(R) 852574L Gigabit
                                          Network Connection
      Physical Address. . . . . . . . . : 00-50-56-B3-7B-06
      DHCP Enabled. . . . . . . . . . . : Yes
      Autoconfiguration Enabled . . . . : Yes
      IPv6 Address. . . . . . . . . . . : 2001:db8:acad3:aaaa:7104:8b7d:54
                                          02(Preferred)
      Lease Obtained. . . . . . . . . . : Sunday, October 6, 2019
                                          3:27:13 PM
      Lease Expires . . . . . . . . . . : Tuesday, October 8, 2019
                                          3:27:13 PM
      Link-local IPv6 Address . . . . . : fe80::a0f3:3d39:f9fb:a020%6
                                          (Preferred)
      IPv4 Address. . . . . . . . . . . : 169.254.160.32(Preferred)
      Subnet Mask . . . . . . . . . . . : 255.255.0.0
      Default Gateway . . . . . . . . . : fe80::2%6
      DHCPv6 IAID . . . . . . . . . . . : 50334761
      DHCPv6 Client DUID. . . . . . . . : 00-01-00-01-24-F2-08-38-00-50-
                                          56-B3-7B-06
      DNS Servers . . . . . . . . . . . : 2001:db8:acad::254
      NetBIOS over Tcpip. . . . . . . . : Enabled
      Connection-specific DNS Suffix Search List  : STATEFUL.com
```

    c.   Test connectivity by pinging R1's G0/0/1 interface IP address.

FHRP Concepts

The "Study Guide" portion of this chapter uses a variety of exercises to test your knowledge of how First Hop Redundancy Protocols (FHRPs) provide default gateway services in a redundant network. The "Labs and Activities" portion of this chapter includes the instructions for a Packet Tracer activity in which you configure and verify the FHRP Host Standby Router Protocol (HSRP).

As you work through this chapter, use Chapter 9 in *Switching, Routing, and Wireless Essentials v7 Companion Guide* or use the corresponding Module 9 in the Switching, Routing, and Wireless Essentials online curriculum for assistance.

Study Guide

First Hop Redundancy Protocols

This section reviews the various FHRPs and the purpose of each one.

Default Gateway Limitations

If a router or router interface (that serves as a default gateway) fails, the hosts configured with that default gateway are isolated from outside networks. FHRPs provide alternate default gateways in switched networks where two or more routers are connected to the same VLANs.

Router Redundancy

As shown in Figure 9-1, by sharing an IP address and a MAC address, two or more routers can act as a single virtual router.

Figure 9-1   Topology with Router Redundancy

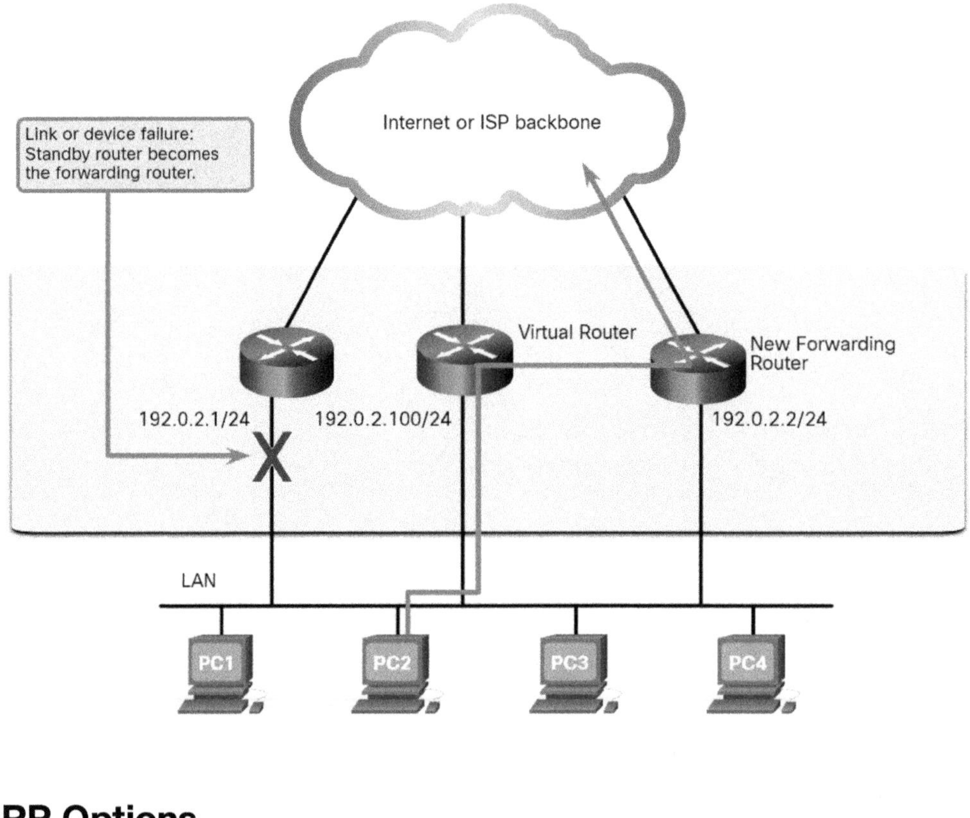

FHRP Options

In Table 9-1, indicate whether each characteristic describes HSRP, Virtual Router Redundancy Protocol (VRRP), Gateway Load Balancing Protocol (GLBP), or ICMP Router Discovery Protocol (IRDP).

Table 9-1   FHRP Characteristic

FHRP Characteristic	HSRP	VRRP	GLBP	IRDP
Used in a group of routers for selecting an active device and a standby device.				
A nonproprietary election protocol that allows several routers on a multiaccess link to use the same virtual IPv4 address.				
A Cisco-proprietary FHRP protocol designed to allow for transparent failover of first hop IP devices.				
A legacy FHRP solution specified in RFC 1256.				
A Cisco-proprietary FHRP protocol that protects data traffic from a failed router or circuit while also allowing load sharing between a group of redundant routers.				
A protocol with which one router is elected as the virtual router master, and the other routers act as backups in case the virtual router master fails.				

Check Your Understanding—First Hop Redundancy Protocols

Check your understanding of first hop redundancy protocols by choosing the BEST answer to each of the following questions.

1. What type of device routes traffic destined to network segments beyond the source network segment for which the sending node may not have explicit routing information?

    a. virtual router

    b. standby router

    c. default gateway

    d. Layer 3 switch

2. What device presents the illusion of a single router to hosts on a LAN segment but actually represents a set of routers working together?

    a. virtual router

    b. forwarding router

    c. default gateway

    d. Layer 3 switch

3. What device is part of a virtual router group assigned the role of alternate default gateway?

    a. virtual router

    b. standby router

    c. default gateway

    d. Layer 3 switch

4. What device that is part of a virtual router group is assigned to the role of default gateway?

    a. virtual router

    b. forwarding router

    c. default gateway

    d. Layer 3 switch

5. Which FHRPs are Cisco proprietary? (Choose two.)

    a. IRDP

    b. HSRP

    c. HSRP for IPv6

    d. VRRPv2

HSRP

In this section, you review how HSRP operates to provide redundant default gateways.

HSRP Priority and Preemption

The role of the active and standby routers is determined during the HSRP election process. By default, the router with the numerically highest IPv4 address is elected the active router. However, HSRP priority can be configured to determine the active router. What is the default priority value?

In Figure 9-2, R1 and R2 have priorities of 50 and 150, respectively. Which router will be the active HSRP router?

Figure 9-2 HSRP Scenario

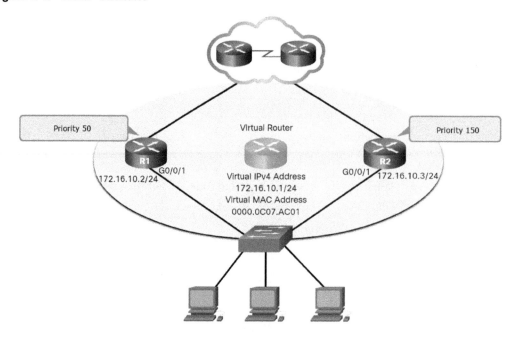

The command to configure a router to be the active router is the **standby** *group* **priority** *priority* interface command. The range of the HSRP priority is 0 to 255. By default, after a router becomes the active router, it remains the active router even if another router with a higher HSRP priority comes online. To make sure the router you want to be the active router is always the active router, configure the **standby** *group* **preempt** interface command.

Example 9-1 shows the configuration for R2 in Figure 9-2 with a priority of 150. This configuration always forces an HSRP election if the router fails and then comes back online. Example 9-1 also shows the commands to configure HSRPv2 and the virtual IPv4 address that both R1 and R2 will use.

Note: HSRP configuration is not a certification objective.

Example 9-1 Configure R2 as the Active HSRP Router

```
R2(config)# interface g0/0/1
R2(config-if)# ip address 172.16.10.3 255.255.255.0
R2(config-if)# standby version 2
R2(config-if)# standby 1 ip 1722.16.10.1
R2(config-if)# standby 1 priority 150
R2(config-if)# standby 1 preempt
R2(config-if)# no shutdown
R2(config-if)# end
R1#
```

HSRP States and Timers

In Table 9-2, indicate the HSRP state based on the scenario description.

Table 9-2 Determine the HSRP State

Scenario	Initial	Learn	Listen	Speak	Standby	Active
The router has not determined the virtual IP address and has not yet seen a hello message from the active router. In this state, the router waits to hear from the active router.						
The router forwards packets that are sent to the group virtual MAC address. The router sends periodic hello messages.						
A new HSRP interface is activated.						
The router becomes active if it does not receive a hello message from the active router after 10 seconds.						
The router knows the virtual IP address, but the router is neither the active router nor the standby router. It listens for hello messages from those routers.						

Scenario	Initial	Learn	Listen	Speak	Standby	Active
The router sends periodic hello messages and actively participates in the election of the active and/or standby router.						
The router is a candidate to become the next active router and sends periodic hello messages.						
The router is configured with a priority of 200. The other router is not configured with an HSRP priority.						
This state is entered through a configuration change.						

Check Your Understanding—HSRP

Check your understanding of HSRP by choosing the BEST answer to each of the following questions.

1. What is the default HSRP priority?

   a. 50

   b. 100

   c. 150

   d. 255

2. True or false: If a router with a higher HSRP priority joins the network, it will take over the active router role from an existing active router that has a lower priority.

   a. true

   b. false

3. During which HSRP state does an interface begin sending periodic hello messages?

   a. initial

   b. listen

   c. speak

   d. active

4. Which is a characteristic of the HSRP learn state?

   a. The router has not determined the virtual IP address.

   b. The router knows the virtual IP address.

   c. The router sends periodic hello messages.

   d. The router actively participates in the active/standby election process.

Labs and Activities

Command Reference

In Table 9-3, record the command, including the correct router prompt, that fits each description.

Table 9-3   Commands for Chapter 9, "FHRP Concepts"

Command	Description
	Configure R1 to use the virtual IP address 10.1.1.1 for group 10.
	Configure R1 with HSRP priority 110.
	Configure R1 to immediately take over the active role when rebooting.

9.3.3 Packet Tracer—HSRP Configuration Guide

Addressing Table

Device	Interface	IP Address	Default Gateway
R1	G0/0	10.1.1.1/30	N/A
	G0/1	192.168.1.1/24	
	G0/2	10.1.1.9/30	
R2	G0/0	10.1.1.2/30	N/A
	G0/1	10.1.1.5/30	
	G0/2	10.100.100.1/30	
R3	G0/0	192.168.1.3/24	N/A
	G0/1	10.1.1.6/30	
	G0/2	10.1.1.10/30	
I-Net	G0/1	10.100.100.2/30	N/A
HSRP Virtual Gateway	Virtual	192.168.1.254/24	N/A
S1	VLAN 1	192.168.1.11/24	192.168.1.1
S3	VLAN 1	192.168.1.13/24	192.168.1.3
PC-A	NIC	192.168.1.101/24	192.168.1.1
PC-B	NIC	192.168.1.103/24	192.168.1.3
Web Server	NIC	209.165.200.226/27	209.165.100.225

Note: The I-Net router is present in the internet cloud and cannot be accessed in this activity.

Objectives

In this Packet Tracer activity, you will learn how to configure Hot Standby Router Protocol (HSRP) to provide redundant default gateway devices to hosts on LANs. After configuring HSRP, you will test the configuration to verify that hosts are able to use the redundant default gateway if the current gateway device becomes unavailable.

- Configure an HSRP active router.
- Configure an HSRP standby router.
- Verify HSRP operation.

Background / Scenario

Spanning Tree Protocol provides loop-free redundancy between switches within a LAN. However, it does not provide redundant default gateways for end-user devices within the network if a gateway router fails. First Hop Redundancy Protocols (FHRPs) provide redundant default gateways for end devices with no additional end-user configuration necessary. By using an FHRP, two or more routers can share the same virtual IP address and MAC address and can act as a single virtual router. Hosts on the network are configured with a shared IP address as their default gateway. In this Packet Tracer activity, you will configure Cisco's Hot Standby Router Protocol (HSRP), which is an FHRP.

You will configure HSRP on routers R1 and R3, which serve as the default gateways for the hosts on LAN 1 and LAN 2. When you configure HSRP, you will create a virtual gateway that uses the same default gateway address for hosts in both LANs. If one gateway router becomes unavailable, the second router will take over using the same default gateway address that was used by the first router. Because the hosts on the LANs are configured with the IP address of the virtual gateway as the default gateway, the hosts will regain connectivity to remote networks after HSRP activates the remaining router.

Instructions

Part 1: Verify Connectivity

Step 1:   Trace the path to the Web Server from PC-A.

    a. Go to the desktop of PC-A and open a command prompt.

    b. Trace the path from PC-A to the Web Server by executing the **tracert 209.165.200.226** command.

    Question:

    Which devices are on the path from PC-A to the Web Server? Use the addressing table to determine the device names.

_____

Step 2:   Trace the path to the Web Server from PC-B.

    Repeat the process in Step 1 from PC-B.

    Question:

    Which devices are on the path from PC-B to the Web Server?

_____

Step 3:   Observe the network behavior when R3 becomes unavailable.

    a.   Select the delete tool from the Packet Tracer tool bar and delete the link between **R3** and **S3**.

    b.   Open a command prompt on PC-B. Execute the **tracert** command with the Web Server as the destination.

    c.   Compare the current output with the output of the command from Step 2.

      Question:

      What are the results?

---

    d.   Click the **Connections** icon in the lower left corner of the PT window. Locate and select the **Copper Straight-Through** icon in the pallet of connection types.

    e.   Click on S3 and select port **GigbitEthernet0/2**. Click **R3** and select port **GigabitEthernet0/0**.

    f.   After the link lights on the connection are both green, test the connection by pinging the Web Server. The ping should be successful.

Part 2: Configure HSRP Active and Standby Routers

Step 1:   Configure HSRP on R1.

    a.   Configure HSRP on the G0/1 LAN interface of R1.

```
R1(config)# interface g0/1
```

    b.   Specify the HSRP protocol version number. The most recent version is version **2**.

Note: Standby version 1 only supports IPv4 addressing.

```
R1(config-if)# standby version 2
```

    c.   Configure the IP address of the virtual default gateway. This address must be configured on any hosts that require the services of the default gateway. It replaces the physical interface address of the router that has been previously configured on the hosts.

      Multiple instances of HSRP can be configured on a router. You must specify the HSRP group number to identify the virtual interface between routers in a HSRP group. This number must be consistent between the routers in the group. The group number for this configuration is 1.

```
R1(config-if)# standby 1 ip 192.168.1.254
```

    d.   Designate the active router for the HSRP group. It is the router that will be used as the gateway device unless it fails or the path to it becomes inactive or unusable. Specify the priority for the router interface. The default value is 100. A higher value will determine which router is the active router. If the priorities of the routers in the HSRP group are the same, then the router with the highest configured IP address will become the active router.

```
R1(config-if)# standby 1 priority 150
```

      R1 will operate as the active router and traffic from the two LANs will use it as the default gateway.

e. If it is desirable that the active router resume that role when it becomes available again, configure it to preempt the service of the standby router. The active router will take over the gateway role when it becomes operable again.

```
R1(config-if)# standby 1 preempt
```

Question:

What will the HSRP priority of R3 be when it is added to HSRP group 1?

_____

Step 2:   Configure HSRP on R3.

Configure R3 as the standby router.

a. Configure the R3 interface that is connected to LAN 2.

b. Repeat only steps 1b and 1c above.

Step 3:   Verify HSRP Configuration.

a. Verify HSRP by issuing the **show standby** command on R1 and R3. Verify the values for HSRP role, group, virtual IP address of the gateway, preemption, and priority. Note that HSRP also identifies the active and standby router IP addresses for the group.

```
R1# show standby
GigabitEthernet0/1 - Group 1 (version 2)
  State is Active
    4 state changes, last state change 00:00:30
  Virtual IP address is 192.168.1.254
  Active virtual MAC address is 0000.0C9F.F001
    Local virtual MAC address is 0000.0C9F.F001 (v2 default)
  Hello time 3 sec, hold time 10 sec
    Next hello sent in 1.696 secs
  Preemption enabled
  Active router is local
  Standby router is 192.168.1.3
  Priority 150 (configured 150)
  Group name is "hsrp-Gi0/1-1" (default)
R3# show standby
GigabitEthernet0/0 - Group 1 (version 2)
  State is Standby
    4 state changes, last state change 00:02:29
  Virtual IP address is 192.168.1.254
  Active virtual MAC address is 0000.0C9F.F001
    Local virtual MAC address is 0000.0C9F.F001 (v2 default)
  Hello time 3 sec, hold time 10 sec
    Next hello sent in 0.720 secs
  Preemption disabled
  Active router is 192.168.1.1
    MAC address is d48c.b5ce.a0c1
  Standby router is local
  Priority 100 (default 100)
  Group name is "hsrp-Gi0/0-1" (default)
```

Using the output shown above, answer the following questions:

Questions:

Which router is the active router?

_____

What is the MAC address for the virtual IP address?

_____

What is the IP address and priority of the standby router?

_____

b. Use the **show standby brief** command on R1 and R3 to view an HSRP status summary. Sample output is shown below.

```
R1# show standby brief
                     P indicates configured to preempt.
                     |
Interface   Grp  Pri P State   Active      Standby       Virtual IP
Gi0/1       1    150 P Active  local       192.168.1.3   192.168.1.254


R3# show standby brief
                     P indicates configured to preempt.
                     |
Interface   Grp  Pri P State   Active      Standby       Virtual IP
Gi0/0       1    100   Standby 192.168.1.1 local         192.168.1.254
```

c. Change the default gateway address for PC-A, PC-C, S1, and S3.

Questions:

Which address should you use?

_____

Verify the new settings. Issue a ping from both PC-A and PC-C to the Web Server. Are the pings successful?

_____

Part 3: Observe HSRP Operation

Step 1: Make the active router become unavailable.

Open a command prompt on **PC-B** and enter the command **tracert 209.165.200.226.**

Question:

Does the path differ from the path used before HSRP was configured?

_____

Step 2: Break the link to R1.

a. Select the delete tool from the Packet Tracer toolbar and delete the cable that connects R1 to S1.

b. Immediately return to PC-B and execute the **tracert 209.165.200.226** command again. Observe the output of the command until the command completes execution. You may need to repeat the trace to see the full path.

Question:

How was this trace different from the previous trace?

_____

HSRP undergoes a process to determine which router should take over when the active router becomes unavailable. This process takes time. Once the process is complete, the R3 standby router becomes active and is used as the default gateway for hosts on LAN 1 and LAN 2.

Step 3:   Restore the link to R1.

a. Re-connect R1 to S1 with a copper straight-through cable.

b. Execute a trace from PC-B to the Web Server. You may need to repeat the trace to see the full path.

Questions:

What path is used to reach the Web Server?

_____

If the preempt command was not configured for the HSRP group on R1, would the results have been the same?

_____

LAN Security Concepts

The "Study Guide" portion of this chapter uses a variety of exercises to test your knowledge of how vulnerabilities compromise LAN security. There are no labs or Packet Tracer activities for this chapter.

As you work through this chapter, use Chapter 10 in *Switching, Routing, and Wireless Essentials v7 Companion Guide* or use the corresponding Module 10 in the Switching, Routing, and Wireless Essentials online curriculum for assistance.

Study Guide

Endpoint Security

In this section, you review how to use endpoint security to mitigate attacks.

Network Security Devices

Various network security devices are required to protect the network perimeter from outside access. Fill in the name of each network security device described.

- _____ Provides a secure connection to remote users across a public network and into the enterprise network. These services can also be integrated into a firewall.

- _____ Provides stateful packet inspection, application visibility and control, a next-generation intrusion prevention system (NGIPS), advanced malware protection (AMP), and URL filtering.

- _____ A device that includes authentication, authorization, and accounting (AAA) services. It might be incorporated into an appliance that can manage access policies across a wide variety of users and device types.

Check Your Understanding—Endpoint Security

Check your understanding of endpoint security by choosing the BEST option to each of the following questions.

1. Which attack encrypts the data on hosts in an attempt to extract a monetary payment from the victim?

   a. DDoS

   b. data breach

   c. malware

   d. ransomware

2. Which devices are specifically designed for network security? (Choose three)

   a. VPN-enabled router

   b. NGFW

   c. switch

   d. WLC

   e. NAC

3. Which device monitors Simple Mail Transfer Protocol (SMTP) traffic to block threats and encrypt outgoing messages to prevent data loss?

   a. NGFW

   b. ESA

   c. NAC

   d. WSA

4. Which device monitors Hypertext Transfer Protocol (HTTP) traffic to block access to risky sites and encrypt outgoing messages?

   a. NGFW

   b. ESA

   c. NAC

   d. WSA

Access Control

In this section, you review how AAA and 802.1X are used to authenticate LAN endpoints and devices.

Authentication with a Local Password

The simplest method of remote access authentication is to configure a login and password combination on console, vty lines, and aux ports. This method is the weakest and least secure. Secure Shell (SSH) is a more secure form of remote access. List the commands to configure Secure Shell version 2 (SSHv2) on R1 and apply it to the vty lines with the following requirements.

- The domain is srwelsg.com.

- The modulus size is 2048.

- The user is student and the password is Cisco12345!.

    R1(config)# _____

    _____

    _____

    _____

    _____

    _____

    _____

List two limitations of using the local database for user authentication:

- _____

- _____

AAA Components

Authentication, authorization, and accounting (AAA) provides the primary framework to set up access control on a network device. AAA provides a way to control who is permitted to access a network (authenticate) and what they can do while they are there (authorize) and to audit what actions they performed while accessing the network (accounting).

Authentication

Local and server-based are two common methods of implementing AAA authentication. Local AAA authentication stores usernames and passwords locally on the device. Server-based AAA authentication uses a central AAA server to authenticate users. What are the two authentication protocols supported by Cisco devices?

_____

_____

Authorization

AAA authorization governs what users can and cannot do on the network after they are authenticated. Authorization uses a set of attributes that describes the user's access to the network. These attributes are used by the AAA server to determine privileges and restrictions for that user.

Accounting

In AAA accounting, the server keeps a detailed log of exactly what the authenticated user does on the device. This includes all EXEC and configuration commands issued by the user. This information is useful when troubleshooting devices. It also provides evidence for when individuals perform malicious acts.

802.1X

The IEEE 802.1X standard is a port-based access control and authentication protocol. This protocol restricts unauthorized workstations from connecting to a LAN through publicly accessible switch ports. With 802.1X port-based authentication, the devices in the network have specific roles. Briefly describe each role.

- Client (supplicant): _____

_____

- Switch or wireless access point (authenticator): _____

_____

_____

- Authentication server: _____

_____

_____

Check Your Understanding—Access Control

Check your understanding of access control by choosing the BEST answer to each of the following questions.

1. Which AAA component is responsible for collecting and reporting usage data for auditing and billing purposes?

    a. authentication

    b. authorization

    c. accounting

2. Which AAA component is responsible for controlling who is permitted to access the network?

   a. authentication

   b. authorization

   c. accounting

3. Which AAA component is responsible for determining what the user can access?

   a. authentication

   b. authorization

   c. accounting

4. In an 802.1X implementation, which device is responsible for relaying responses?

   a. supplicant

   b. authenticator

   c. router

   d. authentication server

   e. client

Layer 2 Security Threats

In this section, you review Layer 2 vulnerabilities. Network administrators routinely implement security solutions to protect the elements in Layer 3 through Layer 7. However, if Layer 2 is compromised, then all the layers above it are also affected.

Switch Attack Categories

Table 10-1 lists attacks against the Layer 2 LAN infrastructure.

Table 10-1   Layer 2 Attacks

Category	Examples
Media Access Control (MAC) table attacks	Includes MAC address flooding attacks.
VLAN attacks	Includes VLAN hopping and VLAN double-tagging attacks. It also includes attacks between devices on a common VLAN.
Dynamic Host Configuration Protocol (DHCP) attacks	Includes DHCP starvation and DHCP spoofing attacks.
Address Resolution Protocol (ARP) attacks	Includes ARP spoofing and ARP poisoning attacks.
Address Spoofing attacks	Includes MAC address and IP address spoofing attacks.
Spanning Tree Protocol (STP) attacks	Includes Spanning Tree Protocol manipulation attacks.

Switch Attack Mitigation Techniques

Table 10-2 provides an overview of Cisco solutions to help mitigate Layer 2 attacks.

Table 10-2   Layer 2 Attack Mitigation

Solution	Description
Port security	Prevents many types of attacks, including MAC address flooding attacks and DHCP starvation attacks.
DHCP snooping	Prevents DHCP starvation and DHCP spoofing attacks.
Dynamic ARP Inspection (DAI)	Prevents ARP spoofing and ARP poisoning attacks.
IP Source Guard (IPSG)	Prevents MAC and IP address spoofing attacks.

Check Your Understanding—Layer 2 Security Threats

Check your understanding of Layer 2 security threats by choosing the BEST answer to each of the following questions.

1. Which of the following mitigation techniques are used to protect Layer 3 through Layer 7 of the OSI model? (Choose three.)

   a. DHCP snooping

   b. VPN

   c. firewalls

   d. IPSG

   e. IPS devices

2. Which of the following mitigation techniques prevents many types of attacks, including MAC address table overflow and DHCP starvation attacks?

   a. IPSG

   b. DHCP snooping

   c. DAI

   d. port security

3. Which of the following mitigation techniques prevents MAC and IP address spoofing?

   a. IPSG

   b. DHCP snooping

   c. DAI

   d. port security

4. Which of the following mitigation techniques prevents ARP spoofing and ARP poisoning attacks?

   a. IPSG

   b. DHCP snooping

   c. DAI

   d. port security

5. Which of the following mitigation techniques prevents DHCP starvation and DHCP spoofing attacks?

   a. IPSG

   b. DHCP snooping

   c. DAI

   d. port security

MAC Address Table Attack

In this section, you review how a MAC address table attack compromises LAN security.

Recall that to make forwarding decisions, a Layer 2 LAN switch builds a table based on the source MAC addresses in received frames. Every MAC table has a fixed size; consequently, a switch can run out of resources in which to store MAC addresses. MAC address flooding attacks take advantage of this limitation by bombarding the switch with fake source MAC addresses until the switch MAC address table is full. To mitigate MAC address table overflow attacks, network administrators must implement port security.

Check Your Understanding—MAC Address Table Attacks

Check your understanding of MAC address table attacks by choosing the BEST answer to each of the following questions.

1. What is the behavior of a switch as a result of a successful MAC address table attack?

   a. The switch shuts down.

   b. The switch interfaces transition to the error-disabled state.

   c. The switch forwards all received frames to all other ports within the VLAN.

   d. The switch drops all received frames.

2. What would be the primary reason a threat actor would launch a MAC address overflow attack?

   a. To see frames that are destined for other devices

   b. To execute arbitrary code on the switch

   c. So the switch stops forwarding traffic

   d. So legitimate hosts cannot obtain a MAC address

3. What mitigation technique must be implemented to prevent MAC address overflow attacks?

   a. IPSG

   b. DAI

   c. port security

   d. DHCP snooping

LAN Attacks

In this section, you review how LAN attacks compromise LAN security.

VLAN Hopping Attacks

In a basic VLAN hopping attack, the threat actor configures a host to spoof 802.1Q signaling and Cisco-proprietary Dynamic Trunking Protocol (DTP) signaling. This allows it to trunk with the connecting switch. The threat actor can then access all the VLANs on the switch. The threat actor can send and receive traffic on any VLAN, effectively hopping between VLANs.

VLAN Double-Tagging Attack

In specific situations, a threat actor could embed a hidden 802.1Q tag inside a frame that already has an 802.1Q tag. This tag allows the frame to go to a VLAN that the original 802.1Q tag did not specify.

What three security guidelines mitigate VLAN hopping and VLAN double-tagging attacks?

_____

_____

_____

DHCP Attacks

Two types of DHCP attacks are DHCP starvation and DHCP spoofing:

- A DHCP starvation attack creates a DoS for connecting clients.
- A DHCP spoofing attack occurs when a rogue DHCP server is connected to the network and provides false IP configuration parameters to legitimate clients.

How are DHCP attacks mitigated?

_____

ARP Attacks

An attacker can send a gratuitous ARP message containing a spoofed MAC address to a switch, and the switch would update its MAC table accordingly. The effect of this ARP spoofing is to poison the MAC table of the switch.

How are ARP spoofing and ARP poisoning attacks mitigated?

_____

Address Spoofing Attack

With IP address spoofing, a threat actor hijacks a valid IP address of another device on the subnet or uses a random IP address. IP address spoofing is difficult to mitigate, especially when it is used inside a subnet in which the IP address belongs.

MAC address spoofing attacks occur when the threat actors alter the MAC address of their host to match another known MAC address of a target host.

How are IP and MAC address spoofing attacks mitigated?

STP Attack

A threat actor can manipulate the Spanning Tree Protocol (STP) to conduct an attack by spoofing the bridge protocol data units (BPDUs) of the root bridge and changing the topology of a network. This allows the threat actor to appear as the root bridge and capture all traffic for the immediate switched domain.

How is this STP attack mitigated?

CDP Reconnaissance

Cisco Discovery Protocol (CDP) information is extremely useful in network troubleshooting. For example, CDP can be used to verify Layer 1 and 2 connectivity. If an administrator cannot ping a directly connected interface but still receives CDP information, the problem is most likely related to the Layer 3 configuration.

However, the information provided by CDP can also be used by a threat actor to discover network infrastructure vulnerabilities.

How do you mitigate the exploitation of CDP?

Check Your Understanding—LAN Attacks

Check your understanding of LAN attacks by choosing the BEST answer to each of the following questions.

1. A threat actor changes the MAC address of the threat actor's device to the MAC address of the default gateway. What type of attack is this?

   a. address spoofing

   b. ARP spoofing

   c. CDP reconnaissance

   d. DHCP starvation

   e. STP attack

   f. VLAN hopping

2. A threat actor sends a BPDU message with priority 0. What type of attack is this?

   a. address spoofing

   b. ARP spoofing

   c. CDP reconnaissance

   d. DHCP starvation

   e. STP attack

   f. VLAN hopping

3. A threat actor leases all the available IP addresses on a subnet. What type of attack is this?

   a. address spoofing

   b. ARP spoofing

   c. CDP reconnaissance

   d. DHCP starvation

   e. STP attack

   f. VLAN hopping

4. A threat actor sends a message that causes all other devices to believe the MAC address of the threat actor's device is the default gateway address. What type of attack is this?

   a. address spoofing

   b. ARP spoofing

   c. CDP reconnaissance

   d. DHCP starvation

   e. STP attack

   f. VLAN hopping

5. A threat actor configures a host with the 802.1Q protocol and forms a trunk with the connected switch. What type of attack is this?

   a. address spoofing

   b. ARP spoofing

   c. CDP reconnaissance

   d. DHCP starvation

   e. STP attack

   f. VLAN hopping

6. A threat actor discovers the IOS version and IP addresses of the local switch. What type of attack is this?

   a. Address spoofing

   b. ARP spoofing

   c. CDP reconnaissance

   d. DHCP starvation

   e. STP attack

   f. VLAN hopping

Labs and Activities

There are no labs or Packet Tracer activities for this chapter.

CHAPTER 11

Switch Security Configuration

The "Study Guide" portion of this chapter uses a variety of exercises to test your knowledge and skills related to configuring switch security to mitigate LAN attacks. The "Labs and Activities" portion of this chapter includes all the online curriculum labs and Packet Tracer activity instructions.

As you work through this chapter, use Chapter 11 in *Switching, Routing, and Wireless Essentials v7 Companion Guide* or use the corresponding Module 11 in the Switching, Routing, and Wireless Essentials online curriculum for assistance.

Study Guide

Implement Port Security

In this section, you review how to implement port security to mitigate Media Access Control (MAC) address table attacks.

Secure Unused Ports

A simple method that many administrators use to help secure the network from unauthorized access is to disable all unused ports on a switch. If a port must be reactivated at a later time, it can be enabled with the **no shutdown** command.

You are logged into S1 in global configuration mode. S1 is a Catalyst 2960 switch. Record the two commands, including switch prompt, to disable ports Fa0/17 through Fa0/24.

_____

_____

Enable Port Security

The simplest and most effective method of preventing MAC address table overflow attacks is to enable port security.

On S1, ports G0/1 and G0/2 are used for trunking with other switches. Record the commands to configure ports Fa0/1 through Fa0/16, based on the following requirements:

- Set the ports to the correct mode.

- Enable port security.

- Specify that each port can learn two MAC addresses.

- Ensure that MAC addresses are added to the running configuration.

- Set the ports to remove secured MAC addresses after 20 minutes of inactivity.

- Ensure that when the MAC address limit is reached, the port drops packets for subsequent unknown MAC addresses and sends a syslog message.

S1(config)# _____

_____

_____

_____

_____

_____

_____

In Table 11-1, each violation mode is listed along with the possible actions that the port will take if there is a violation. Answer with a "yes" or "no" if the violation mode will take the action.

Table 11-1   Security Violation Mode Comparison

Violation Mode	Discards Offending Traffic	Sends Syslog Message	Increases Violation Counter	Shuts Down Port
Protect				
Restrict				
Shutdown				

In Table 11-2, list the default security settings for ports.

Table 11-2   Port Security Default Settings

Feature	Default Setting
Port security	
Maximum number of secure MAC addresses	
Violation mode	
Sticky address learning	

Ports in error-disabled State

What is the error-disabled state, and how do you resolve the problem?

In an error-disabled state, a port security violation has occurred, and the port is shut down. No traffic is sent or received on that port. To restore the port and remove the violation, the administrator should investigate to determine what device caused the problem. After ensuring that all devices connected to the port are authorized, the administrator must then access the affected port and enter the **shutdown** command and then the **no shutdown** command to remove the error-disabled state.

Verify Port Security

In Examples 11-1 through 11-4, record the command that generates the output.

Example 11-1   Verify Port Security for All Interfaces

```
S1# _____

Secure Port  MaxSecureAddr  CurrentAddr  SecurityViolation  Security Action
             (Count)        (Count)      (Count)

-------------------------------------------------------------------
     Fa0/1        1              0                 0          Restrict
     Fa0/2        1              0                 0          Restrict
     Fa0/3        1              0                 0          Restrict
(output omitted)
     Fa0/16       1              0                 0          Restrict
-------------------------------------------------------------------
Total Addresses in System (excluding one mac per port)    : 0
Max Addresses limit in System (excluding one mac per port) : 4096
Switch#
```

Example 11-2   Verify Port Security on FastEthernet 0/10

```
S1# _____
Port Security               : Enabled
Port Status                 : Secure-up
Violation Mode              : Restrict
Aging Time                  : 0 mins
Aging Type                  : Absolute
SecureStatic Address Aging  : Disabled
Maximum MAC Addresses       : 2
Total MAC Addresses         : 1
Configured MAC Addresses    : 0
Sticky MAC Addresses        : 0
Last Source Address:Vlan    : 0025.83e6.4b01:1
Security Violation Count    : 0
S1#
```

Example 11-3   Verify Learned MAC Addresses for FastEthernet 0/10

```
S1# _____
interface FastEthernet 0/10
switchport mode access
switchport port-security maximum 2
switchport port-security
switchport port-security mac-address sticky
switchport port-security mac-address sticky 0025.83e6.4b01
(output omitted)
S1#
```

Example 11-4   Verify All Secure MAC Addresses on S1

```
S1# _____
Secure Mac Address Table
-------------------------------------------------------------
Vlan    Mac Address        Type           Ports     Remaining Age
                                                    (mins)
----    -----------        ----           -----     -------------
1       0025.83e6.4b01     SecureDynamic  Fa0/10        15
1       0025.83e6.4b02     SecureSticky   Fa0/11         9
-------------------------------------------------------------
Total Addresses in System (excluding one mac per port)    : 0
Max Addresses limit in System (excluding one mac per port) : 8192
S1#
```

Mitigate VLAN Attacks

In this section, you review how to configure Dynamic Trunking Protocol (DTP) and native VLANs to mitigate VLAN attacks.

VLAN Attacks Review

Briefly describe the three ways a VLAN hopping attack can be launched.

- _____

- _____

- _____

Steps to Mitigate VLAN Hopping Attacks

Using the following requirements, record the commands necessary to mitigate VLAN attacks on S1:

- Fa0/1–Fa0/16 are active access ports.

- Fa0/17–Fa0/24 are not currently used.

- G0/1–G0/2 are trunks.

Your configuration should include placing inactive ports in unused VLAN 86, and trunks should be assigned to a different native VLAN, VLAN 99.

```
S1(config)# _____
```

_____

_____

_____

_____

_____

_____

Mitigate DHCP Attacks

In this section, you review how to configure Dynamic Host Configuration Protocol (DHCP) snooping to mitigate DHCP attacks.

DHCP Attack Review

How are DHCP starvation attacks effectively mitigated?

_____

How are DHCP spoofing attacks mitigated?

_____

DHCP Snooping

Briefly explain how DHCP snooping mitigates DHCP spoofing.

_____

_____

_____

_____

_____

_____

Steps to Implement DHCP Snooping

Based on the following requirements, record the commands to configure DHCP snooping on S1 in Figure 11-1:

- Enable DHCP snooping globally for S1.

- Configure DHCP snooping to trust VLANs 10, 20, and 30.

- Configure G0/1 and G0/2 as trusted interfaces.

- Rate limit all untrusted interfaces, Fa0/1 through Fa0/24, to a maximum of 10 DHCP messages per second.

Figure 11-1   DHCP Snooping Topology

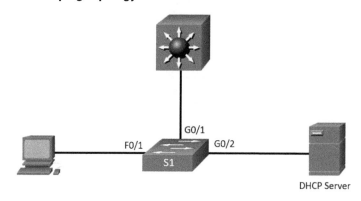

S1(config)# _____

_____

_____

_____

_____

_____

_____

_____

Mitigate ARP Attacks

In this section, you review how to mitigate Address Resolution Protocol (ARP) attacks by configuring Dynamic ARP Inspection (DAI).

Dynamic ARP Inspection

To prevent ARP spoofing and the resulting ARP poisoning, a switch must ensure that only valid ARP requests and replies are relayed. DAI requires DHCP snooping. List the ways DAI prevents ARP attacks.

- _____

- _____

- _____

- _____

- _____

Configure DAI

Using the topology in Figure 11-1 and the following requirements, record the commands to configure DAI on S1:

- Enable DHCP snooping globally for S1.

- Configure DHCP snooping to trust VLANs 10, 20, and 30.

- Configure G0/1 and G0/2 as trusted DHCP interfaces.

- Configure G0/1 and G0/2 as trusted ARP interfaces.

S1(config)# _____

_____

_____

_____

_____

_____

Mitigate STP Attacks

In this section, you review how to configure PortFast and Bridge Protocol Data Unit (BPDU) Guard to mitigate Spanning Tree Protocol (STP) attacks.

PortFast and BPDU Guard

To mitigate STP manipulation attacks, use PortFast and BPDU Guard. Briefly describe these two mitigation techniques.

- PortFast: _____

    _____

    _____

- BPDU Guard: _____

    _____

    _____

Configure PortFast and BPDU Guard

What is the command to configure all access ports for PortFast?

_____

What is the command to configure PortFast on an interface?

_____

What is the command to configure all PortFast-enabled ports for BPDU Guard?

_____

What is the command to configure BPDU Guard on an interface?

_____

What happens when an interface configured for BPDU Guard receives a BPDU?

_____

What command is used to reenable a port after a BPDU Guard violation?

_____

Labs and Activities

Command Reference

In Table 11-3, record the command, including the correct switch prompt, that fits each description.

Table 11-3   Commands for Chapter 11, "Switch Security Configuration"

Command	Description
	Configure a switch interface to be an access port only.
	Enable port security on an interface.
	Specify that an interface can learn up to three MAC addresses.
	Specify that MAC addresses should be added to the running configuration.
	Set the port security on an interface to age out the MAC addresses after 10 minutes.
	Verify the port security settings on all interfaces.
	Verify the port security settings on Fa0/1.
	Verify all the secure MAC addresses on the switch.
	Disable DTP messages on a trunking interface.
	Configure VLAN 99 as the native VLAN.
	Enable DHCP snooping globally.
	Enable DHCP snooping for VLANs 15, 25, and 45.
	Configure the interface to be trusted for DHCP messages.
	Configure the interface to only allow up to 10 DHCP messages per second.
	Configure the interface for DAI.
	Configure PortFast for all access ports.
	Configure PortFast on the interface.
	Configure BPDU Guard for all PortFast-enabled ports.
	Configure BPDU Guard on the interface.
	Verify that PortFast and BPDU Guard are enabled.

11.1.10 Packet Tracer—Implement Port Security

Addressing Table

Device	Interface	IP Address	Subnet Mask
S1	VLAN 1	10.10.10.2	255.255.255.0
PC1	NIC	10.10.10.10	255.255.255.0
PC2	NIC	10.10.10.11	255.255.255.0
Rogue Laptop	NIC	10.10.10.12	255.255.255.0

Objective

Part 1: Configure Port Security

Part 2: Verify Port Security

Background

In this activity, you will configure and verify port security on a switch. Port security allows you to restrict a port's ingress traffic by limiting the MAC addresses that are allowed to send traffic into the port.

Step 1: Configure Port Security

    a. Access the command line for **S1** and enable port security on Fast Ethernet ports 0/1 and 0/2.

```
S1(config)# interface range f0/1 - 2
S1(config-if-range)# switchport port-security
```

    b. Set the maximum so that only one device can access the Fast Ethernet ports 0/1 and 0/2.

```
S1(config-if-range)# switchport port-security maximum 1
```

    c. Secure the ports so that the MAC address of a device is dynamically learned and added to the running configuration.

```
S1(config-if-range)# switchport port-security mac-address sticky
```

    d. Set the violation mode so that the Fast Ethernet ports 0/1 and 0/2 are not disabled when a violation occurs, but a notification of the security violation is generated and packets from the unknown source are dropped.

```
S1(config-if-range)# switchport port-security violation restrict
```

    e. Disable all the remaining unused ports. Use the **range** keyword to apply this configuration to all the ports simultaneously.

```
S1(config-if-range)# interface range f0/3 - 24, g0/1 - 2
S1(config-if-range)# shutdown
```

Step 2: Verify Port Security

a. From **PC1**, ping **PC2**.

b. Verify that port security is enabled and the MAC addresses of **PC1** and **PC2** were added to the running configuration.

```
S1# show run | begin interface
```

c. Use port-security show commands to display configuration information.

```
S1# show port-security
S1# show port-security address
```

d. Attach **Rogue Laptop** to any unused switch port and notice that the link lights are red.

e. Enable the port and verify that **Rogue Laptop** can ping **PC1** and **PC2**. After verification, shut down the port connected to **Rogue Laptop**.

f. Disconnect **PC2** and connect **Rogue Laptop** to F0/2, which is the port to which PC2 was originally connected. Verify that **Rogue Laptop** is unable to ping **PC1**.

g. Display the port security violations for the port to which **Rogue Laptop** is connected.

```
S1# show port-security interface f0/2
```

Question:

How many violations have occurred?

_____

h. Disconnect **Rogue Laptop** and reconnect **PC2**. Verify **PC2** can ping **PC1**.

Question:

Why is **PC2** able to ping PC1, but the **Rogue Laptop** is not?

_____

11.6.1 Packet Tracer—Switch Security Configuration

VLAN Table

Switch	VLAN Number	VLAN Name	Port Membership	Network
SW-1	10	Admin	F0/1, F0/2	192.168.10.0/24
	20	Sales	F0/10	192.168.20.0/24
	99	Management	F0/24	192.168.99.0/24
	100	Native	G0/1, G0/2	None
	999	BlackHole	All unused	None
SW-2	10	Admin	F0/1, F0/22	192.168.10.0/24
	20	Sales	F0/10	192.168.20.0/24
	99	Management	F0/24	192.168.99.0/24
	100	Native	None	None
	999	BlackHole	All unused	None

Objectives

Part 1: Create a Secure Trunk

Part 2: Secure Unused Switchports

Part 3: Implement Port Security

Part 4: Enable DHCP Snooping

Part 5: Configure Rapid PVST PortFast and BPDU Guard

Background

You are enhancing security on two access switches in a partially configured network. You will implement the range of security measures that were covered in this module according to the requirements below. Note that routing has been configured on this network, so connectivity between hosts on different VLANs should function when completed.

Instructions

Step 1: Create a Secure Trunk.

    a. Connect the G0/2 ports of the two access layer switches.

    b. Configure ports G0/1 and G0/2 as static trunks on both switches.

    c. Disable DTP negotiation on both sides of the link.

    d. Create VLAN 100 and give it the name **Native** on both switches.

    e. Configure all trunk ports on both switches to use VLAN 100 as the native VLAN.

Step 2:   Secure Unused Switchports.

    a. Shut down all unused switch ports on SW-1.

    b. On SW-1, create a VLAN 999 and name it BlackHole. The configured name must match the requirement exactly.

    c. Move all unused switch ports to the BlackHole VLAN.

Step 3:   Implement Port Security.

    a. Activate port security on all the active access ports on switch SW-1.

    b. Configure the active ports to allow a maximum of 4 MAC addresses to be learned on the ports.

    c. For ports F0/1 on SW-1, statically configure the MAC address of the PC using port security.

    d. Configure each active access port so that it will automatically add the MAC addresses learned on the port to the running configuration.

    e. Configure the port security violation mode to drop packets from MAC addresses that exceed the maximum, generate a Syslog entry, but not disable the ports.

Step 4:   Configure DHCP Snooping.

    a. Configure the trunk ports on SW-1 as trusted ports.

    b. Limit the untrusted ports on SW-1 to five DHCP packets per second.

    c. On SW-2, enable DHCP snooping globally and for VLANs 10, 20, and 99.

Note: The DHCP snooping configuration may not score properly in Packet Tracer.

Step 5:   Configure PortFast, and BPDU Guard.

    a. Enable PortFast on all the access ports that are in use on SW-1.

    b. Enable BPDU Guard on all the access ports that are in use on SW-1.

    c. Configure SW-2 so that all access ports will use PortFast by default.

11.6.2 Lab—Switch Security Configuration

Topology

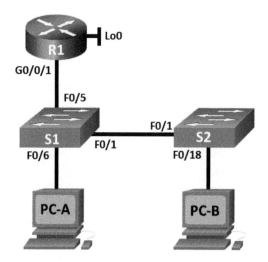

Addressing Table

Device	Interface / VLAN	IP Address	Subnet Mask
R1	G0/0/1	192.168.10.1	255.255.255.0
	Loopback 0	10.10.1.1	255.255.255.0
S1	VLAN 10	192.168.10.201	255.255.255.0
S2	VLAN 10	192.168.10.202	255.255.255.0
PC-A	NIC	DHCP	255.255.255.0
PC-B	NIC	DHCP	255.255.255.0

Objectives

Part 1: Configure the Network Devices.

- Cable the network.

- Configure R1.

- Configure and verify basic switch settings.

Part 2: Configure VLANs on Switches.

- Configure VLAN 10.

- Configure the SVI for VLAN 10.

- Configure VLAN 333 with the name Native on S1 and S2.

- Configure VLAN 999 with the name ParkingLot on S1 and S2.

Part 3: Configure Switch Security.

- Implement 802.1Q trunking.

- Configure access ports.

- Secure and disable unused switchports.

- Document and implement port security features.

- Implement DHCP snooping security.

- Implement PortFast and BPDU guard.

- Verify end-to-end-connectivity.

Background / Scenario

This is a comprehensive lab to review previously covered Layer 2 security features.

Note: The routers used with CCNA hands-on labs are Cisco 4221 with Cisco IOS XE Release 16.9.3 (universalk9 image). The switches used in the labs are Cisco Catalyst 2960s with Cisco IOS Release 15.0(2) (lanbasek9 image). Other routers, switches, and Cisco IOS versions can be used. Depending on the model and Cisco IOS version, the commands available and the output produced might vary from what is shown in the labs. Refer to the Router Interface Summary Table at the end of the lab for the correct interface identifiers.

Note: Make sure that the switches have been erased and have no startup configurations. If you are unsure, contact your instructor.

Required Resources

- 1 Router (Cisco 4221 with Cisco IOS XE Release 16.9.3 universal image or comparable)

- 2 Switches (Cisco 2960 with Cisco IOS Release 15.0(2) lanbasek9 image or comparable)

- 2 PCs (Windows with a terminal emulation program, such as Tera Term)

- Console cables to configure the Cisco IOS devices via the console ports

- Ethernet cables as shown in the topology

Instructions

Part 1: Configure the Network Devices.

Step 1: Cable the network.

a. Cable the network as shown in the topology.

b. Initialize the devices.

Step 2: Configure R1.

a. Load the following configuration script on R1.

```
enable
configure terminal
hostname R1
no ip domain lookup
ip dhcp excluded-address 192.168.10.1 192.168.10.9
ip dhcp excluded-address 192.168.10.201 192.168.10.202
!
```

```
ip dhcp pool Students
 network 192.168.10.0 255.255.255.0
 default-router 192.168.10.1
 domain-name CCNA2.Lab-11.6.1
!
interface Loopback0
 ip address 10.10.1.1 255.255.255.0
!
interface GigabitEthernet0/0/1
 description Link to S1 Port 5
 ip dhcp relay information trusted
 ip address 192.168.10.1 255.255.255.0
 no shutdown
!
line con 0
 logging synchronous
 exec-timeout 0 0
```

b. Verify the running-configuration on R1 using the following command:

```
R1# show ip interface brief
```

c. Verify IP addressing and interfaces are in an up / up state (troubleshoot as necessary).

Step 3:   Configure and verify basic switch settings.

a. Configure the hostname for switches S1 and S2.

b. Prevent unwanted DNS lookups on both switches.

c. Configure interface descriptions for the ports that are in use in S1 and S2.

d. Set the default-gateway for the Management VLAN to 192.168.10.1 on both switches.

Part 2: Configure VLANs on Switches.

Step 1:   Configure VLAN 10.

Add VLAN 10 to S1 and S2 and name the VLAN **Management**.

Step 2:   Configure the SVI for VLAN 10.

Configure the IP address according to the Addressing Table for SVI for VLAN 10 on S1 and S2. Enable the SVI interfaces and provide a description for the interface.

Step 3:   Configure VLAN 333 with the name Native on S1 and S2.

Step 4:   Configure VLAN 999 with the name ParkingLot on S1 and S2.

Part 3: Configure Switch Security.

Step 1:   Implement 802.1Q trunking.

   a.   On both switches, configure trunking on F0/1 to use VLAN 333 as the native VLAN.

   b.   Verify that trunking is configured on both switches.

```
S1# show interface trunk
```

Port	Mode	Encapsulation	Status	Native vlan
Fa0/1	on	802.1q	trunking	333

Port	Vlans allowed on trunk
Fa0/1	1-4094

Port	Vlans allowed and active in management domain
Fa0/1	1,10,333,999

Port	Vlans in spanning tree forwarding state and not pruned
Fa0/1	1,10,333,999

```
S2# show interface trunk
```

Port	Mode	Encapsulation	Status	Native vlan
Fa0/1	on	802.1q	trunking	333

Port	Vlans allowed on trunk
Fa0/1	1-4094

Port	Vlans allowed and active in management domain
Fa0/1	1,10,333,999

Port	Vlans in spanning tree forwarding state and not pruned
Fa0/1	1,10,333,999

   c.   Disable DTP negotiation on F0/1 on S1 and S2.

   d.   Verify with the **show interfaces** command.

```
S1# show interfaces f0/1 switchport | include Negotiation
Negotiation of Trunking: Off
```

```
S2# show interfaces f0/1 switchport | include Negotiation
Negotiation of Trunking: Off
```

Step 2:   Configure access ports.

   a.   On S1, configure F0/5 and F0/6 as access ports that are associated with VLAN 10.

   b.   On S2, configure F0/18 as an access port that is associated with VLAN 10.

Step 3:   Secure and disable unused switchports.

   a.   On S1 and S2, move the unused ports from VLAN 1 to VLAN 999 and disable the unused ports.

b. Verify that unused ports are disabled and associated with VLAN 999 by issuing the **show** command.

```
S1# show interfaces status
```

Port	Name	Status	Vlan	Duplex	Speed	Type
Fa0/1	Link to S2	connected	trunk	a-full	a-100	10/100BaseTX
Fa0/2		disabled	999	auto	auto	10/100BaseTX
Fa0/3		disabled	999	auto	auto	10/100BaseTX
Fa0/4		disabled	999	auto	auto	10/100BaseTX
Fa0/5	Link to R1	connected	10	a-full	a-100	10/100BaseTX
Fa0/6	Link to PC-A	connected	10	a-full	a-100	10/100BaseTX
Fa0/7		disabled	999	auto	auto	10/100BaseTX
Fa0/8		disabled	999	auto	auto	10/100BaseTX
Fa0/9		disabled	999	auto	auto	10/100BaseTX
Fa0/10		disabled	999	auto	auto	10/100BaseTX

```
<output omitted>
S2# show interfaces status
```

Port	Name	Status	Vlan	Duplex	Speed	Type
Fa0/1	Link to S1	connected	trunk	a-full	a-100	10/100BaseTX
Fa0/2		disabled	999	auto	auto	10/100BaseTX
Fa0/3		disabled	999	auto	auto	10/100BaseTX

```
<output omitted>
```

Fa0/14		disabled	999	auto	auto	10/100BaseTX
Fa0/15		disabled	999	auto	auto	10/100BaseTX
Fa0/16		disabled	999	auto	auto	10/100BaseTX
Fa0/17		disabled	999	auto	auto	10/100BaseTX
Fa0/18	Link to PC-B	connected	10	a-full	a-100	10/100BaseTX
Fa0/19		disabled	999	auto	auto	10/100BaseTX
Fa0/20		disabled	999	auto	auto	10/100BaseTX
Fa0/21		disabled	999	auto	auto	10/100BaseTX
Fa0/22		disabled	999	auto	auto	10/100BaseTX
Fa0/23		disabled	999	auto	auto	10/100BaseTX
Fa0/24		disabled	999	auto	auto	10/100BaseTX
Gi0/1		disabled	999	auto	auto	10/100/1000BaseTX
Gi0/2		disabled	999	auto	auto	10/100/1000BaseTX

Step 4:   Document and implement port security features.

The interfaces F0/6 on S1 and F0/18 on S2 are configured as access ports. In this step, you will also configure port security on these two access ports.

a. On S1, issue the **show port-security interface f0/6** command to display the default port security settings for interface F0/6. Record your answers in the table below.

Default Port Security Configuration	
Feature	**Default Setting**
Port Security	
Maximum number of MAC addresses	
Violation Mode	

Default Port Security Configuration
Aging Time
Aging Type
Secure Static Address Aging
Sticky MAC Address

b. On S1, enable port security on F0/6 with the following settings:

- Maximum number of MAC addresses: **3**

- Violation type: **restrict**

- Aging time: **60 min**

- Aging type: **inactivity**

c. Verify port security on S1 F0/6.

```
S1# show port-security interface f0/6
Port Security              : Enabled
Port Status                : Secure-up
Violation Mode             : Restrict
Aging Time                 : 60 mins
Aging Type                 : Inactivity
SecureStatic Address Aging : Disabled
Maximum MAC Addresses      : 3
Total MAC Addresses        : 1
Configured MAC Addresses   : 0
Sticky MAC Addresses       : 0
Last Source Address:Vlan   : 0022.5646.3411:10
Security Violation Count   : 0


S1# show port-security address
              Secure Mac Address Table
-------------------------------------------------------------------
Vlan    Mac Address      Type            Ports   Remaining Age
                                                    (mins)

----    -----------      ----            -----   ------------
  10    0022.5646.3411   SecureDynamic   Fa0/6      60 (I)

-------------------------------------------------------------------
Total Addresses in System (excluding one mac per port)     : 0
Max Addresses limit in System (excluding one mac per port) : 8192
```

d. Enable port security for F0/18 on S2. Configure the port to add MAC addresses learned on the port automatically to the running configuration.

e. Configure the following port security settings on S2 F/18:

- Maximum number of MAC addresses: **2**

- Violation type: **Protect**

- Aging time: **60 min**

f. Verify port security on S2 F0/18.

```
S2# show port-security interface f0/18
```

```
Port Security                : Enabled
Port Status                  : Secure-up
Violation Mode               : Protect
Aging Time                   : 60 mins
Aging Type                   : Absolute
SecureStatic Address Aging   : Disabled
Maximum MAC Addresses        : 2
Total MAC Addresses          : 1
Configured MAC Addresses     : 0
Sticky MAC Addresses         : 0
Last Source Address:Vlan     : 0022.5646.3413:10
Security Violation Count     : 0
```

```
S2# show port-security address
              Secure Mac Address Table
----------------------------------------------------------------------
Vlan    Mac Address      Type            Ports    Remaining Age
                                                     (mins)
----    -----------      ----            -----    -------------
  10    0022.5646.3413   SecureSticky    Fa0/18       -
----------------------------------------------------------------------
Total Addresses in System (excluding one mac per port)     : 0
Max Addresses limit in System (excluding one mac per port) : 8192
```

Step 5: Implement DHCP snooping security.

a. On S2, enable DHCP snooping and configure DHCP snooping on VLAN 10.

b. Configure the trunk port on S2 as a trusted port.

c. Limit the untrusted port, F18 on S2, to five DHCP packets per second.

d. Verify DHCP Snooping on S2.

```
S2# show ip dhcp snooping
Switch DHCP snooping is enabled
DHCP snooping is configured on following VLANs:
10
DHCP snooping is operational on following VLANs:
10
DHCP snooping is configured on the following L3 Interfaces:
Insertion of option 82 is enabled
   circuit-id default format: vlan-mod-port
   remote-id: 0cd9.96d2.3f80 (MAC)
Option 82 on untrusted port is not allowed
Verification of hwaddr field is enabled
Verification of giaddr field is enabled
DHCP snooping trust/rate is configured on the following Interfaces:

Interface              Trusted    Allow option    Rate limit (pps)
---------------------  -------    ------------    ----------------
FastEthernet0/1        yes        yes             unlimited
   Custom circuit-ids:
FastEthernet0/18       no         no              5
   Custom circuit-ids:
```

e. From the command prompt on PC-B, release and then renew the IP address.

```
C:\Users\Student> ipconfig /release
C:\Users\Student> ipconfig /renew
```

f. Verify the DHCP snooping binding using the **show ip dhcp snooping binding** command.

```
S2# show ip dhcp snooping binding

MacAddress          IpAddress       Lease(sec) Type          VLAN Interface
------------------  ------------    ---------  -------       ---- ---------

00:50:56:90:D0:8E   192.168.10.11  86213       dhcp-snooping  10   FastEthernet0/18
Total number of bindings: 1
```

Step 6: Implement PortFast and BPDU guard.

a. Configure PortFast on all the access ports that are in use on both switches.

b. Enable BPDU guard on S1 and S2 VLAN 10 access ports connected to PC-A and PC-B.

c. Verify that BPDU guard and PortFast are enabled on the appropriate ports.

```
S1# show spanning-tree interface f0/6 detail
 Port 8 (FastEthernet0/6) of VLAN0010 is designated forwarding
   Port path cost 19, Port priority 128, Port Identifier 128.6.
   <output omitted for brevity>
   Number of transitions to forwarding state: 1
   The port is in the portfast mode
   Link type is point-to-point by default
   Bpdu guard is enabled
   BPDU: sent 128, received 0
```

Step 7: Verify end-to-end connectivity.

Verify PING connectivity between all devices in the IP Addressing Table. If the pings fail, you may need to disable the firewall on the PC hosts.

Reflection Questions

1. In reference to Port Security on S2, why is there no timer value for the remaining age in minutes when sticky learning was configured?

2. In reference to Port Security on S2, if you load the running-config script on S2, why will PC-B on port 18 never get an IP address via DHCP?

3. In reference to Port Security, what is the difference between the absolute aging type and inactivity aging type?

The "Study Guide" portion of this chapter uses a variety of exercises to test your knowledge of how WLANs enable network connectivity. This chapter does not include any labs or Packet Tracer activities.

As you work through this chapter, use Chapter 12 in *Switching, Routing, and Wireless Essentials v7 Companion Guide* or use the corresponding Module 12 in the Switching, Routing, and Wireless Essentials online curriculum for assistance.

Study Guide

Introduction to Wireless

In this section, you review WLAN technologies and standards.

Wireless Terminology

A wireless LAN (WLAN) is a type of wireless network that is commonly used in homes, offices, and campus environments. WLANs make mobility possible within home and business environments. Wireless networks encompass WLANs but also include other wireless network types and technologies.

Match each definition with the appropriate term. This exercise is a one-to-one matching: Each definition has exactly one matching term.

Definitions

   a. A network that uses transmitters to cover a medium-sized network, usually up to 300 feet, that is based on the 802.11 standard and a 2.4 GHz or 5 GHz radio frequency

   b. An IEEE 802.15 wireless personal-area network (WPAN) standard that uses a device-pairing process to communicate over distances up to 300 ft

   c. A network that uses low-powered transmitters for a short-range network, usually 20 to 30 ft, and is based on the 802.15 standard and a 2.4 GHz radio frequency

   d. Uses a dish pointing to a geosynchronous device and provides wireless network access for rural homeowners and businesses where cable and DSL are not available

   e. Wireless mobile networks carrying both data and voice communications and used by phones, automobiles, tablets, and laptops

   f. An alternative to broadband wired internet connections that uses the 802.16 wireless wide area network (WWAN) standard to provide wireless broadband access for up to 30 miles

   g. A network that uses transmitters to provide coverage for national and global communications and that uses specific licensed frequencies

   h. A network that uses transmitters to provide wireless service over a metropolitan area and that uses specific licensed frequencies

Wireless Terms

_____ Bluetooth

_____ Cellular broadband

_____ Satellite broadband

_____ WiMAX (Worldwide Interoperability for Microwave Access)

_____ Wireless LAN (WLAN)

_____ Wireless MAN (WMAN)

_____ Wireless personal-area network (WPAN)

_____ Wireless wide-area network (WWAN)

Check Your Understanding—Introduction to Wireless

Check your understanding of wireless networks, technologies, and standards by choosing the BEST answer to each of the following questions.

1. Which of the following wireless networks typically uses lower-powered transmitters for short ranges?

   a. WPAN

   b. WLAN

   c. WMAN

   d. WWAN

2. Which of the following wireless networks is specified in the IEEE 802.11 standards for the 2.4 GHz and 5 GHz radio frequencies?

   a. WPAN

   b. WLAN

   c. WMAN

   d. WWAN

3. Which of the following is an IEEE 802.15 WPAN standard that uses a device-pairing process to communicate?

   a. cellular

   b. WiMAX

   c. Wi-Fi

   d. Bluetooth

4. Which 802.11 standards exclusively use the 5 GHz radio frequency? (Choose two.)

   a. 802.11a

   b. 802.11g

   c. 802.11n

   d. 802.11ac

   e. 802.11ax

5. Which standards organization is responsible for allocating radio frequencies?

   a. IEEE

   b. ITU-R

   c. Wi-Fi Alliance

WLAN Components

In this section, you review the components of a WLAN infrastructure.

WLAN Component Terminology

Match each definition with the appropriate term. This exercise is a one-to-one matching: Each definition has exactly one matching term.

Definitions

a. A device typically used to extend the range of a WLAN

b. A standalone device, such as a home router, that includes an entire WLAN's configuration

c. Uses up to eight transmit and receive antennas and can be used to increase throughput on IEEE 802.11n/ac/ax wireless networks

d. A device commonly implemented to provide a WLAN and access to the internet for a small business or home office

e. A radio transmitter/receiver used in laptops, tablets, and smartphones to connect to a wireless network

f. Typically uses Lightweight Access Point Protocol (LWAPP) to communicate with a WLAN controller (WLC)

g. Focuses the radio signal, typically by pointing at another access point (AP) device, and includes a Yagi antenna and a parabolic dish

h. Provides 360-degree coverage and is ideal in houses, open office areas, conference rooms, and outside areas

WLAN Component

_____ Autonomous AP

_____ Controller-based AP

_____ Directional antenna

_____ Multiple input/multiple output (MIMO) antenna

_____ Omnidirectional antenna

_____ Wireless access point

_____ Wireless NIC

_____ Wireless router

Check Your Understanding—WLAN Components

Check your understanding of WLAN components by choosing the BEST answer to each of the following questions.

1. True or false: A laptop that does not have an integrated wireless NIC can only be attached to a network through a wired connection.

   a. true

   b. false

2. Which of the following components are integrated in a wireless home router? (Choose three.)

   a. access point

   b. switch

   c. router

   d. range extender

3. True or false: When you need to expand the coverage of a small network, the best solution is to use a range extender.

   a. true

   b. false

4. Which of the following is a standalone device, like a home router, where the entire WLAN configuration resides on the device?

   a. range extender

   b. autonomous AP

   c. controller-based AP

   d. USB wireless NIC

5. Which of the following antennas provides 360 degrees of coverage?

   a. wireless NIC

   b. directional

   c. omnidirectional

   d. MIMO

WLAN Operation

In this section, you review how wireless technology enables WLAN operation.

WLAN Operation Terminology

Match each definition with the appropriate term. This exercise is a one-to-one matching: Each definition has exactly one matching term.

Definitions

   a. Selection of either Wired Equivalent Privacy (WEP), Wi-Fi Protected Access (WPA), or WPA2

   b. Consists of a single AP interconnecting all associated wireless clients in a basic service area

   c. A peer-to-peer wireless network that does not use an AP or wireless router

   d. Wireless clients connect to a wireless router or AP which are connected to a wired distribution system

   e. Method used in wireless networks to determine which client is clear to send

   f. AP periodically broadcasting a beacon containing its service set identifier (SSID), supported standards, and security settings

   g. The name of a WLAN, typically mapped to a VLAN, that clients use to associate to an AP

   h. A mode in which the wireless client must know the SSID for the AP and send a probe request before joining the WLAN

   i. Determines which 802.11 standard a client is connecting to

    j. Connects multiple basic service areas through a common distribution system

    k. Uses a smartphone or tablet to provide a connection to the internet

    l. Selection of the frequency band that the client will use with the 802.11 network

Term

_____ Active mode

_____ Ad hoc mode

_____ Basic Service Set (BSS)

_____ Channel setting

_____ Carrier sense multiple access with collision avoidance (CSMA/CA)

_____ Extended Service Set (ESS)

_____ Infrastructure mode

_____ Network mode

_____ Passive mode

_____ Security mode

_____ SSID

_____ Tethering

Check Your Understanding—WLAN Operation

Check your understanding of WLAN operation by choosing the BEST answer to each of the following questions.

    1. Which wireless topology mode is used by two devices to connect in a peer-to-peer network?

        a. ad hoc

        b. infrastructure

        c. tethering

    2. True or false: An ESS is created when two or more BSSs need to be joined to support roaming clients.

        a. true

        b. false

    3. How many address fields are in the 802.11 wireless frame?

        a. 2

        b. 3

        c. 4

        d. 5

    4. What is the term for an AP that openly advertises its service periodically?

        a. active

        b. infrastructure

        c. ad hoc

        d. passive

5. What is the term for an AP that does not send a beacon but waits for clients to send probes?

   a. active

   b. infrastructure

   c. ad hoc

   d. passive

CAPWAP Operation

In this section, you review how a WLC uses CAPWAP to manage multiple APs.

CAPWAP Review

What is the purpose of the Control and Provisioning of Wireless Access Points (CAPWAP) protocol?

_____

What security technology does CAPWAP use?

_____

CAPWAP can operate either over IPv4 or IPv6. Which one is the default?

_____

What User Datagram Protocol (UDP) ports and IP protocols does CAPWAP use?

_____

Split MAC Architecture

The CAPWAP split MAC concept does all of the functions normally performed by individual APs and distributes them between AP MAC functions and WLC MAC functions. In Table 12-1, indicate whether the AP or WLC is responsible for each MAC function.

Table 12-1   AP and WLC MAC Functions

MAC Function	AP	WLC
Termination of 802.11 traffic on a wired interface		
Frame queueing and packet prioritization		
Beacons and probe responses		
Association and re-association of roaming clients		
MAC layer data encryption and decryption		
Frame translation to other protocols		
Authentication		
Packet acknowledgments and retransmissions		

Check Your Understanding—CAPWAP Operation

Check your understanding of CAPWAP by choosing the BEST answer to each of the following questions.

1. What IP version or versions does CAPWAP support?

   a. IPv4 only

   b. IPv6 only

   c. IPv4 by default but can configure IPv6

   d. IPv6 by default but can configure IPv4

2. What UDP ports and IP protocols in the frame header are used with CAPWAP for IPv4? (Choose three.)

   a. 17

   b. 136

   c. 5246

   d. 5247

   e. 802.11

3. What UDP ports and IP protocols in the frame header are used with CAPWAP for IPv6? (Choose three.)

   a. 17

   b. 136

   c. 5246

   d. 5247

   e. 802.11

4. In the split MAC architecture for CAPWAP, which of the following are the responsibility of the AP? (Choose four.)

   a. authentication

   b. packet acknowledgments and retransmissions

   c. beacons and probe responses

   d. association and re-association of roaming clients

   e. MAC layer data encryption and decryption

   f. termination of 802.11 traffic on a wired interface

   g. frame translation to other protocols

   h. frame queueing and packet prioritization

5. In the split MAC architecture for CAPWAP, which of the following are the responsibility of the WLC? (Choose four.)

   a. authentication

   b. packet acknowledgments and retransmissions

   c. beacons and probe responses

   d. association and re-association of roaming clients

    e. MAC layer data encryption and decryption

    f. termination of 802.11 traffic on a wired interface

    g. frame translation to other protocols

    h. frame queueing and packet prioritization

6. True or false: Datagram Transport Layer Security (DTLS) is enabled by default on the control and data CAPWAP tunnels.

    a. true

    b. false

7. Which of the following statements are true about modes of operation for a FlexConnect AP? (Choose two.)

    a. In connect mode, the WLC is unreachable, and the AP switches local traffic and performs client authentication locally.

    b. In standalone mode, the WLC is unreachable, and the AP switches local traffic and performs client authentication locally.

    c. In connect mode, the WLC is reachable and performs all its CAPWAP functions.

    d. In standalone mode, the WLC is reachable and performs all its CAPWAP functions

Channel Management

In this section, you review channel management in a WLAN.

Frequency Channel Saturation

Over the years, a number of techniques have been created to improve wireless communication and alleviate channel saturation. Briefly describe each technique and name the devices that use it.

- Direct-Sequence Spread Spectrum (DSSS): _____

  _____

  _____

- Frequency-Hopping Spread Spectrum (FHSS): _____

  _____

  _____

  _____

- Orthogonal Frequency-Division Multiplexing (OFDM): _____

  _____

  _____

  _____

Channel Selection

A best practice for WLANs requiring multiple APs is to use non-overlapping channels. For the 2.4 GHz band, what are the non-overlapping channels?

For the 5 GHz band, what are the first eight channel identifiers?

Check Your Understanding—Channel Management

Check your understanding of channel management by choosing the BEST answer to each of the following questions.

1. Which of the following modulation techniques rapidly switches a signal among frequency channels?

   a. DSSS

   b. FHSS

   c. OFDM

   d. OFDMA

2. Which of the following modulation techniques spreads a signal over a larger frequency band?

   a. DSSS

   b. FHSS

   c. OFDM

   d. OFDMA

3. Which of the following modulation techniques is used in the 802.11ax standard?

   a. DSSS

   b. FHSS

   c. OFDM

   d. OFDMA

4. How many channels are available for the 2.4 GHz band in Europe?

   a. 11

   b. 13

   c. 14

   d. 24

5. How many channels are available for the 5 GHz band?

   a. 11

   b. 13

   c. 14

   d. 24

WLAN Threats

In this section, you review threats to WLANs.

DoS Attacks

Describe three ways wireless networks can experience DoS attacks.

- _____

- _____

- _____

Rogue Access Points

Briefly describe how a rogue access point (AP) is a threat to a WLAN.

_____

_____

_____

_____

Man-in-the-Middle Attack

Briefly describe the "evil twin" man-in-the-middle attack in a wireless network.

_____

_____

_____

_____

Check Your Understanding—WLAN Threats

Check your understanding of WLAN threats by choosing the BEST answer to each of the following questions.

1. Which of the following is most likely NOT the source of a wireless DoS attack?

   a. radio interference

   b. improperly configured devices

   c. rogue AP

   d. malicious user

2. True or false: A rogue AP is a misconfigured AP connected to the network and a possible source of DoS attacks.

   a. true

   b. false

3. What type of attack is an "evil twin AP" attack?

   a. DoS

   b. MITM

   c. wireless intruder

   d. radio interference

Secure WLANs

In this section, you review WLAN security mechanisms.

SSID Cloaking and MAC Address Filtering

To address the threats of keeping wireless intruders out and protecting data, two early security features were used and are still available on most routers and APs: SSID cloaking and MAC address filtering. Briefly describe each of them.

_____

_____

_____

_____

Open and Shared Key Authentication Methods

Two types of authentication were introduced with the original 802.11 standard:

- **Open system authentication:** Should be used only in situations where security is of no concern. The wireless client is responsible for providing security, such as by using a virtual private network (VPN) to connect securely.

- **Shared key authentication:** Provides mechanisms to authenticate and encrypt data between a wireless client and an AP. The password must be pre-shared between the parties in order for them to connect.

In Table 12-2, provide the name of each of the four shared key authentication techniques described.

Table 12-2 Share Key Authentication Methods

Authentication Method	Description
	The original 802.11 specification, designed to secure the data using the Rivest Cipher 4 (RC4) encryption method with a static key. However, the key never changes when exchanging packets. This makes it easy to hack. This method is no longer recommended and should never be used.
	Secures data with the Temporal Key Integrity Protocol (TKIP) encryption algorithm. TKIP changes the key for each packet, making it difficult to hack.
	The current industry standard for securing wireless networks. It uses the Advanced Encryption Standard (AES) for encryption. AES is currently considered the strongest encryption protocol.
	The next generation of Wi-Fi security. All devices that use this method require the use of Protected Management Frames (PMF).

Authentication in the Enterprise

The enterprise security mode choice requires an authentication, authorization, and accounting (AAA) RADIUS server. In the list below, fill in the missing information.

- **RADIUS server IP address:** This is the reachable address of the RADIUS server.

- **UDP port numbers:** _____

- **Shared key (what is this used for?):** _____

    _____

WPA3

WPA3 includes four features. Briefly describe each of them.

- **WPA3-Personal:** _____

    _____

    _____

- **WPA3-Enterprise:** _____

    _____

    _____

- **Open Networks:** _____

    _____

    _____

- **IoT Onboarding:** _____

    _____

Check Your Understanding—Secure WLANs

Check your understanding of techniques for securing WLANs by choosing the BEST answer to each of the following questions.

1. What are the best ways to secure WLANs? (Choose two.)

    a. authentication

    b. SSID cloaking

    c. encryption

    d. MAC address filtering

2. Which of the following authentication methods does NOT use a password shared between the wireless client and the AP?

    a. WEP

    b. WPA

    c. WPA2

    d. WPA3

    e. Open

3. Which encryption method is used by the original 802.11 specification?

    a. AES

    b. TKIP

    c. AES or TKIP

    d. RC4

4. Which of the following encryption methods uses CCMP to recognize whether the encrypted and non-encrypted bits have been altered?

    a. RC4

    b. TKIP

    c. AES

5. Which of the following authentication methods has the user enter a pre-shared password? (Choose two.)

    a. WPA Personal

    b. WPA Enterprise

    c. WPA2 Personal

    d. WPA2 Enterprise

Labs and Activities

There are no labs or Packet Tracer activities for this chapter.

CHAPTER 13

WLAN Configuration

The "Study Guide" portion of this chapter uses a variety of exercises to test your knowledge and skills related to implementing a wireless LAN (WLAN), using a wireless router and a wireless LAN controller (WLC). The "Labs and Activities" portion of this chapter includes all the online curriculum labs and Packet Tracer activity instructions.

As you work through this chapter, use Chapter 13 in *Switching, Routing, and Wireless Essentials v7 Companion Guide* or use the corresponding Module 13 in the Switching, Routing, and Wireless Essentials online curriculum for assistance.

Study Guide

Remote Site WLAN Configuration

In this section, you review how to configure a WLAN to support a remote site.

Video—Configure a Wireless Network

Be sure you review the video in the online curriculum, which covers the following:

- Using the wireless router web page

- Changing the password

- Changing the WAN and LAN settings

- Connecting to the wireless network

The Wireless Router

Remote workers, small branch offices, and home networks often use wireless routers. In addition to wired and wireless access for clients, list at least three other services typically offered by these devices.

_____

_____

Basic Network Setup

Most wireless routers are ready for service out of the box. They are preconfigured to be connected to the network and provide services. However, wireless router default IP addresses, usernames, and passwords can easily be found on the internet. Therefore, your first priority should be to change these defaults for security reasons.

In Table 13-1, describe each of the six steps for changing the default settings on a wireless router.

Table 13-1   Steps to Change the Default Settings on a Wireless Router

Step	Description
1	
2	
3	
4	
5	
6	

Basic Wireless Setup

The specific steps for setting up a wireless router vary depending on the router model. However, most models require variations of the steps shown in Table 13-2. Fill in your answers for the questions asked for each step.

Table 13-2   Steps to Set Up a Wireless Router

Step	Brief Description	Questions
1	View the WLAN defaults.	Out of the box, a wireless router provides wireless access to devices using a default wireless network name and password. What is the network name called?
2	Change the network mode.	What is the network mode?
		What are some examples of modes supported by wireless routers?
3	Configure the SSID.	Assign an SSID to the WLANs. What does the wireless router do with the SSID?
		What is the purpose of the SSID?
		What happens if SSID broadcast is disabled?
4	Configure the channel.	Why is it important to configure the channel?
		What are the non-overlapping channels for 2.4 GHz?
5	Configure the security mode.	What security mode and encryption that are widely available on wireless routers and clients are currently the strongest?
6	Configure the passphrase.	What is the passphrase used for?

Other Services Provided by a Wireless Router

Wireless routers typically provide additional services, including NAT, QoS, and port forwarding.

Briefly describe the purpose of NAT.

_____

_____

_____

_____

Briefly describe the benefits of configuring QoS.

_____

_____

_____

Briefly describe port forwarding and port triggering.

_____

_____

_____

_____

_____

Configure a Basic WLAN on the WLC

In this section, you review how to configure a WLC WLAN to use the management interface and Wi-Fi Protected Access version 2 (WPA2) with pre-shared key (PSK) authentication.

Note: This section reviews some important configuration screens for the Cisco 3504 Wireless Controller. However, for hands-on review, be sure to view the video and complete the Packet Tracer activity for this section in the online curriculum.

Video—Configure a Basic WLAN on the WLC

This video covers the following:

- The topology
- Accessing the GUI of the WLAN controller
- Information about the wireless network on the Network Summary screen
- Configuring a new WLAN
- Securing a new WLAN

Overview of the Cisco 3504 Wireless Controller

The online curriculum uses the Cisco 3504 Wireless Controller shown in Figure 13-1. Other WLC models have similar menus and features.

Figure 13-1   Cisco 3504 Wireless Controller

Configuring a WLC is very similar to configuring a wireless router. Briefly summarize the difference between the two.

_____

_____

Figure 13-2 shows the Network Summary page for the Cisco 3504 Wireless Controller.

Figure 13-2   Network Summary

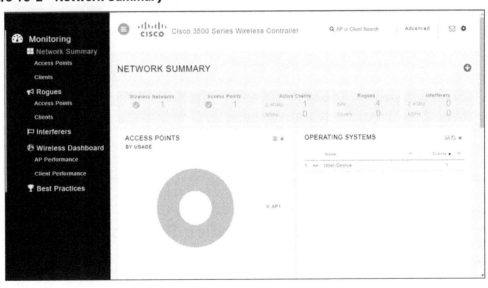

Figure 13-3 shows the Access Point View page, which provides overall information for the AP, including its IP address.

Figure 13-3   Access Point View

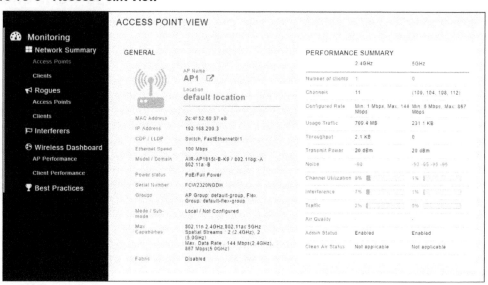

Figure 13-4 shows the Summary page for advanced settings. From here, you can access all the features of the WLC.

Figure 13-4   Advanced Settings Summary Page

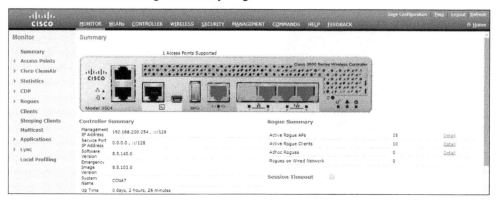

Basic WLAN Configuration Steps on the WLC

Basic WLAN configuration on the WLC involves the following steps:

Step 1.   Create the WLAN.

Step 2.   Apply and enable the WLAN.

Step 3.   Select the interface.

Step 4.   Secure the WLAN.

Step 5.   Verify that the WLAN is operational.

Step 6.   Monitor the WLAN.

Step 7.   View the wireless client information.

Figures 13-5 through 13-11 review the Cisco 3560 Wireless Controller screens for completing these steps.

Figure 13-5 shows the page where you create a new WLAN.

Figure 13-5   Step 1: Create a New WLAN

Figure 13-6 shows the page where you must enable the WLAN before it can be used.

Figure 13-6   Step 2: Apply and Enable the WLAN

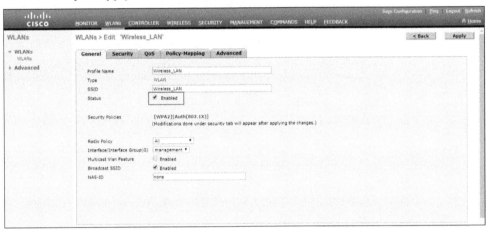

Figure 13-7 shows where you select the interface this WLAN will use.

Figure 13-7   Step 3: Select the Interface

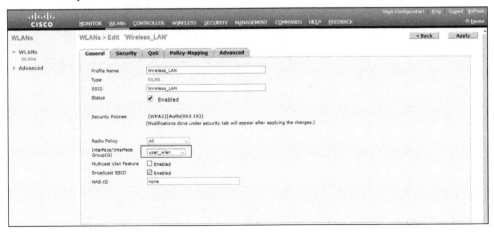

Figure 13-8 shows where you configure the security method as WPA2 with Advanced Encryption Standard (AES).

Figure 13-8   Step 4: Secure the WLAN

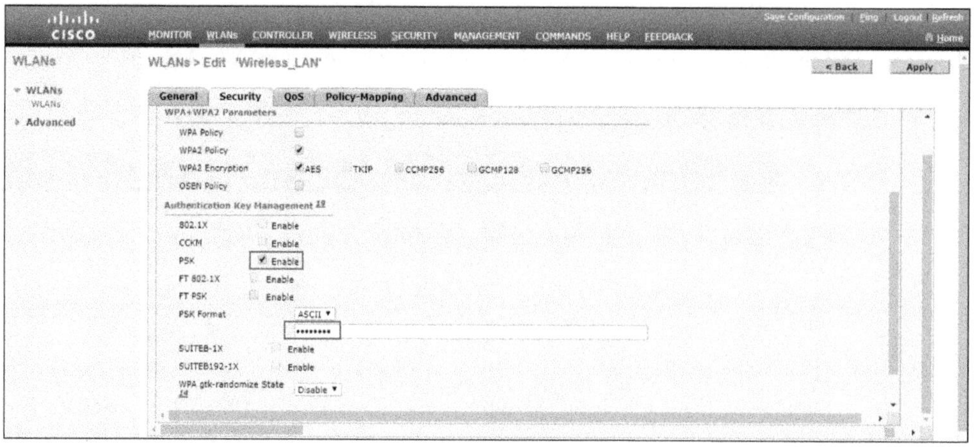

Figure 13-9 shows the page where you can verify that the new WLAN is operational.

Figure 13-9   Step 5: Verify that the WLAN Is Operational

Figure 13-10 shows the Summary page, where you can see the number of clients that are using the WLAN.

Figure 13-10   Step 6: Monitor the WLAN

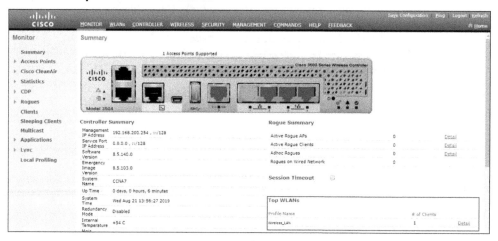

Figure 13-11 shows the page where you can see the details of all the clients managed by the WLC.

Figure 13-11   Step 7: View the Wireless Client Information

Configure a WPA2 Enterprise WLAN on the WLC

In this section, you review how to configure a WLC WLAN to use a VLAN interface, a DHCP server, and WPA2 Enterprise authentication.

Note: This section reviews some important configuration screens for the Cisco 3504 Wireless Controller. However, for hands-on review, be sure to view the videos and complete the Packet Tracer activity for this section in the online curriculum.

Video—Define an SNMP and RADIUS Server on the WLC

This video covers the following:

- Configuring the WLAN controller to send SNMP traps to an external server

- Configuring the WLAN controller to use an external RADIUS server to authenticate WLAN users

- Verifying connectivity with the RADIUS server

Configure SNMP and RADIUS Servers

Simple Network Management Protocol (SNMP) can be used to trap log messages on network devices. Remote Authentication Dial-In User Service (RADIUS) can be used to provide authentication, authorization, and accounting (AAA) services. In addition to WLAN configuration, a WLC can forward SNMP log messages to an SNMP server and forward user login requests to a RADIUS server.

Figures 13-12 and 13-13 show the SNMP configuration pages for the Cisco 3560 Wireless Controller.

Figure 13-12   SNMP Configuration Options

In Figure 13-12, the steps indicated by the circled numerals are as follows:

Step 1. Click **MANAGEMENT**.

Step 2. Click **SNMP**.

Step 3. Click **Trap Receivers**.

Step 4. Click **New**. The screen shown in Figure 13-13 appears.

Figure 13-13 Configuring the Details of the Remote SNMP Server

Figures 13-14 and 13-15 show the configuration pages for the RADIUS server.

Figure 13-14 RADIUS Configuration Options

In Figure 13-14, the steps indicated by the circled numerals are as follows:

Step 1. Click **SECURITY**.

Step 2. Click **RADIUS**.

Step 3. Click **Authentication**.

Step 4. Click **New**. The screen shown in Figure 13-15 appears.

Figure 13-15 Configuring the Details of the Remote RADIUS Server

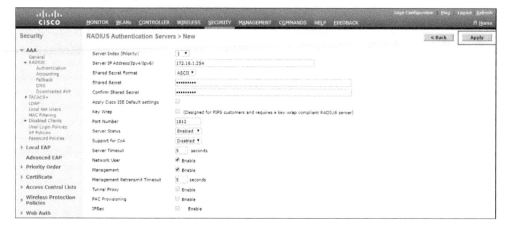

Figure 13-16 shows the page where you can verify your new RADIUS server configuration.

Figure 13-16   Verifying the RADIUS Server Configuration

Video—Configure a VLAN for a New WLAN

This video covers the following:

- Reviewing the topology
- Deploying a new VLAN interface
- Associating the new VLAN interface with a WLAN

Configure a New Interface

Each WLAN configured on a WLC needs its own virtual interface. VLAN interface configuration on the WLC involves the following steps:

Step 1.   Create a new interface.

Step 2.   Configure the VLAN name and ID.

Step 3.   Configure the port and interface address.

Step 4.   Configure the DHCP server address.

Step 5.   Apply and confirm the new interface.

Step 6.   Verify the new interface.

Figures 13-17 through 13-22 show the VLAN interface configuration pages on the Cisco 3560 Wireless Controller.

Figure 13-17 shows the steps to create a new interface.

Figure 13-17   Step 1: Create a New Interface

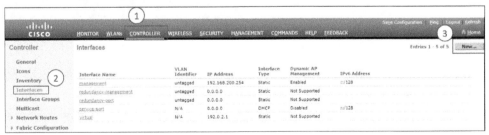

In Figure 13-17, the steps indicated by the circled numerals are as follows:

Step 1.   Click **CONTROLLER.**

Step 2.   Click **Interfaces.**

Step 3.   Click **New.**

Figure 13-18 shows the page that appears, where you specify the interface name and VLAN ID.

Figure 13-18   Step 2: Configure the VLAN Name and ID

Figure 13-19 shows the page where you configure the port number and IP address information for the new interface.

Figure 13-19   Step 3: Configure the Port and Interface Address

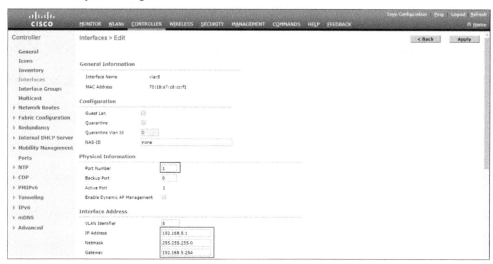

Figure 13-20 shows the bottom half of the interface configuration page, where you configure the DHCP server address for this interface.

Figure 13-20   Step 4: Configure the DHCP Server Address

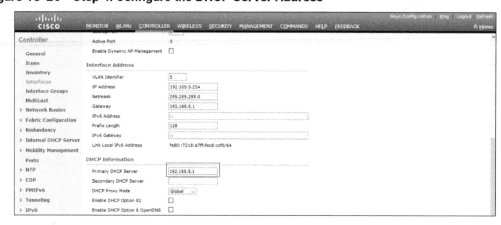

Figure 13-21 shows how to apply the new interface configuration.

Figure 13-21   Step 5: Apply and Confirm the New Interface

Figure 13-22 shows the page where you can verify all the interfaces on the WLC, including the new interface.

Figure 13-22   Step 6: Verify the New Interface.

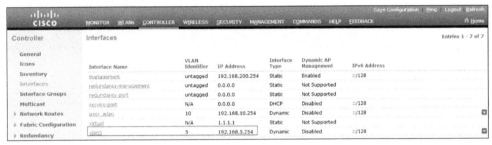

Video—Configure a DHCP Scope

This video covers the following:

- Reviewing the topology
- Explaining the role of the WLC DHCP server
- Creating a new DHCP scope

Configure a DHCP Scope

DHCP scope configuration involves the following steps:

Step 1.   Create a new DHCP scope.

Step 2.   Name the DHCP scope.

Step 3.   Verify the new DHCP scope.

Step 4.   Configure and enable the new DHCP scope.

Step 5.   Verify the enabled DHCP scope.

Figures 13-23 through 13-27 show the DHCP scope configuration pages for the Cisco 3560 Wireless Controller.

Figure 13-23 shows the page where you create a new DHCP scope.

Figure 13-23 Step 1: Create a New DHCP Scope

Figure 13-24 shows the page where you name the new DHCP scope.

Figure 13-24 Step 2: Name the DHCP Scope

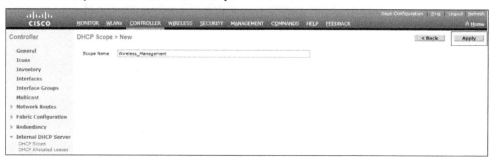

Figure 13-25 shows the page where you can verify that the new DHCP scope is created. You can see that it does not have any addressing information yet.

Figure 13-25 Step 3: Verify the New DHCP Scope

Figure 13-26 shows the page where you configure and enable the new DHCP scope.

Figure 13-26 Step 4: Configure and Enable the New DHCP Scope

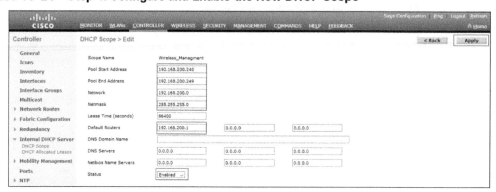

Figure 13-27 shows the page where you can now verify that the new DHCP scope is configured and enabled.

Figure 13-27   Step 5: Verify the Enabled DHCP Scope

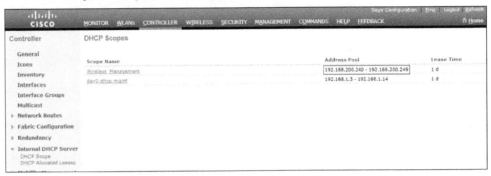

Video—Configure a WPA2 Enterprise WLAN

This video covers the following:

- Reviewing the topology

- Creating a WLAN

- Configuring the WLC to use the RADIUS server

- Securing the new WLAN with WPA2-Enterprise

- Verifying the WPA2-Enterprise security

Configure a WPA2-Enterprise WLAN

Configuring a new WLAN to use WPA2-Enterprise involves the following steps:

Step 1.   Create a new WLAN.

Step 2.   Configure the WLAN name and service set identifier (SSID).

Step 3.   Enable the WLAN for VLAN 5.

Step 4.   Verify the AES and 802.1X defaults.

Step 5.   Configure WLAN security to use the RADIUS server.

Step 6.   Verify that the new WLAN is available.

Figures 13-28 through 13-33 show the WPA2 Enterprise configuration pages for the Cisco 3560 Wireless Controller.

Figure 13-28 shows the page used to create a new WLAN.

Figure 13-28   Step 1: Create a New WLAN

Figure 13-29 shows the page used to configure the WLAN name and SSID.

Figure 13-29   Step 2: Configure the WLAN Name and SSID

Figure 13-30 shows the page to enable the WLAN, assign it to a VLAN interface, and apply the configuration.

Figure 13-30   Step 3: Enable the WLAN for VLAN 5

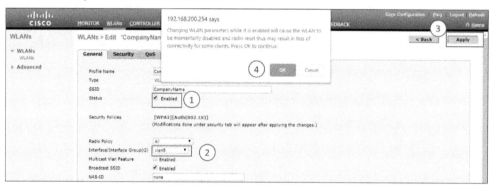

In Figure 13-30, the steps indicated by the circled numerals are as follows:

Step 1.   Click **Enabled.**

Step 2.   Choose an interface.

Step 3.   Click **Apply.**

Step 4.   Click **OK.**

Figure 13-31 shows the tab to configure WLAN security.

Figure 13-31   Step 4: Verify the AES and 802.1X Defaults

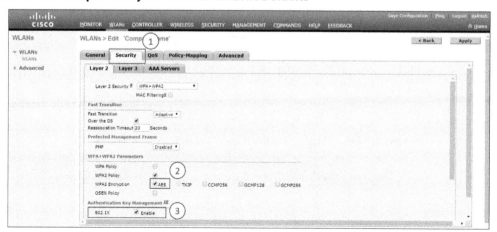

In Figure 13-31, the steps indicated by the circled numerals are as follows:

Step 1. Click the **Security** tab.

Step 2. Verify that **AES** is selected as the encryption method.

Step 3. Verify that **802.1X** is selected as the authentication key management protocol.

Figure 13-32 shows the tab where you configure the AAA server.

Figure 13-32   Step 5: Configure WLAN Security to Use the RADIUS Server

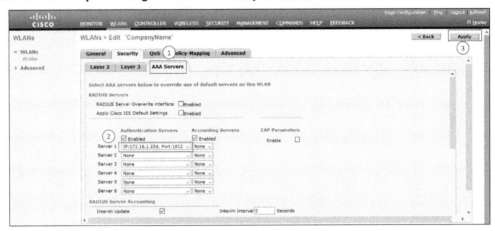

In Figure 13-32, the steps indicated by the circled numerals are as follows:

Step 1. Click the **AAA Servers** tab.

Step 2. From the **Server 1** drop-down list, select a RADIUS server that has been previously configured on the WLC.

Step 3. Click **Apply** to apply your changes.

Figure 13-33 shows the page where you can verify that the new WLAN is enabled with WPA2 and 802.1X authentication.

Figure 13-33   Step 6: Verify That the New WLAN Is Available

Troubleshoot WLAN Issues

In this section, you review how to troubleshoot common wireless configuration issues.

Troubleshooting Approaches

Troubleshooting for any sort of network problem should follow a systematic approach. A common and efficient troubleshooting methodology is based on the scientific method and can be broken into the six main steps. In Table 13-3, fill in the title for each step.

Table 13-3   Troubleshooting Steps

Step	Title	Description
1		The first step in the troubleshooting process is to identify the problem. While tools can be used in this step, a conversation with the user is often very helpful.
2		After you have talked to the user and identified the problem, you can try to establish a theory of probable causes. This step often yields more than a few probable causes to the problem.
3		Based on the probable causes, test your theories to determine which one is the cause of the problem. A technician will often apply a quick procedure to test and see if it solves the problem. If a quick procedure does not correct the problem, you might need to research the problem further to establish the exact cause.
4		After you have determined the exact cause of the problem, establish a plan of action to resolve the problem and implement the solution.
5		After you have corrected the problem, verify full functionality and, if applicable, implement preventive measures.
6		In the final step of the troubleshooting process, document your findings, actions, and outcomes. This is very important for future reference.

Wireless Client Not Connecting

When troubleshooting a WLAN, a process of elimination is recommended. For example, if a wireless client has no connectivity, check the following:

- Verify that the client received an IP address via DHCP or is configured with a static IP address.

- If possible, connect the device to the wired LAN and ping a known IP address.

- If necessary, reload drivers as appropriate for the client. It may be necessary to try a different wireless NIC.

- If the wireless NIC of the client is working, check the security mode and encryption settings on the client. If the security settings do not match, the client cannot gain access to the WLAN.

If the client is operational but the wireless connection is performing poorly, check the following:

- How far is the client from an AP? Is the client out of the planned coverage area (BSA)?

- Check the channel settings on the wireless client. The client software should detect the appropriate channel as long as the SSID is correct.

- Check for the presence of other devices in the area that may be interfering with the 2.4 GHz band.

Troubleshooting When the Network Is Slow

List and briefly describe two strategies to optimize the bandwidth on 802.11 dual-band wireless routers and APs.

- _____

- _____

Labs and Activities

13.1.10 Packet Tracer—Configure a Wireless Network

Objectives

- Connect to a wireless router
- Configure the wireless router
- Connect a wired device to the wireless router
- Connect a wireless device to the wireless router
- Add an AP to the network to extend wireless coverage
- Update default router settings

Introduction

In this activity, you will configure a wireless router and an access point to accept wireless clients and route IP packets. Furthermore, you will also update some of the default settings.

Instructions

Part 1: Connect to a Wireless Router

Step 1:   Connect Admin to WR.

a. Connect **Admin** to **WR** using a straight-through Ethernet cable through the Ethernet ports. Select **Connections**, represented by a lightning bolt, from the bottom-left side of Packet Tracer. Click **Copper Straight-Through**, represented by a solid black line.

b. When the cursor changes to connection mode, click **Admin** and choose **FastEthernet0**. Click **WR** and choose an available Ethernet port to connect the other end of the cable.

WR will act as a switch to the devices connected to the LAN and as a router to the internet. **Admin** is now connected to the LAN (**GigabitEthernet 1**). When Packet Tracer displays green triangles on both sides of the connection between **Admin** and **WR**, continue to the next step.

Note: If no green triangles are shown, make sure to enable **Show Link Lights** under **Options > Preferences**. You may also click **Fast Forward Time** just above the **Connections** selection box in the yellow bar.

Step 2:   Configure Admin to use DHCP.

To reach the **WR** management page, **Admin** must communicate on the network. A wireless router usually includes a DHCP server, and the DHCP server is usually enabled by default on the LAN. **Admin** will receive IP address information from the DHCP server on **WR**.

a.   Click **Admin**, and select the **Desktop** tab.

b.   Click **IP Configuration** and select **DHCP**.

Questions:

What is the IP address of the computer?

_____

What is the subnet mask of the computer?

_____

What is the default gateway of the computer?

_____

c.   Close the **IP Configuration** window.

Note: Values can vary within the network range due to normal DHCP operation.

Step 3:   Connect to the WR Web Interface.

a.   In the **Desktop** tab on **Admin**, choose **Web Browser**.

b.   Enter **192.168.0.1** in the URL field to open the web configuration page of the wireless router.

c.   Use **admin** for both the username and password.

d.   Under the Network Setup heading on the **Basic Setup** page, notice the IP address range for the DHCP server.

Question:

Is the IP address for **Admin** within this range? Is it expected? Explain your answer.

_____

Step 4:   Configure the Internet Port of WR.

In this step, **WR** is configured to route the packets from the wireless clients to internet. You will configure the **Internet** port on **WR** to connect to the internet.

a.   Under the **Internet Setup** at the top of the **Basic Setup** page, change the Internet IP address method from **Automatic Configuration – DHCP** to **Static IP**.

b.   Type the IP address to be assigned to the Internet interface as follows:

Internet IP Address:	209.165.200.225
Subnet Mask:	255.255.255.252
Default Gateway:	209.165.200.226
DNS Server:	209.165.201.1

c. Scroll down the page and click **Save Settings.**

Note: If you get a **Request Timeout** message, close the Admin window and wait for the orange lights to turn into green triangles. Click the fast forward button to make this happen faster. Then reconnect to **WR** from **Admin's** browser using the process explained in Step 3.

---

d. To verify connectivity, open a new web browser and navigate to the **www.cisco. pka** server.

Note: It may take a few seconds for the network to converge. Click **Fast Forward Time** or **Alt+D** to speed up the process.

Part 2: Configure the Wireless Settings

In this activity, you will only configure the wireless settings for 2.4 GHz.

Step 1:   Configure the WR SSID.

a. Navigate to the **WR** GUI interface at **192.168.0.1** in a web browser on **Admin.**

b. Navigate to **Wireless > Basic Wireless Settings.**

c. Change **Network Name (SSID)** to **aCompany** for only 2.4 GHz. Notice that SSIDs are case-sensitive.

d. Change the **Standard Channel** to **6 - 2.437GHz.**

e. For this activity, disable both 5 GHz frequencies. Leave the rest of the settings unchanged.

f. Scroll to the bottom of the window and click **Save Settings.**

Step 2:   Configure wireless security settings.

In this step, you configure the wireless security settings using WPA2 security mode with encryption and passphrase.

a. Navigate to **Wireless > Wireless Security.**

b. Under the 2.4 GHz heading, select **WPA2 Personal** for the Security Mode.

c. For the Encryption field, keep the default **AES** setting.

d. In the Passphrase field, enter **Cisco123!** as the passphrase.

e. Click **Save Settings.**

f. Verify that the settings in the **Basic Wireless Settings** and **Wireless Security** pages are correct and saved.

Step 3:   Connect the Wireless Clients.

a. Open **Laptop1.** Select the **Desktop** tab. Click **PC Wireless.**

b. Select the **Connect** tab. Click **Refresh** as necessary. Select the Wireless Network Name **aCompany.**

   c. Enter the passphrase configured in the previous step. Enter **Cisco123!** In the pre-shared key field and click **Connect**. Close the PC Wireless window.

   d. Open a web browser and verify that you can navigate to **www.cisco.pka** server.

   e. Repeat the above steps to connect **Laptop2** to the wireless network.

Part 3: Connect Wireless Clients to an Access Point

An access point (AP) is a device that extends the wireless local area network. An access point is connected to a wired router using an Ethernet cable to project the signal to a desired location.

Step 1:   Configure the Access Point.

   a. Connect **Port 0** of **AP** to an available Ethernet port of **WR** using a straight-through Ethernet cable.

   b. Click **AP**. Select the **Config** tab.

   c. Under the INTERFACE heading, select **Port 1**.

   d. In the SSID field, enter **aCompany**.

   e. Select **WPA2-PSK**. Enter the passphrase **Cisco123!** In the Pass Phrase field.

   f. Keep **AES** as the default Encryption Type.

Step 2:   Connect the Wireless Clients.

   a. Open **Laptop3**. Select **Desktop** tab. Click **PC Wireless**.

   b. Select the **Connect** tab. Click **Refresh** as necessary. Select the Wireless Network Name **aCompany** with the stronger signal (Channel 1) and click **Connect**.

   c. Open a web browser and verify that you can navigate to the **www.cisco.pka** server.

Part 4: Other Administrative Tasks

Step 1:   Change the WR Access Password.

   a. On **Admin**, navigate to the WR GUI interface at **192.168.0.1**.

   b. Navigate to **Administration > Management** and change the current **Router Password** to **cisco**.

   c. Scroll to the bottom of the window and click **Save Settings**.

   d. Use the username **admin** and the new password **cisco** when prompted to log in to the wireless router. Click **OK** to continue.

   e. Click **Continue** and move on to the next step.

Step 2:   Change the DHCP address range in WR.

   In this step, you will change the internal network address from 192.168.0.0/24 to 192.168.50.0/24. When the LAN network address changes, the IP addresses on the devices in the LAN and WLAN must be renewed to receive new IP addresses before the lease is timed out.

   a. Navigate to **Setup > Basic Setup**.

   b. Scroll down the page to **Network Setup**.

c. The IP address assigned to **Router IP** is 192.168.0.1. Change it to 192.168.50.1. Verify that IP addresses still start at .100, and there are 50 available IP addresses in the DHCP pool.

d. Add **209.165.201.1** as the DNS server with the DHCP settings.

e. Scroll to the bottom of the window and click **Save Settings**.

f. Note that the DHCP range of addresses has been automatically updated to reflect the interface IP address change. The Web Browser will display a **Request Timeout** after a short time.

Question:

Why?

---

g. Close the **Admin** web browser.

h. In the **Admin Desktop** tab, click **Command Prompt**.

i. Type **ipconfig /renew** to force **Admin** to re-acquire its IP information via DHCP.

Question:

What is the new IP address information for **Admin**?

---

j. Verify that you can still navigate to the **www.cisco.pka** server.

k. Renew the IP address on other laptops to verify that you can still navigate to the **www.cisco.pka** server.

l. Notice that **Laptop1** connected to the AP instead of **WR**.

Question:

Why?

13.1.11 Lab—Configure a Wireless Network

Introduction

In this lab, you will configure basic settings on a wireless router and connect a PC to router wirelessly.

Recommended Equipment

- A Windows computer with wired and wireless network cards installed
- Wireless router
- Ethernet patch cable

Note: All wireless settings in this lab are for a 2.4 GHz wireless connection. Follow the same steps for setting up a 5 GHz wireless connection or when setting up both 2.4 GHz and 5 GHz connections.

Instructions

Part 1: Log into the Wireless Router

Step 1:   Connect the computer to the router.

a. Ask the instructor for the following information that is used during the lab.

Router Address Information:

IP address:

_____

Subnet mask:

_____

Router name:

_____

DHCP Server Setting Information:

Start IP address:

_____

Maximum number of users:

_____

Default Router Access:

Router Username / Password:

_____

Assigned SSID:

Your Assigned SSID:

_____

_____

Note: Only use configurations assigned by the instructor.

b. Plug in the power for the wireless router. Boot the computer and log in as an administrator.

c. Connect the computer to one of the **Ethernet** ports on the wireless router with an Ethernet patch cable.

Note: If this is the first time connecting to the lab router, follow these instructions to set a network location. This will be explained later in the course.

d. If prompted by the **Set Network Location** window, select **Public network**. Click **Close** to accept the network location Public.

e. Open a command prompt and type **ipconfig** to determine the IP address of the default gateway, which should be the IP address of your wireless router. If it is necessary to renew the IP address, enter **ipconfig /all** at the prompt.

Question:

What is the default gateway for the computer?

_____

Step 2: Log in to the router.

a. Open **Microsoft Edge** or other web browsers. Enter the IP address of your default gateway in the **Address** field, and then press **Enter**.

b. In the **Windows Security** window, enter administrative user credentials provided by your instructor.

Part 2: Configure Basic Wireless Settings

In this lab, you will not be configuring the wireless router to the internet. You will configure the SSID or network name and security in the wireless settings, configure DHCP settings, and set a new administrative password.

Step 1: Configure SSID.

a. Locate the wireless settings. In the SSID or network name field, enter your assigned SSID.

b. Save the settings.

Step 2: Configure wireless security.

a. Locate the wireless security settings.

b. Select **WPA2** security option. Select **AES cipher** and **personal** if available.

c. Enter a passphrase or password as assigned by your instructor or use **Cisco456!** as an example.

      d. Save the settings.

Step 3:   Configure DHCP settings.

      a. Locate the LAN settings.

      b. Configure router device name if available.

      c. Configure the router's IP address and subnet mask as assigned by your instructor.

      d. Verify that the wireless router is used as the DHCP server.

      e. Configure the LAN information for your assigned subnet. If possible, you may be providing the starting and end IP addresses or the maximum number of IP addresses available for connecting hosts wirelessly.

      f. Save the settings.

      g. The router may need to reboot at this time. If necessary, reboot the router.

Step 4:   Change the default administrative password.

      a. Locate the password settings for the administrative account.

      b. Provide the current password and the new password as assigned by your instructor or Cisco123!.

      c. Save the settings.

      d. Log into the wireless using the new credentials: **admin / Cisco123!** or the credentials that were assigned to you.

      e. At this time, you can disconnect the Ethernet cable if desired.

Part 3: Connect a Wireless Client

  a. Click **Start**, enter **wireless**. Select **Change Wi-Fi Settings**.

  b. In the Wi-Fi settings window, select **Show available networks**.

  c. Select the configured SSID that you configured in a previous step.

  d. Enter the password or passphrase configured in a previous step.

  e. Open a command prompt. Type **ipconfig** and record the following information.

Computer IP information:

IP address:

_____

Subnet mask:

_____

Default Gateway:

_____

Part 4: Connect an Access Point (Optional)

In this part, you will add a wireless access point (AP) to the network. An AP is connected directly to a wireless router using an Ethernet cable. The purpose of an AP is to extend the wireless LAN where the wireless users cannot reach the wireless router otherwise.

In this part, you may need to partner with another group with a wireless router that can be converted to an access point. Or your instructor may also provide an access point. Unless instructed to connect the wireless router the internet, you do not need to connect the Internet port of the wireless router to a cable or DSL connection.

Note: If you are converting a wireless router to an AP, please follow the instructions provided by your instructor or manufacturer's documentations.

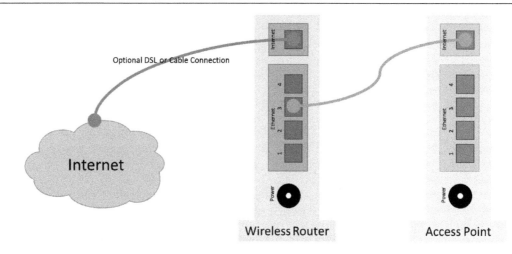

Optional DSL or Cable Connection

Internet

Wireless Router

Access Point

Step 1:   Connect the access point to the wireless network.

    a.   Connect the wireless router via the Ethernet port. Navigate to the wireless router using a web browser using the IP address of the default gateway and log in as the administrator.

    b.   To prevent interference, navigate to the wireless settings. Change the wireless channel from the default channel 1 to channel 6 or 11 on the wireless router. Save the new settings.

    c.   Connect the Internet port of the access point to one of LAN ports on the existing wireless router.

Step 2:   Configure access point wireless settings.

    a.   In the web page of the wireless router, navigate to the LAN settings to determine the IP address of the access point. The IP address of the access point can be listed in the address reservation table or DHCP client list.

    b.   In another web browser, navigate to the IP address of the access point.

    c.   In the access point settings, navigate to the wireless settings and configure the AP with the same wireless SSID and security options as the wireless router. For example, **ITE** as the SSID and WPA2 Personal AES with **Cisco456!** as the passphrase.

    d. Verify that the wireless router and AP are not using the same wireless channels.

    e. Attempt to connect a wireless client to the wireless network.

Step 3: Turn off wireless radio on the wireless router.

After you have successfully connected to the wireless network, you will attempt to disable the wireless router radio, and a wireless client will attempt to connect to the wireless network through the AP.

Depending on the wireless router model, you may be able to switch off the wireless radio using the on/off switch.

    a. Navigate to the wireless router using a web browser. If necessary, connect to the wireless router using a wired Ethernet connection.

    b. Navigate to the wireless settings. Turn off the wireless router radio if available. The option to enable wireless radio may be in the advanced wireless settings.

    c. Save the settings.

    d. Attempt to connect a wireless client to the AP.

Part 5: Reset to the original configuration

Unless stated otherwise by the instructor, restore the router back to factory default if the option is available.

Note: Some wireless models have a reset button to reset the router to its default factory settings.

---

    a. Locate the Maintenance or System settings.

    b. Click the selection to revert to factory default settings.

    c. Provide your administrative credentials if prompted.

    d. Wait for your router to finish reboot before shutting down the wireless router.

13.2.7 Packet Tracer—Configure a Basic WLAN on the WLC

Addressing Table

Device	Interface	IP Address
R-1	G/0/0	172.31.1.1/24
	G0/0/1.5	192.168.5.1/24
	G0/0/1.200	192.168.200.1/24
SW-1	VLAN 200	192.168.200.100/24
LAP-1	G0	DHCP
WLC-1	Management	192.168.200.254/24
Server	NIC	172.31.1.254/24
Admin PC	NIC	192.168.200.200/24
Wireless Host	Wireless NIC	DHCP

Objectives

In this lab, you will explore some of the features of a wireless LAN controller. You will create a new WLAN on the controller and implement security on that LAN. Then you will configure a wireless host to connect to the new WLAN through an AP that is under the control of the WLC. Finally, you will verify connectivity.

- Connect to a wireless LAN controller GUI.

- Explain some of the information that is available on the WLC Monitor screen.

- Configure a WLAN on a wireless LAN controller.

- Implement security on a WLAN.

- Configure a wireless host to connect to a wireless LAN.

Background / Scenario

An organization is centralizing control of their wireless LAN by replacing their standalone access points with lightweight access points (LAP) and a wireless LAN controller (WLC). You will be leading this project and you want to become familiar with the WLC and any potential challenges that may occur during the project. You will configure a WLC by adding a new wireless network and securing it with WPA-2 PSK security. To test the configuration, you will connect a laptop to the WLAN and ping devices on the network.

Instructions

Part 1: Monitor the WLC

Wait until STP has converged on the network. You can click the Packet Tracer Fast Forward Time button to speed up the process. Continue when all link lights are green.

a. Go the desktop of **Admin PC** and open a browser. Enter the management IP address of **WLC-1** from the addressing table into the address bar. You must specify the **HTTPS** protocol.

b. Click **Login** and enter these credentials: User Name: **admin**, Password: **Cisco123**. After a short delay, you will see the WLC Monitor Summary screen.

Note: Packet Tracer does not support the initial dashboard that has been demonstrated in this module.

c. Scroll through the Monitor Summary screen.

What can be learned from this screen?

Is the WLC connected to an AP?

d. Click **Detail** next to the All APs entry in the Access Point Summary section of the page. What information can you find about APs on the All APs screen?

Part 2: Create a Wireless LAN

Now you will create a new wireless LAN on the WLC. You will configure the settings that are required for hosts to join the WLAN.

Step 1:   Create and enable the WLAN.

a. Click **WLANs** in the WLC menu bar. Locate the dropdown box in the upper right had corner of the WLANs screen. It will say **Create New**. Click **Go** to create a new WLAN.

b. Enter the **Profile Name** of the new WLAN. Use the profile name **Floor 2 Employees**. Assign an SSID of **SSID-5** to the WLAN. Hosts will need to use this SSID to join the network.

c. Select the **ID** for the WLAN. This value is a label that will be used to identify the WLAN in other displays. Select a value of **5** to keep it consistent with the VLAN number and SSID. This is not a requirement but it helps with understanding the topology.

d. Click **Apply** so that the settings go into effect.

e. Now that the WLAN has been created, you can configure features of the network. Click **Enabled** to make the WLAN functional. It is a common mistake to accidentally skip this step.

f. Choose the VLAN interface that will be used for the WLAN. The WLC will use this interface for user traffic on the network. Click the drop-down box for Interface/Interface Group (G). Select the **WLAN-5** interface. This interface was previously configured on the WLC for this activity.

g. Click the **Advanced** tab.

h. Scroll down to the FlexConnect portion of the page. Click to enable **FlexConnect Local Switching** and **FlexConnect Local Auth**.

i. Click **Apply** to enable the new WLAN. If you forget to do this, the WLAN will not operate.

Step 2:   Secure the WLAN.

The new WLAN currently has no security in place. This WLAN will initially use WPA2-PSK security. In another activity, you will configure the WLAN to use WPA2-Enterprise, a much better solution for larger wireless networks.

a. In the WLANs Edit screen for the Floor 2 Employees WLAN, click the **Security** tab. Under the **Layer 2** tab, select **WPA+WPA2** from the **Layer 2 Security** drop down box. This will reveal the WPA parameters.

b. Click the checkbox next to **WPA2 Policy**. This will reveal additional security settings. Under **Authentication Key Management**, enable **PSK**.

c. Now you can enter the pre-shared key that will be used by hosts to join the WLAN. Use **Cisco123** as the passphrase.

d. Click **Apply** to save these settings.

Note: It is not a good practice to reuse passwords when configuring security. We have reused passwords in this activity to simplify configuration.

Step 3:   Verify the Settings.

a. After applying the configuration, click **Back**. This will take you back to the WLANs screen.

Question:

What information about the new WLAN is available on this screen?

---

b. If you click the WLAN ID, you will be taken to the WLANs Edit screen. Use this to verify and change the details of the settings.

Part 3: Connect a Host to the WLAN

Step 1:   Connect to the network and verify connectivity.

a. Go to the desktop of **Wireless Host** and click the **PC Wireless** tile.

b. Click the **Connect** tab. After a brief delay you should see the SSID for the WLAN appear in the table of wireless network names. Select the **SSID-5** network and click the **Connect** button.

c. Enter the pre-shared key that you configured for the WLAN and click **Connect**.

d. Click the **Link Information** tab. You should see a message that confirms that you have successfully connected to the access point. You should also see a wireless wave in the topology showing the connection to LAP-1.

e. Click the **More Information** button to see details about the connection.

f. Close the PC Wireless app and open the IP Configuration app. Verify that Wireless Host has received a non-APIPA IP address over DHCP. If not, click the **Fast Forward Time** button a few times.

g. From Wireless Host, ping the WLAN default gateway and the Server to verify that the laptop has full connectivity.

13.3.12 Packet Tracer—Configure a WPA2 Enterprise WLAN on the WLC

Addressing Table

Device	Interface	IP Address
R1	G0/0/0.5	192.168.5.1/24
	G0/0/0.200	192.168.200.1/24
	G0/0/1	172.31.1.1/24
SW1	VLAN 200	192.168.200.100/24
LAP-1	G0	DHCP
WLC-1	Management	192.168.200.254/24
RADIUS/SNMP Server	NIC	172.31.1.254/24
Admin PC	NIC	192.168.200.200/24

Objectives

In this activity, you will configure a new WLAN on a wireless LAN controller (WLC), including the VLAN interface that it will use. You will configure the WLAN to use a RADIUS server and WPA2-Enterprise to authenticate users. You will also configure the WLC to use an SNMP server.

- Configure a new VLAN interface on a WLC.

- Configure a new WLAN on a WLC.

- Configure a new scope on the WLC internal DHCP server.

- Configure the WLC with SNMP settings.

- Configure the WLC to use a RADIUS server to authenticate WLAN users.

- Secure a WLAN with WPA2-Enterprise.

- Connect hosts to the new WLC.

Background / Scenario

You have already configured and tested the WLC with an existing WLAN. You configured WPA2-PSK for that WLAN because it was to be used in a smaller business. You have been asked to configure and test a WLC topology that will be used in a larger enterprise. You know that WPA2-PSK does not scale well and is not appropriate to use in an enterprise network. This new topology will use a RADIUS server and WPA2-Enterprise to authenticate WLAN users. This allows administration of the user accounts from a central location and provides enhanced security and transparency because each account has its own username and password. In addition, user activity is logged on the server.

In this lab, you will create a new VLAN interface, use that interface to create a new WLAN, and secure that WLAN with WPA2-Enterprise. You will also configure the WLC to use the enterprise RADIUS server to authenticate users. In addition, you will configure the WLC to use a SNMP server.

Instructions

Part 1: Create a new WLAN

Step 1:   Create a new VLAN interface.

Each WLAN requires a virtual interface on the WLC. These interfaces are known as dynamic interfaces. The virtual interface is assigned a VLAN ID and traffic that uses the interface will be tagged as VLAN traffic. This is why connections between the APs, the WLC, and the router are over trunk ports. For the traffic from multiple WLANs to be transported through the network, traffic for the WLAN VLANs must be trunked.

a.   Open the browser from the desktop of Admin PC. Connect to the IP address of the WLC over HTTPS.

b.   Log in with the username **admin** and password **Cisco123**.

c.   Click the **Controller** menu and then click **Interfaces** from the menu on the left. You will see the default virtual interface and the management interface to which you are connected.

d.   Click the **New** button in the upper right-hand corner of the page. You may need to scroll the page to the right to see it.

e.   Enter the name of the new interface. We will call it **WLAN-5**. Configure the VLAN ID as **5**. This is the VLAN that will carry traffic for the WLAN that we create later. Click **Apply**. This leads to a configuration screen for the VLAN interface.

f.   First, configure the interface to use physical port number **1**. Multiple VLAN interfaces can use the same physical port because the physical interfaces are like dedicated trunk ports.

g.   Address the interface as follows:

IP Address: **192.168.5.254**

Netmask: **255.255.255.0**

Gateway: **192.168.5.1**

Primary DHCP server: **192.168.5.1**

User traffic for the WLAN that uses this VLAN interface will be on the 192.168.5.0/24 network. The default gateway is the address of an interface on router **R-1**. A DHCP pool has been configured on the router. The address that we configure here for DHCP tells the WLC to forward all DHCP requests that it receives from hosts on the WLAN to the DHCP server on the router.

h.   Be sure to click **Apply** to enact your changes and click **OK** to respond to the warning message. Click **Save Configuration** so that your configuration will be in effect when the WLC restarts.

Step 2:   Configure the WLC to use a RADIUS server.

WPA2-Enterprise uses an external RADIUS server to authenticate WLAN users. Individual user accounts with unique usernames and passwords can be configured on the RADIUS server. Before the WLC can use the services of the RADIUS server, the WLC must be configured with the server address.

a. Click the **Security** menu on the WLC.

b. Click the **New** button and enter the IP address of the RADIUS server in the **Server IP Address** field.

c. The RADIUS server will authenticate the WLC before it will allow the WLC to access the user account information that is on the server. This requires a shared secret value. Use **Cisco123**. Confirm the shared secret and click **Apply.**

Note: It is not a good practice to reuse passwords. This activity reuses passwords only to make the activity easier for you to complete and review.

Step 3:   Create a new WLAN.

Create a new WLAN. Use the newly created VLAN interface for the new WLAN.

a. Click the **WLANs** entry in the menu bar. Locate the dropdown box in the upper right-had corner of the WLANs screen. It will say **Create New.** Click **Go** to create a new WLAN.

b. Enter the **Profile Name** of the new WLAN. Use the profile name **Floor 2 Employees.** Assign an SSID of **SSID-5** to the WLAN. Change the ID drop down to **5.** Hosts will need to use this SSID to join the network. When you are done, click **Apply** to accept your settings.

Note: The ID is an arbitrary value that is used as a label for the WLAN. In this case, we configured it as **5** to be consistent with the VLAN for the WLAN. It could be any available value.

---

c. Click **Apply** so that the settings go into effect.

d. Now that the WLAN has been created you can configure features of the network. Click **Enabled** to make the WLAN functional. It is a common mistake to accidentally skip this step.

e. Choose the VLAN interface that will be used for the new WLAN. The WLC will use this interface for user traffic on the network. Click the drop-down box for Interface/Interface Group (G). Select the interface that we created in Step 1.

f. Go to the Advanced tab. Scroll to **FlexConnect** section of the interface.

g. Click to enable **FlexConnect Local Switching** and **FlexConnect Local Auth.**

h. Click **Apply** to enable the new WLAN. If you forget to do this, the WLAN will not operate.

Step 4:   Configure WLAN security.

Instead of WPA2-PSK, we will configure the new WLAN to use WPA2-Enterprise.

a. Click the WLAN ID of the newly created WLAN to continue configuring it, if necessary.

b. Click the Security tab. Under the Layer 2 tab, select **WPA+WPA2** from the drop-down box.

c. Under WPA+WPA2 Parameters, enable **WPA2 Policy**. Click **802.1X** under Authentication Key Management. This tells the WLC to use the 802.1X protocol to authenticate users externally.

d. Click the **AAA Servers** tab. Open the drop-down next to Server 1 in the Authentication Servers column and select the server that we configured in Step 2.

e. Click **Apply** to enact this configuration. You have now configured the WLC to use the RADIUS sever to authenticate users that attempt to connect to the WLAN.

Part 2: Configure a DHCP Scope and SNMP

Step 1:   Configure a DHCP Scope.

The WLC offers its own internal DHCP server. Cisco recommends that the WLAN DHCP server not be used for high-volume DHCP services, such as that required by larger user WLANs. However, in smaller networks, the DHCP server can be used to provide IP addresses to LAPs that are connected to the wired management network. In this step, we will configure a DHCP scope on the WLC and use it to address LAP-1.

a. Should be connected to the WLC GUI from Admin PC.

b. Click the **Controller** menu and then click **Interfaces**.

Question:

What interfaces are present?

_____

c. Click the **management** interface. Record its addressing information here.

Questions:

IP address:

_____

Netmask:

_____

Gateway:

_____

Primary DHCP server:

_____

d. We want the WLC to use its own DHCP sever to provide addressing to devices on the wireless management network, such as lightweight APs. For this reason, enter the IP address of the WLC management interface as the primary DHCP server address. Click **Apply**. Click **OK** to acknowledge any warning messages that appear.

e. In the left-hand menu, expand the **Internal DHCP Server** section. Click **DHCP Scope.**

f. To create a DHCP scope, click the **New** button.

g. Name the scope **Wired Management.** You will configure this DHCP scope to provide addresses to the wired infrastructure network that connects the Admin PC, **WLC-1,** and **LAP-1.**

h. Click **Apply** to create the new DHCP scope.

i. Click the new scope in the DHCP Scopes table to configure addressing information for the scope. Enter the following information.

Pool Start Address: **192.168.200.240**

Pool End Address: **192.168.200.249**

Status: **Enabled**

Provide the values for **Network, Netmask,** and **Default Routers** from the information you gathered in Step 1c.

j. Click **Apply** to activate the configuration. Click **Save Configuration** in the upper-right-hand corner of the WLC interface to save your work so that it is available when the WLC restarts.

The internal DHCP server will now provide an address to LAP-1 after a brief delay. When LAP-1 has its IP address, the CAPWAP tunnel will be established and LAP-1 will be able to provide access to the Floor 2 Employees (SSID-5) WLAN. If you move the mouse over LAP-1 in the topology, you should see its IP address, the status of the CAPWAP tunnel, and the WLAN that LAP-1 is providing access to.

Step 2: Configure SNMP.

a. Click the **Management** menu in the WLC GUI and expand the entry for **SNMP** in the left-hand menu.

b. Click **Trap Receivers** and then **New.**

c. Enter the community string as **WLAN_SNMP** and the IP address of the server at **172.31.1.254.**

d. Click **Apply** to finish the configuration.

Part 3: Connect Hosts to the Network

Step 1: Configure a host to connect to the enterprise network.

In the Packet Tracer PC Wireless client app, you must configure a WLAN Profile in order to attach to a WPA2-Enterprise WLAN.

a. Click Wireless Host and open the **PC Wireless** app.

b. Click the **Profiles** tab and then click **New** to create a new profile. Name the profile **WLC NET.**

c. Highlight the Wireless Network Name for the WLAN that we created earlier and click **Advanced Setup.**

    d. Verify that the SSID for the wireless LAN is present and then click **Next**. Wireless Host should see SSID-5. If it does not, move the mouse over LAP-1 to verify that it is communicating with the WLC. The popup box should indicate that LAP-1 is aware of SSID-5. If it is not, check the WLC configuration. You can also manually enter the SSID.

    e. Verify that the DHCP network setting is selected and click **Next**.

    f. In the Security drop down box, select **WPA2-Enterprise**. Click **Next**.

    g. Enter login name **user1** and the password **User1Pass** and click **Next**.

    h. Verify the Profile Settings and click **Save**.

    i. Select the **WLC NET** profile and click the **Connect to Network** button. After a brief delay, you should see the Wireless Host connect to LAP-1. You can click the Fast Forward Time button to speed up the process if it seems to be taking too long.

    j. Confirm that Wireless Host has connected to the WLAN. Wireless Host should receive an IP address from the DHCP server that is configured for hosts on **R1**. The address will be in the 192.168.5.0/24 network. You may need to click the Fast Forward Time button speed up the process.

Step 2: Test Connectivity.

    a. Close the PC Wireless app.

    b. Open a command prompt and confirm that **Wireless Host** laptop has obtained an IP address from the WLAN network.

    Question:

    What network should the address be in? Explain.

    c. Ping the default gateway, SW1, and the RADIUS server. Success indicates full connectivity within this topology.

Reflection Questions

  1. The RADIUS server uses a dual authentication mechanism. What two things are authenticated by the RADIUS server? Why do think this is necessary?

  2. What are the advantages of WPA2-Enterprise over WPA2-PSK?

13.4.5 Packet Tracer—Troubleshoot WLAN Issues

Addressing Table

Device	Interface	IP Address
Home Wireless Router	Internet	DHCP
	LAN	192.168.0.1
R1	G0/0/0.10	192.168.10.1/24
	G0/0/0.20	192.168.20.1/24
	G0/0/0.200	192.168.200.1/24
	G0/0/1	172.31.1.1/24
SW1	VLAN 200	192.168.200.100/24
LAP-1	G0	DHCP
WLC-1	Management	192.168.200.254/24
RADIUS Server	NIC	172.31.1.254/24
Admin PC	NIC	192.168.200.200/24
Web Server	NIC	203.0.113.78/24
DNS Server	NIC	10.100.100.254
Home Admin	NIC	DHCP
Laptop	NIC	DHCP
Laptop1	Wireless0	DHCP
Laptop2	Wireless0	DHCP
Tablet PC	Wireless0	DHCP
Smartphone	Wireless0	DHCP

WLAN Information

WLAN	SSID	Authentication	Username	Password
Home Network	HomeSSID	WPA2-Personal	N/A	Cisco123
WLAN VLAN 10	SSID-10	WPA-2 PSK/Personal	N/A	Cisco123
WLAN VLAN 20	SSID-20	WPA-2 802.1x/Enterprise	user2	user2Pass

Objectives

In this activity, you will troubleshoot various issues in home wireless and enterprise wireless networks.

- Troubleshoot wireless LAN connectivity issues in a home network.
- Troubleshoot wireless LAN connectivity issues in an enterprise network.

Background / Scenario

Now that you have learned how to configure wireless in home and enterprise networks, you need to learn how to troubleshoot in both wireless environments. Your goal is to enable connectivity between hosts on the networks to the web server by both IP address and URL. Connectivity between the home and enterprise networks is not required.

To access the Home Wireless Router, the username and password is **admin.**

The WLC management interface username is **admin** and the password is **Cisco123.**

Instructions

Part 1: Troubleshoot the Network

Note: You will only be troubleshooting the Home Wireless Router, WLC and wireless host devices in this activity.

Step 1: Test connectivity.

    a. Test connectivity between the various wireless hosts and the web server by both IP and URL **www.netacad.pt.**

    b. Record the hosts that cannot access the web server in the table in Step 2.

Step 2: Investigate issues and record findings.

    a. Investigate the connectivity issues with each host. Issues may be with the host configuration, or with other wireless network components.

    b. Complete the table.

Device	Network Home/ Enterprise	Issue	Remedy

Part 2: Fix Issues

Make changes to the device configurations so hosts can achieve connectivity with the network. Test to ensure all hosts can reach the communication goal of connecting to the web server by both IP address and URL.

Packet Tracer
☐ Activity

13.5.1 Packet Tracer—WLAN Configuration

Addressing Table

Device	Interface	IP Address
Home Wireless Router	Internet	DHCP
	LAN	192.168.6.1/27
RTR-1	G0/0/0.2	192.168.2.1/24
	G0/0/0.5	192.168.5.1/24
	G0/0/0.100	192.168.100.1/24
	G0/0/1	10.6.0.1/24
SW1	VLAN 200	192.168.100.100/24
LAP-1	G0	DHCP
WLC-1	Management	192.168.100.254/24
RADIUS Server	NIC	10.6.0.254/24
Home Admin	NIC	DHCP
Enterprise Admin	NIC	192.168.100.200/24
Web Server	NIC	203.0.113.78/24
DNS Server	NIC	10.100.100.252
Laptop	NIC	DHCP
Tablet PC	Wireless0	DHCP
Smartphone	Wireless0	DHCP
Wireless Host 1	Wireless0	DHCP
Wireless Host 2	Wireless0	DHCP

WLAN Information

WLAN	SSID	Authentication	Username	Password
Home Network	HomeSSID	WPA2-Personal	N/A	Cisco123
WLAN VLAN 2	SSID-2	WPA2-Personal	N/A	Cisco123
WLAN VLAN 5	SSID-5	WPA2-Enterprise	userWLAN5	userW5pass

Note: It is not a good practice to reuse passwords as is done in this activity. Passwords have been reused to make it easier to work through the tasks.

Objectives

In this activity, you will configure both a wireless home router and a WLC-based network. You will implement both WPA2-PSK and WPA2-Enterprise security.

- Configure a home router to provide Wi-Fi connectivity to a variety of devices.
- Configure WPA2-PSK security on a home router.
- Configure interfaces on a WLC.

- Configure WLANs on a WLC.
- Configure WPA2-PSK security on a WLAN and connect hosts to WLAN.
- Configure WPA2-Enteprise on a WLAN and connect hosts to the WLAN.
- Verify connectivity WLAN connectivity.

Background / Scenario

You will apply your WLAN skills and knowledge by configuring a home wireless router and an enterprise WLC. You will implement both WPA2-PSK and WPA2-Enterprise security. Finally, you will connect hosts to each WLAN and verify connectivity.

Instructions

Part 1: Configure a Home Wireless Router.

You are installing a new home wireless router at a friend's house. You will need to change settings on the router to enhance security and meet your friend's requirements.

Step 1:   Change DHCP settings.

a.   Open the Home Wireless Router GUI and change the router IP and DHCP settings according to the information in the Addressing Table.

b.   Permit a maximum of **20** addresses to be issued by the router.

c.   Configure the DHCP server to start with IP address .3 of the LAN network.

d.   Configure the internet interface of the router to receive its IP address over DHCP.

Question:

Verify the address. What address did it receive?

---

e.   Configure the static DNS server to the address in the Addressing Table.

Step 2:   Configure the Wireless LAN.

a.   The network will use the 2.4 GHz Wireless LAN interface. Configure the interface with the SSID shown in the Wireless LAN information table.

b.   Use **channel 6.**

c.   Be sure that all wireless hosts in the home will be able to see the SSID.

Step 3:   Configure security.

a.   Configure wireless LAN security. Use WPA2-Personal and the passphrase shown in the Wireless LAN information table.

b.   Secure the router by changing the default password to the value shown in the Wireless LAN information table.

Step 4:   Connect clients to the network.

a.   Open the PC Wireless app on the desktop of the laptop and configure the client to connect to the network.

b. Open the Config tab on the Tablet PC and Smartphone and configure the wireless interfaces to connect to the wireless network.

c. Verify connectivity. The hosts should be able to ping each other and the web server. They should also be able to reach the web server URL.

Part 2: Configure a WLC Controller Network

Configure the wireless LAN controller with two WLANs. One WLAN will use WPA2-PSK authentication. The other WLAN will use WPA2-Enterprise authentication. You will also configure the WLC to use an SNMP server and configure a DHCP scope that will be used by the wireless management network.

Step 1: Configure VLAN interfaces.

a. From the Enterprise Admin, navigate to the WLC-1 management interface via a web browser. To log into WLC-1, use **admin** as the username and **Cisco123** as the password.

b. Configure an interface for the first WLAN.

Name: **WLAN 2**

VLAN Identifier: **2**

Port Number: **1**

Interface IP Address: **192.168.2.254**

Netmask: **255.255.255.0**

Gateway: **RTR-1 G0/0/0.2 address**

Primary DHCP Server: **Gateway address**

c. Configure an interface for the second WLAN.

Name: **WLAN 5**

VLAN Identifier: **5**

Port Number: **1**

Interface IP Address: **192.168.5.254**

Netmask: **255.255.255.0**

Gateway: **RTR-1 interface G0/0/0.5 address**

Primary DHCP Server: **Gateway address**

Step 2: Configure a DHCP scope for the wireless management network.

Configure and enable an internal DHCP scope as follows:

Scope Name: **management**

Pool Start Address: **192.168.100.235**

Pool End Address: **192.168.100.245**

Network: **192.168.100.0**

Netmask: **255.255.255.0**

Default Routers: **192.168.100.1**

Step 3:   Configure the WLC with external server addresses.

    a.   Configure the RADIUS server information as follows:

    Server Index: **1**

    Server Address: **10.6.0.254**

    Shared Secret: **RadiusPW**

    b.   Configure the WLC to send log information to an SNMP server.

    Community Name: **WLAN**

    IP Address: **10.6.0.254**

Step 4:   Create the WLANs.

    a.   Create the first WLAN:

    Profile Name: **Wireless VLAN 2**

    WLAN SSID: **SSID-2**

    ID: **2**

    Interface: **WLAN 2**

    Security: **WPA2-PSK**

    Passphrase: **Cisco123**

    Under the Advanced tab, go to the FlexConnect section. Enable **FlexConnect Local Switching** and **FlexConnect Local Auth.**

    b.   Create the second WLAN:

    Profile Name: **Wireless VLAN 5**

    WLAN SSID: **SSID-5**

    Interface: **WLAN 5**

    ID: **5**

    Security: **802.1x - WPA2-Enterprise**

    Configure the WLAN to use the RADIUS server for authentication.

    Make the **FlexConnect** settings as was done in Step 4a.

Step 5:   Configure the hosts to connect to the WLANs.

    Use the desktop PC Wireless app to configure the hosts as follows:

    a.   Wireless Host 1 should connect to Wireless VLAN 2.

    b.   Wireless Host 2 should connect to Wireless VLAN 5 using the credentials in the WLAN information table.

Step 6:   Test connectivity.

    Test connectivity between the wireless hosts and the Web Server by ping and URL.

CHAPTER 14

Routing Concepts

The "Study Guide" portion of this chapter uses a variety of exercises to test your knowledge of how routers use information in packets to make forwarding decisions. The "Labs and Activities" portion of this chapter includes the instructions for the one Packet Tracer activity in this module in the online curriculum.

As you work through this chapter, use Chapter 14 in *Switching, Routing, and Wireless Essentials v7 Companion Guide* or use the corresponding Module 14 in the Switching, Routing, and Wireless Essentials online curriculum for assistance.

Study Guide

Path Determination

In this section, you will review how routers determine the best path.

Two Functions of a Router

A router connects multiple networks, which means that it has multiple interfaces that each belong to a different IP network.

Briefly describe the process of routing.

_____

_____

The interface that the router uses to forward the packet may be the final destination, or it may be a network connected to another router that is used to reach the destination network. Each network that a router connects to typically requires a separate interface, but this may not always be the case.

What are the two functions of a router?

_____

_____

Best Path Equals Longest Match

The best path in the routing table is also known as the longest match. The prefix length of the route in the routing table is used to determine the minimum number of far-left bits that must match. Remember that an IP packet contains only the destination IP address and not the prefix length.

For an IPv4 packet with the destination address **172.16.0.26**, which route will the router choose from the following routing table entries?

Route Entry	Prefix/Prefix Length
1	172.16.0.0/14
2	172.16.0.0/24
3	172.16.0.0/18

_____

For an IPv6 packet with the destination address **2001:db8:acad::45**, which route will the router choose from the from the following routing table entries?

Route Entry	Prefix/Prefix Length
1	2001:db8:acad::/40
2	2001:db8:acad::/48
3	2001:db8:acad:1::/64

_____

Build the Routing Table

A router learns routes in three ways:

- Directly connected networks are added to the routing table when an interface is configured with an IP address and subnet mask (prefix length) and is active (up and up).

- Remote networks are added to the routing table in two ways: using static routes and through dynamic routing protocols.

- A default route, which is used if there are no other routes that match the destination IP address, can be entered manually as a static route or learned automatically from a dynamic routing protocol.

Check Your Understanding—Path Determination

Check your understanding of routers by choosing the BEST answer to each of the following questions.

1. What table does a router use to determine how to forward an IP packet?

   a. ARP table

   b. MAC address table

   c. neighbor cache

   d. routing table

2. What action does a router take on a packet with a destination IP address that is on a remote network?

   a. It forwards the packet directly to the device with the destination IP address of the packet.

   b. It forwards the packet to a next-hop router.

   c. It forwards the packet to an Ethernet switch.

   d. It drops the packet.

3. Which of the following routes may be found in a routing table? (Choose all that apply.)

   a. directly connected networks

   b. static routes

   c. dynamic routing protocol routes

   d. default route

4. What is used to determine the minimum number of far-left bits that must match between the prefix in the route entry and the destination IP address?

   a. prefix length in the routing table entry

   b. prefix length of the destination IP address

   c. classful address of the network address

Packet Forwarding

In this section, you will review how routers forward packets to the destination.

Packet Forwarding Decision Process

Figure 14-1 demonstrates how a router first determines the best path and then forwards the packet.

Figure 14-1   Path Determination and Packet Forwarding Flowchart

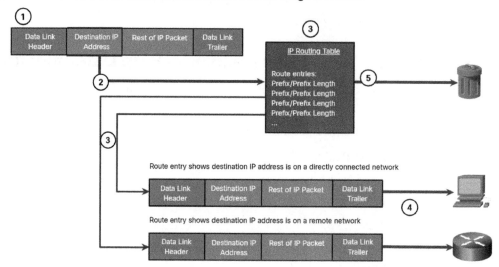

Briefly describe the five steps shown in Figure 14-1.

_____

_____

_____

_____

_____

End-to-End Packet Forwarding

The primary responsibility of the packet forwarding function is to encapsulate packets in the appropriate data link frame type for the outgoing interface. For example, the data link frame format for a serial link could be Point-to-Point Protocol (PPP), High-Level Data Link Control (HDLC), or some other Layer 2 protocol.

Refer to Figure 14-2 to answer the following questions.

Figure 14-2   Mapping Layer 2 and Layer 3 Addresses

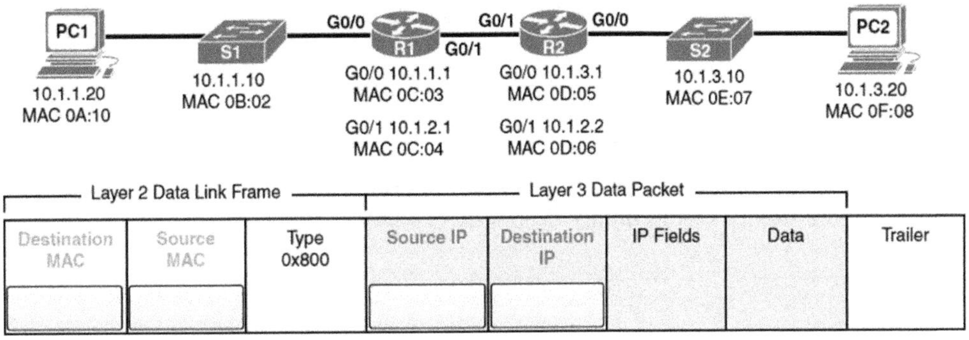

PC1 sends a ping to PC2. What are the Layer 2 and Layer 3 addresses that PC1 will use to encapsulate the packet and frame before sending it to R1?

■ Destination MAC: _____

■ Source MAC: _____

■ Source IP: _____

■ Destination IP: _____

R1 receives the ping from PC1. What are the Layer 2 and Layer 3 addresses that R1 will use to encapsulate the packet and frame before sending it to R2?

■ Destination MAC: _____

■ Source MAC: _____

■ Source IP: _____

■ Destination IP:_____

R2 receives the ping from R1. What are the Layer 2 and Layer 3 addresses that R2 will use to encapsulate the packet and frame before sending it to PC2?

■ Destination MAC:_____

■ Source MAC: _____

■ Source IP: _____

■ Destination IP:_____

PC2 receives the ping from R2. What are the Layer 2 and Layer 3 addresses that PC2 will use to encapsulate the reply packet and frame before sending it to R2?

■ Destination MAC:_____

■ Source MAC: _____

■ Source IP: _____

■ Destination IP: _____

What role do the switches have in relationship to addressing in this scenario?

_____

_____

_____

As packets are forwarded from source to destination, what do you notice about the Layer 2 addresses compared to the Layer 3 addresses?

_____

_____

Packet Forwarding Mechanisms

Briefly describe the math analogy used to compare process switching, fast switching, and Cisco Express Forwarding (CEF).

_____

_____

_____

In Figure 14-3, draw the path that each packet will take through a router that is using process switching.

Figure 14-3   Process Switching Diagram

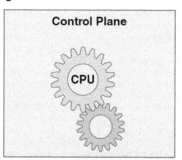

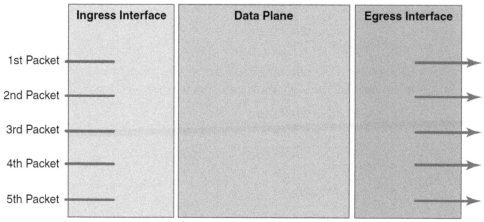

In Figure 14-4, draw the path that each packet will take through a router that is using fast switching.

Figure 14-4   Fast Switching Diagram

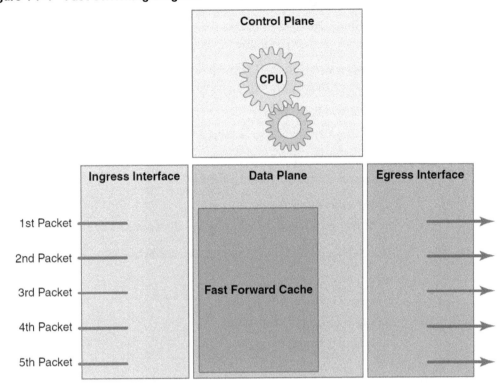

In Figure 14-5, draw the path that each packet will take through a router that is using CEF.

Figure 14-5   Cisco Express Forwarding Diagram

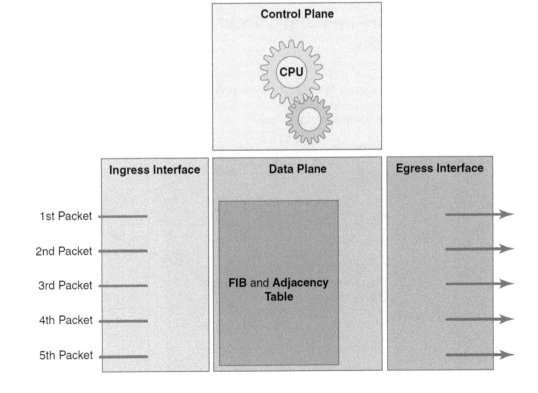

Check Your Understanding—Packet Forwarding

Check your understanding of packet forwarding from source to destination by choosing the BEST answer to each of the following questions.

1. If a router needs to send an ARP request for the destination IPv4 address of a packet, this means the packet will be forwarded _____.

   a. to a next-hop router

   b. to the device with the destination IPv4 address of the packet

2. If a router needs to send an ARP request for the IPv4 address in one of its route entries, this means the packet will be forwarded _____.

   a. to a next-hop router

   b. to the device with the destination IPv4 address of the packet

3. Which packet forwarding method is used by default on Cisco routers?

   a. process switching

   b. fast switching

   c. Cisco Express Forwarding

   d. Ethernet switching

Basic Router Configuration Review

In this section, you will review how to configure basic settings on a router.

Configure and Verify Dual Stack IPv4 and IPv6 Addressing

In this activity, you document the configuration for a router that is running both IPv4 and IPv6 (dual stack). Figure 14-6 shows the topology, and Table 14-1 documents the addressing scheme.

Figure 14-6   Dual Stack Topology

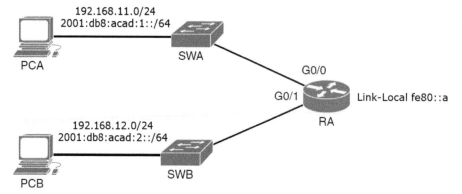

Table 14-1   Addressing Table for Figure 14-6

Device	Interface	IP Address/Prefix	Default Gateway
RA	G0/0/0	192.168.11.1/24	N/A
		2001:db8:acad:1::1/64	N/A
	G0/0/1	192.168.12.1/24	N/A
		2001:db8:acad:2::1/64	N/A
	Link local	fe80::a	N/A
PCA	NIC	192.168.11.10/24	192.168.11.1
		2001:db8:acad:1::3/64	fe80::a
PCA	NIC	192.168.12.10/24	192.168.12.1
		2001:db8:acad:2::3/64	fe80::a

In the space provided, document the script for configuring RA, including the following:

- Hostname

- Passwords

- Banner

- Interface addressing and descriptions

Packet Tracer Exercise 14-1: Dual Stack Addressing

To use Packet Tracer to apply your documented configuration, download and open the file LSG02-1401.pka from the companion website for this book. Refer to the Introduction of this book for specifics on accessing files.

Note: The following instructions are also contained within the Packet Tracer Exercise.

In this Packet Tracer activity, you will configure the RA router with basic configurations and dual stack addressing. You will then verify that PCA and PCB can ping each other using IPv4 and IPv6 addresses. Use the addressing table and the commands you documented in the section "Configure and Verify Dual Stack IPv4 and IPv6 Addressing."

Requirements

Configure RA with the following settings:

- The name of the router is **RA**.

- The privileged EXEC password is **class**.

- The line password is **cisco**.

- The message of the day is **Authorized Access Only**.

- Configure and activate the RA interfaces according to Table 14-1.

- Save the configurations.

- Verify IPv4 and IPv6 connectivity between PCA and PCB.

Your completion percentage should be 100%. All the connectivity tests should show a status of "successful." If they do not, click Check Results to see which required components are not yet completed.

Verify Connectivity of Directly Connected Networks

After completing the Packet Tracer exercise, you can verify the configuration with a number of commands. Record the commands that generated the following output:

RA# _____

Interface	IP-Address	OK?	Method	Status	Protocol
GigabitEthernet0/0/0	192.168.11.1	YES	manual	up	up
GigabitEthernet0/0/1	192.168.12.1	YES	manual	up	up
Vlan1	unassigned	YES	unset	administratively down	down

RA# _____

```
GigabitEthernet0/0/0      [up/up]
    FE80::A
    2001:DB8:ACAD:1::1
GigabitEthernet0/0/1      [up/up]
    FE80::A
    2001:DB8:ACAD:2::1
Vlan1                     [administratively down/down]
    unassigned
```

RA# _____

```
GigabitEthernet0/0/0 is up, line protocol is up (connected)
  Hardware is Lance, address is 0030.a313.2301 (bia 0030.a313.2301)
  Internet address is 192.168.11.1/24
  MTU 1500 bytes, BW 1000000 Kbit, DLY 10 usec,
      reliability 255/255, txload 1/255, rxload 1/255
  Encapsulation ARPA, loopback not set
  Full-duplex, 100Mb/s, media type is RJ45
<output omitted>
```

RA# _____

```
GigabitEthernet0/0/0 is up, line protocol is up (connected)
  Internet address is 192.168.11.1/24
  Broadcast address is 255.255.255.255
  Address determined by setup command
  MTU is 1500 bytes
  Helper address is not set
  Directed broadcast forwarding is disabled
  Outgoing access list is not set
  Inbound  access list is not set
  Proxy ARP is enabled
  Security level is default
  Split horizon is enabled
  ICMP redirects are always sent
```

```
      ICMP unreachables are always sent

      ICMP mask replies are never sent

      IP fast switching is disabled

      IP fast switching on the same interface is disabled

      IP Flow switching is disabled

<output omitted>
```

```
RA# _____

GigabitEthernet0/0/0 is up, line protocol is up

   IPv6 is enabled, link-local address is FE80::A

   No Virtual link-local address(es):

   Global unicast address(es):

     2001:DB8:ACAD:1::1, subnet is 2001:DB8:ACAD:1::/64

   Joined group address(es):

     FF02::1

     FF02::2

     FF02::1:FF00:1

     FF02::1:FF00:A

   MTU is 1500 bytes

   ICMP error messages limited to one every 100 milliseconds

   ICMP redirects are enabled

   ICMP unreachables are sent

   ND DAD is enabled, number of DAD attempts: 1

   ND reachable time is 30000 milliseconds

   ND advertised reachable time is 0 (unspecified)

   ND advertised retransmit interval is 0 (unspecified)

   ND router advertisements are sent every 200 seconds

   ND router advertisements live for 1800 seconds

   ND advertised default router preference is Medium

   Hosts use stateless autoconfig for addresses.
```

```
RA# _____

Codes: L - local, C - connected, S - static, R - RIP, M - mobile, B - BGP

       D - EIGRP, EX - EIGRP external, O - OSPF, IA - OSPF inter area

       N1 - OSPF NSSA external type 1, N2 - OSPF NSSA external type 2

       E1 - OSPF external type 1, E2 - OSPF external type 2, E - EGP

       i - IS-IS, L1 - IS-IS level-1, L2 - IS-IS level-2, ia - IS-IS inter area

       * - candidate default, U - per-user static route, o - ODR

       P - periodic downloaded static route


Gateway of last resort is not set


      192.168.11.0/24 is variably subnetted, 2 subnets, 2 masks

C        192.168.11.0/24 is directly connected, GigabitEthernet0/0/0
```

```
L       192.168.11.1/32 is directly connected, GigabitEthernet0/0/0
        192.168.12.0/24 is variably subnetted, 2 subnets, 2 masks
C       192.168.12.0/24 is directly connected, GigabitEthernet0/0/1
L       192.168.12.1/32 is directly connected, GigabitEthernet0/0/1
```

RA# _____

```
IPv6 Routing Table - 5 entries
Codes: C - Connected, L - Local, S - Static, R - RIP, B - BGP
       U - Per-user Static route, M - MIPv6
       I1 - ISIS L1, I2 - ISIS L2, IA - ISIS interarea, IS - ISIS summary
       O - OSPF intra, OI - OSPF inter, OE1 - OSPF ext 1, OE2 - OSPF ext 2
       ON1 - OSPF NSSA ext 1, ON2 - OSPF NSSA ext 2
       D - EIGRP, EX - EIGRP external
C    2001:DB8:ACAD:1::/64 [0/0]
     via GigabitEthernet0/0/0, directly connected
L    2001:DB8:ACAD:1::1/128 [0/0]
     via GigabitEthernet0/0/0, receive
C    2001:DB8:ACAD:2::/64 [0/0]
     via GigabitEthernet0/0/1, directly connected
L    2001:DB8:ACAD:2::1/128 [0/0]
     via GigabitEthernet0/0/1, receive
L    FF00::/8 [0/0]
     via Null0, receive
```

Filter Command Output

Filtering commands can be used to display specific sections of output. Record the commands and filtering parameters used to display the following output.

RA# _____

```
line vty 0 4
 password cisco
 login
line vty 5 15
 password cisco
 login
RA#
```

RA# _____

```
GigabitEthernet0/0/0       [up/up]
GigabitEthernet0/0/1       [up/up]
RA#
R1#
```

R1# _____

```
Interface            IP-Address      OK? Method Status              Protocol
GigabitEthernet0/0/0 192.168.11.1    YES manual up                  up
GigabitEthernet0/0/1 192.168.12.1    YES manual up                  up
```

```
RA#
RA# _____
Gateway of last resort is not set

      192.168.11.0/24 is variably subnetted, 2 subnets, 2 masks
C        192.168.11.0/24 is directly connected, GigabitEthernet0/0/0
L        192.168.11.1/32 is directly connected, GigabitEthernet0/0/0
      192.168.12.0/24 is variably subnetted, 2 subnets, 2 masks
C        192.168.12.0/24 is directly connected, GigabitEthernet0/0/1
L        192.168.12.1/32 is directly connected, GigabitEthernet0/0/1
RA#
```

IP Routing Table

In this section, you will review the structure of a routing table.

Routing Table Principles

Briefly describe the three routing table principles.

- _____
- _____
- _____

Routing Table Entries

Figure 14-7 displays IPv4 and IPv6 routing table entries for the route to remote network 10.0.4.0/24 and 2001:db8:acad:4::/64.

Figure 14-7   IPv4 and IPv6 Routing Table Entries

IPv4 Routing Table

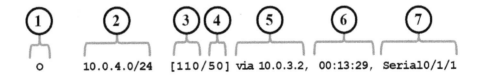

IPv6 Routing Table

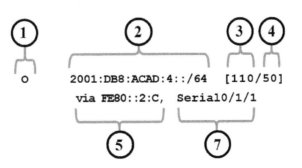

Briefly describe the information that each number in Figure 14-7 identifies.

_____

_____

_____

_____

_____

_____

_____

Administrative Distance Exercise

A router can learn about a route from multiple sources. If a router learns about two or more routes from different sources, the router must use administrative distance to help make the path determination decision.

Complete Table 14-2 for the default administrative distances used by a Cisco router.

Table 14-2   Default Administrative Distances

Route Source	Administrative Distance
Directly connected	
Static route	
EIGRP summary route	
External BGP	
Internal EIGRP	
OSPF	
IS-IS	
RIP	
External EIGRP	
Internal BGP	

Check Your Understanding—IP Routing Table

Check your understanding of the IP routing table by choosing the BEST answer to each of the following questions.

1. Which routing table principle is NOT correct?

    a. Every router makes its decision alone, based on the information it has in its own routing table.

    b. The fact that one router has certain information in its routing table does not mean that other routers have the same information.

    c. Routing information about a path from one network to another also provides routing information about the reverse, or return, path.

2. Which route entry would be used for a packet with a destination IP address that matches an IP address of one of the router interfaces?

    a. C for Directly Connected

    b. L for Local

    c. S for Static

    d. depends on the source of the route

3. What type of network is accessed by a single route, where the router has only one neighbor?

    a. stub network

    b. directly connected network

    c. next-hop network

    d. local network

4. Which two route sources have the ability to automatically discover a new best path when there is a change in the topology? (Choose two.)

    a. static route

    b. OSPF

    c. EIGRP

    d. default route

5. True or false: A default route can only be a static route.

    a. true

    b. false

6. A network administrator configures a static route for the same destination network that was learned automatically by the router using OSPF. Which route will be installed, and why?

    a. static route because it has a lower metric

    b. static route because it has a lower administrative distance

    c. OSPF route because it has a lower metric

    d. OSPF route because it has a lower administrative distance

Static and Dynamic Routing

In this section, you will review static and dynamic routing concepts.

Static or Dynamic?

Briefly describe at least three reasons to use static routing.

- _____

- _____

- _____

- _____

In Table 14-3, indicate the type of routing for each characteristic.

Table 14-3   Dynamic vs. Static Routing

Characteristic	Dynamic Routing	Static Routing
This type of routing is more secure.		
The route to the destination depends on the current topology.		
Administrator intervention is required when there is a topology change.		
Uses no extra router resources.		
Suitable for simple and complex topologies.		
This type of routing is less secure.		
Configuration complexity increases with network size.		
Configuration complexity is generally independent of the network size.		
Uses more CPU, memory, and link bandwidth.		
The route to the destination is always the same.		
Suitable for simple topologies.		
Automatically adapts to topology changes.		

Dynamic Routing Protocol Concepts

List at least three purposes of dynamic routing protocols.

- _____

- _____

- _____

- _____

List and briefly describe the main components of dynamic routing protocols.

- _____

- _____

- _____

In Table 14-4, list and describe the metrics used by each routing protocol.

Table 14-4   RIP, OSPF, and EIGRP Routing Metrics

Routing Protocol	Metric
Routing Information Protocol (RIP)	■ _____ ■ _____ ■ _____
Open Shortest Path First (OSPF)	■ _____ ■ _____
Enhanced Interior Gateway Routing Protocol (EIGRP)	■ _____ ■ _____

Check Your Understanding—Dynamic and Static Routing

Check your understanding of dynamic and static routing by choosing the BEST answer to each of the following questions.

1. Which type of routing automatically adapts to topology changes?

    a. static routing

    b. dynamic routing protocols

    c. both static routing and dynamic routing protocols

2. What type of routing is typically used with a stub network?

    a. static routing

    b. dynamic routing protocol

3. What metric does OSPF use to determine the best path?

    a. hop count

    b. cost

    c. bandwidth and delay

    d. decided by the network administrator

4. What term is used to describe routing over two or more paths to a destination with equal cost metrics?

    a. equal path selection

    b. equal packet forwarding

    c. equal-cost load balancing

    d. equal-cost routing

Labs and Activities

Command Reference

In Table 14-5, record the command, including the correct router or switch prompt, that fits each description.

Table 14-5   Commands for Chapter 14, "Routing Concepts"

Command	Description
	Enter privileged EXEC mode.
	Exit privileged EXEC mode.
	Enter global configuration mode.
	Configure R1 as the hostname for the router.
	Enter line configuration mode for the console.
	Configure the console password to be cisco123.
	Require a password for user EXEC mode.
	Configure Authorized Access Only as the message of the day. Use $ as the delimiting character.
	Enter interface configuration mode for g0/0/0.
	Configure the IPv4 address 172.16.1.1 255.255.255.0 on interface g0/0/0.
	Configure the IPv6 address 2001:db8:acad:1::1/64 on interface g0/0/0.
	Configure the IPv6 link-local address fe80::1 on interface g0/0/0.
	Activate the interface.
	Describe the interface as R1 LAN1.
	Display the routing table that IOS is currently using to choose the best path to its destination networks.
	Display all the interface configuration parameters and statistics.
	Display abbreviated interface configuration information, including IP address and interface status.

14.3.5 Packet Tracer—Basic Router Configuration Review

Addressing Table

Device	Interface	IP Address / Prefix	Default Gateway
R2	G0/0/0	10.0.4.1 /24	N/A
		2001:db8:acad:4::1 /64	
		fe80::2:a	
	G0/0/1	10.0.5.1 /24	
		2001:db8:acad:5::1 /64	
		fe80::2:b	
	S0/1/0	10.0.3.2 /24	
		2001:db8:acad:3::2 /64	
		fe80::1:c	
	S0/1/1	209.165.200.225 /30	
		2001:db8:feed:224::1 /64	
		fe80::1:d	
PC1	NIC	10.0.1.10 /24	10.0.1.1
		2001:db8:acad:1::10 /64	fe80::1:a
PC2	NIC	10.0.2.10 /24	10.0.2.1
		2001:db8:acad:2::10 /64	fe80::1:b
PC3	NIC	10.0.4.10 /24	10.0.4.1
		2001:db8:acad:4::10 /64	fe80::2:a
PC4	NIC	10.0.5.10 /24	10.0.5.1
		2001:db8:acad:5::10 /64	fe80::2:b

Objectives

Part 1: Configure Devices and Verify Connectivity

- Assign static IPv4 and IPv6 addresses to the PC interfaces.

- Configure basic router settings.

- Configure the router for SSH.

- Verify network connectivity.

Part 2: Display Router Information

- Retrieve hardware and software information from the router.

- Interpret the startup configuration.

- Interpret the routing table.

- Verify the status of the interfaces.

Background / Scenario

This activity requires you to configure the **R2** router using the settings from the Addressing Table and the specifications listed. The **R1** router and the devices connected to it have been configured. This is a comprehensive review of previously covered IOS router commands. In Part 1, you will complete basic configurations and interface settings on the router. In Part 2, you will use SSH to connect to the router remotely and utilize the IOS commands to retrieve information from the device to answer questions about the router. For review purposes, this lab provides the commands necessary for specific router configurations.

Instructions

Part 1: Configure Devices and Verify Connectivity

Step 1: Configure the PC interfaces.

   a. Configure the IPv4 and IPv6 addresses on PC3 as listed in the Addressing Table.

   b. Configure the IPv4 and IPv6 addresses on PC4 as listed in the Addressing Table.

Step 2: Configure the router.

   a. On the **R2** router, open a terminal. Move to privileged EXEC mode.

   b. Enter configuration mode.

   c. Assign a device name of **R2** to the router.

   d. Configure **c1sco1234** as the encrypted privileged EXEC mode password.

   e. Set the domain name of the router to **ccna-lab.com**.

   f. Disable DNS lookup to prevent the router from attempting to translate incorrectly entered commands as though they were host names.

   g. Encrypt the plaintext passwords.

   h. Configure the username **SSHadmin** with an encrypted password of **55Hadm!n**.

   i. Generate a set of crypto keys with a 1024 bit modulus.

   j. Assign **cisco** as the console password, configure sessions to disconnect after six minutes of inactivity, and enable login. To prevent console messages from interrupting commands, use the **logging synchronous** command.

   k. Assign **cisco** as the VTY password, configure the vty lines to accept SSH connections only, configure sessions to disconnect after six minutes of inactivity, and enable login using the local database.

   l. Create a banner that warns anyone accessing the device that unauthorized access is prohibited.

   m. Enable IPv6 Routing.

   n. Configure all four interfaces on the router with the IPv4 and IPv6 addressing information from the addressing table above. Configure all four interfaces with descriptions. Activate all four interfaces.

   o. Save the running configuration to the startup configuration file.

Step 3: Verify network connectivity.

    a. Using the command line at **PC3**, ping the IPv4 and IPv6 addresses for **PC4**.

    Question:

    Were the pings successful?

---

    b. From the CLI on **R2** ping the S0/1/1 address of **R1** for both IPv4 and IPv6. The addresses assigned to the S0/1/1 interface on R1 are:

    IPv4 address = 10.0.3.1

    IPv6 address = 2001:db8:acad:3::1

    Question:

    Were the pings successful?

    From the command line of **PC3** ping the ISP address 209.165.200.226.

    Question:

    Were the pings successful?

    From **PC3** attempt to ping an address on the ISP for testing, 64.100.1.1.

    Question:

    Were the pings successful?

---

    c. From the command line of **PC3** open an SSH session to the R2 G0/0/0 IPv4 address and log in as **SSHadmin** with the password **55Hadm!n**.

```
C:\> ssh -l SSHadmin 10.0.4.1

Password:
```

    Question:

    Was remote access successful?

Part 2: Display Router Information

In Part 2, you will use **show** commands from an SSH session to retrieve information from the router.

Step 1: Establish an SSH session to R2.

    From the command line of PC3 open an SSH session to the **R2** G0/0/0 IPv6 address and log in as **SSHadmin** with the password **55Hadm!n**.

Step 2:   Retrieve important hardware and software information.

   a.   Use the **show version** command to answer questions about the router.

   Questions:

   What is the name of the IOS image that the router is running?

   _____

   How much non-volatile random-access memory (NVRAM) does the router have?

   _____

   How much Flash memory does the router have?

   _____

   b.   The **show** commands often provide multiple screens of outputs. Filtering the output allows a user to display certain sections of the output. To enable the filtering command, enter a pipe (I) character after a **show** command, followed by a filtering parameter and a filtering expression. You can match the output to the filtering statement by using the **include** keyword to display all lines from the output that contain the filtering expression. Filter the **show version** command, using **show version | include register** to answer the following question.

   Question:

   What is the boot process for the router on the next reload?

   _____

Step 3:   Display the running configuration.

   Use the **show running-config** command on the router to answer the following questions filtering for lines containing the word "password".

   Question:

   How are passwords presented in the output?

   _____

   Use the **show running-config | begin vty** command.

   Question:

   What is the result of using this command?

   _____

   _____

   Note: A more specific command would be **show running-config | section vty**; however, the current version of Packet Tracer does not support the **section** filtering command.

Step 4:   Display the routing table on the router.

   Use the **show ip route** command on the router to answer the following questions.

   Question:

   What code is used in the routing table to indicate a directly connected network?

   _____

How many route entries are coded with a C code in the routing table?

<hr/>

Step 5:   Display a summary list of the interfaces on the router.

a. Use the **show ip interface brief** command on the router to answer the following question.

```
R2# show ip interface brief
Interface            IP-Address        OK? Method Status                 Protocol
GigabitEthernet0/0/0 10.0.4.1          YES manual up                     up
GigabitEthernet0/0/1 10.0.5.1          YES manual up                     up
Serial0/1/0          10.0.3.2          YES manual                        up
Serial0/1/1          209.165.200.225   YES manual up                     up
Vlan1                unassigned        YES unset  administratively down  down
```

Questions:

What command changed the status of the Gigabit Ethernet ports from administratively down to up?

<hr/>

What filtering command would you use to display only the interfaces with addresses assigned?

<hr/>

b. Use the **show ipv6 int brief** command to verify IPv6 settings on R2.

Question:

What is the meaning of the [up/up] part of the output?

<hr/>

CHAPTER 15

IP Static Routing

The "Study Guide" portion of this chapter uses a variety of exercises to test your knowledge and skills related to configuring IPv4 and IPv6 static routes. The "Labs and Activities" portion of this chapter includes all the online curriculum labs and Packet Tracer activity instructions.

As you work through this chapter, use Chapter 15 in *Switching, Routing, and Wireless Essentials v7 Companion Guide* or use the corresponding Module 15 in the Switching, Routing, and Wireless Essentials online curriculum for assistance.

Study Guide

Static Routes

In this section, you review the command syntax for static routes.

Types of Static Routes

Static routes can be configured for IPv4 and IPv6. List the types of static routes supported by both protocols.

- _____
- _____
- _____
- _____

List the three next-hop options when configuring a static route.

- _____
- _____
- _____

IPv4 Static Route Command

Review the IPv4 static route command syntax and details of the parameters in Table 15-1.

```
Router(config)# ip route network-address subnet-mask
{ip-address | exit-intf [ip-address]} [distance]
```

Table 15-1   IPv4 Static Route Parameters

Parameter	Description
network-address	Identifies the destination IPv4 network address of the remote network to add to the routing table.
subnet-mask	■ Identifies the subnet mask of the remote network. ■ The subnet mask can be modified to summarize a group of networks and create a summary static route.
ip-address	■ Identifies the next-hop router IPv4 address. ■ Typically used with broadcast networks (such as Ethernet). ■ Could create a recursive static route where the router performs an additional lookup to find the exit interface.
exit-intf	■ Identifies the exit interface for forwarding packets. ■ Creates a directly connected static route. ■ Typically used in point-to-point configuration.
exit-intf ip-address	Creates a fully specified static route because it specifies the exit interface and next-hop IPv4 address.

Parameter	Description
distance	■ Optional command that can be used to assign an administrative distance value between 1 and 255. ■ Typically used to configure a floating static route by setting an administrative distance that is higher than that of a dynamically learned route.

IPv6 Static Route Command

Review the IPv6 static route command syntax and details of the parameters in Table 15-2.

```
Router(config)# ipv6 route ipv6-prefix/prefix-length
{ipv6-address | exit-intf [ipv6-address]} [distance]
```

Table 15-2   IPv6 Static Route Parameters

Parameter	Description
ipv6-prefix	Identifies the destination IPv6 network address of the remote network to add to the routing table.
/prefix-length	Identifies the prefix length of the remote network.
ipv6-address	■ Identifies the next-hop router IPv6 address. ■ Typically used with broadcast networks (such as Ethernet). ■ Could create a recursive static route where the router performs an additional lookup to find the exit interface.
exit-intf	■ Identifies the exit interface for forwarding packets. ■ Creates a directly connected static route. Typically used in a point-to-point configuration.
exit-intf ipv6-address	Creates a fully specified static route because it specifies the exit interface and next-hop IPv6 address.
distance	■ Optional command that can be used to assign an administrative distance value between 1 and 255. ■ Typically used to configure a floating static route by setting an administrative distance that is higher than that of a dynamically learned route.

Check Your Understanding—Static Routes

Check your understanding of static routes by choosing the BEST answer to each of the following questions.

1. Which two methods can be used to identify the next hop in a static route? (Choose two.)

   a. destination interface

   b. destination IP address

   c. destination network address

   d. exit interface

   e. source IP address

2. Which IPv4 static route statement is true?

   a. The destination network is identified using the network address and wildcard mask.

   b. The distance keyword is used to create a fully specified static route.

   c. The source network is identified using the network address and wildcard mask.

   d. Using the exit interface only is common in a point-to-point configuration.

3. How is the destination network in an IPv6 static route identified?

   a. using an IPv6 prefix and prefix length

   b. using an IPv6 prefix and subnet mask

   c. using an IPv6 prefix and wildcard mask

   d. using an IPv6 prefix only

Configure IP Static Route Types

In this section, you review how to configure IPv4 and IPv6 static routes, default static routes, floating static routes, and static host routes.

Configure Static and Default Routes

Figure 15-1 shows the dual stack topology used in this section for configuring static routes. Table 15-3 shows the addressing scheme.

Note: The topology in Figure 15-1 uses loopback interfaces to simulate directly connected LANs. By using loopback interfaces, you can build rather complex scenarios without the need for a physical interface for every network.

Figure 15-1   Dual Stack Static Routing Topology

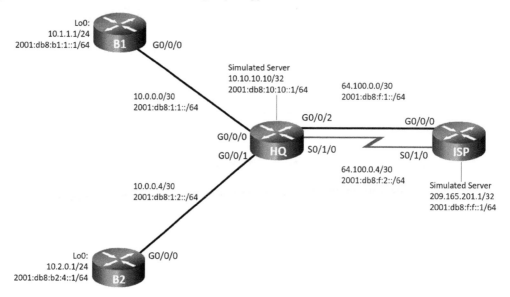

Table 15-3   Addressing Table

Device	Interface	IPv4 Address/Prefix	IPv6 Address/Prefix
ISP	G0/0/0	64.100.0.1/30	2001:db8:f:1::1/64
	S0/1/0	64.100.0.5/30	2001:db8:f:2::1/64
	Lo0	209.165.201.1/32	2001:db8:f:f::1/64
HQ	G0/0/0	10.0.0.1/30	2001:db8:1:1::1/64
	G0/0/1	10.0.0.5/30	2001:db8:1:2::1/64
	G0/0/2	64.100.0.2/30	2001:db8:f:1::2/64
	S0/1/0	64.100.0.6/30	2001:db8:f:2::2/64
B1	G0/0/0	10.0.0.2/30	2001:db8:1:1::2/64
	Lo0	10.1.1.1/24	2001:db8:b1:1::1/64
B2	G0/0/0	10.0.0.6/30	2001:db8:1:2::2/64
	Lo0	10.2.0.1/24	2001:db8:b2:4::1/64

B1 and B2 Routing Strategy

B1 and B2 are both stub routers. What type of static route would you configure on these routers?

Record the commands to configure the appropriate type of IPv4 and IPv6 static routes on B1 and B2 using the next-hop IP address argument.

```
B1# configure terminal
```

```
B2# configure terminal
```

HQ Routing Strategy

HQ operates as a hub router for B1 and B2 and provides access to the Internet through the ISP. What type of static routes would you configure on HQ?

Record the commands to configure the appropriate type of static routes on HQ. Assume that HQ will use both links to the ISP. Consider the following in your configuration:

- Configure the IPv4 and IPv6 static routes to B1 and B2 with the next-hop IP address argument.
- Configure the IPv4 routes to the ISP with the exit interface argument.

■ Configure the IPv6 routes to the ISP with fully specified arguments, using the link-local address as the next-hop address.

```
HQ# configure terminal
```

_____

_____

_____

_____

_____

_____

_____

_____

_____

Configure Floating Static Routes

As you recall from the previous chapter, a router uses administrative distance to choose a route when more than one route exists for a given destination. We can leverage this route decision process to create a floating static route that will not be installed in the routing table unless the primary static route fails.

For example, refer to the topology in Figure 15-1. HQ has two connections to the ISP. The link attached to G0/0/2 is the high-speed primary route that HQ uses as the primary route to send traffic to the ISP. The other link, attached to Serial 0/1/0, is a much slower connection and is used only as a backup route in the event that the primary route fails.

To configure this backup route as a floating static route, we must manually set the administrative distance to be higher than the default administrative distance of a static route. Because a static route's default administrative distance is 1, anything higher than 1 will suffice to create the floating static route. The command syntax for both IPv4 and IPv6 static and default routes with the administrative distance option follows:

```
Router(config)# ip route network mask {next-hop-ip | exit-intf} [admin-dist]
```

```
Router(config)# ip route 0.0.0.0 0.0.0.0 {next-hop-ip | exit-intf} [admin-dist]
```

```
Router(config)# ipv6 route ::/0 {ipv6-address | exit-intf} [admin-dist]
```

```
Router(config)# ipv6 route ipv6-prefix/prefix-length {ipv6-address | exit-intf}
[admin-dist]
```

Refer to Figure 15-1. Record the command to change the HQ IPv4 and IPv6 static default routes to the ISP to floating static routes.

```
HQ# configure terminal
```

_____

_____

Configure Static Host Routes

A host route is an IPv4 address with a 32-bit mask or an IPv6 address with a 128-bit mask. A host route can be added to the routing table three ways:

■ Automatically installed when an IP address is configured on the router

■ Configured as a static host route

■ Automatically obtained through other methods (discussed in later courses)

In the routing tables in Example 15-1, indicate which route entries are host routes.

Example 15-1   Host Routes Automatically Installed in the Routing Table

```
R1# show ip route | begin Gateway
Gateway of last resort is not set
     172.16.0.0/16 is variably subnetted, 4 subnets, 2 masks
C       172.16.2.0/24 is directly connected, Serial0/1/0
L       172.16.2.1/32 is directly connected, Serial0/1/0
C       172.16.3.0/24 is directly connected, GigabitEthernet0/0/0
L       172.16.3.1/32 is directly connected, GigabitEthernet0/0/0
R1#
R1# show ipv6 route | begin C
C   2001:DB8:ACAD:2::/64 [0/0]
     via Serial0/1/0, directly connected
L   2001:DB8:ACAD:2::1/128 [0/0]
     via Serial0/1/0, receive
C   2001:DB8:ACAD:3::/64 [0/0]
     via GigabitEthernet0/0/0, directly connected
L   2001:DB8:ACAD:3::1/128 [0/0]
     via GigabitEthernet0/0/0, receive
L   FF00::/8 [0/0]
     via Null0, receive
R1#
```

To configure a static host route, use a destination IP address and a 255.255.255.255 (/32) mask for IPv4 host routes and a /128 prefix length for IPv6 host routes.

Record the static host routes to configure B1 to access the server on HQ. Both routes should use the next-hop IP address. For the IPv6 static host route, use the link-local address as the next hop and record the command to fully specify the route.

```
B1# configure terminal
```

Packet Tracer Exercise 15-1: Configure Static and Default Routes

To use Packet Tracer to apply your knowledge about static and default routing, download and open the file LSG02-1501.pka from the companion website for this book. Refer to the Introduction of this book for specifics on accessing files.

Note: The following instructions are also contained within the Packet Tracer Exercise: "In this Packet Tracer activity, you will configure B1, B2, and HQ with a variety of static routes."

Requirements

Configure B1 using the following requirements:

- Next-hop IPv4 static default route to HQ
- Next-hop IPv6 static default route to HQ
- Next-hop IPv4 static host route to the HQ simulated server
- Fully specified IPv6 static host route to the HQ simulated server

Configure B2 using the following requirements:

- Next-hop IPv4 static default route to HQ
- Next-hop IPv6 static default route to HQ

Configure HQ using the following requirements:

- Next-hop IPv4 static route to the B1 LAN
- Next-hop IPv4 static route to the B2 LAN
- Next-hop IPv6 static route to the B1 LAN
- Next-hop IPv6 static route to the B2 LAN
- Exit interface (G0/0/2) IPv4 static default route to the ISP
- Exit interface (Serial 0/1/0) IPv4 floating static default route to the ISP with AD of 5
- Fully specified (G0/0/2) IPv6 static default route to the ISP using the link-local address
- Fully specified (Serial 0/1/0) IPv6 floating static default route to the ISP using the link-local address and an AD of 5

Test your floating static route configurations by disabling one of the interfaces on HQ. All routers should still be able to ping the ISP's simulated web server. Your completion percentage should be 100%. If it is not, click Check Results to see which required components are not yet completed.

Labs and Activities

Command Reference

In Table 15-4, record the command, including the correct router or switch prompt, that fits each description.

Table 15-4   Commands for Chapter 15, "IP Static Routing"

Command	Description
	Configure a static route to IPv4 network 192.168.1.0/24, using 172.16.1.2 as the next-hop IPv4 address.
	Configure a static route to the IPv6 network 2001:DB8:A::/64, using 2001:DB8:1::2 as the next-hop IPv6 address.
	Configure an IPv4 default route using Serial 0/0/0 as the exit interface.
	Configure an IPv6 fully specified default route using Serial 0/0/0 as the exit interface and fe80::1 as the next-hop address.
	Configure an IPv4 floating static route to network 10.0.0.0/24 using Serial 0/0/0 as the exit interface and an AD of 10.
	Configure an IPv6 fully specified floating static default route using Serial 0/0/0 as the exit, fe80::1 as the next-hop address, and an AD of 10.

15.6.1 Packet Tracer—Configure IPv4 and IPv6 Static and Default Routes

Addressing Table

Device	Interface	IP Address / Prefix
Edge_Router	S0/0/0	10.10.10.2/30
		2001:db8:a:1::2/64
	S0/0/1	10.10.10.6/30
		2001:db8:a:2::2/64
	G0/0	192.168.10.17/28
		2001:db8:1:10::1/64
	G0/1	192.168.11.33/27
		2001:db8:1:11::1/64
ISP1	S0/0/0	10.10.10.1/30
		2001:db8:a:1::1/64
	G0/0	198.0.0.1/24
		2001:db8:f:f::1/64
ISP2	S0/0/1	10.10.10.5/30
		2001:db8:a:2::1/64
	G0/0	198.0.0.2/24
		2001:db8:f:f::2/64
PC-A	NIC	192.168.10.19/28
		2001:db8:1:10::19/64
PC-B	NIC	192.168.11.4/27
		2001:db8:1:11::45
Customer Server	NIC	198.0.0.10
		2001:db8:f:f::10

Objectives

In this Packet Tracer summary activity, you will configure static, default, and floating static routes for both the IPv4 and IPv6 protocols.

- Configure IPv4 static and floating static default routes.
- Configure IPv6 static and floating static default routes.
- Configure IPv4 static and floating static routes to internal LANs.
- Configure IPv6 static and floating static routes to internal LANS.
- Configure IPv4 host routes.
- Configure IPv6 host routes.

Background / Scenario

In this activity, you will configure IPv4 and IPv6 default static and floating static routes.

Note: The static routing approach that is used in this lab is used to assess your ability to configure different types of static routes only. This approach may not reflect networking best practices.

Instructions

Part 1: Configure IPv4 Static and Floating Static Default Routes

The PT network requires static routes to provide internet access to the internal LAN users through the ISPs. In addition, the ISP routers require static routes to reach the internal LANs. In this part of the activity, you will configure an IPv4 static default route and a floating default route to add redundancy to the network.

Step 1:   Configure an IPv4 static default route.

On **Edge_Router**, configure a **directly connected** IPv4 default static route. This primary default route should be through router **ISP1**.

Step 2:   Configure an IPv4 floating static default route.

On Edge_Router, configure a **directly connected** IPv4 floating static default route. This default route should be through router **ISP2**. It should have an administrative distance of **5**.

Part 2: Configure IPv6 Static and Floating Static Default Routes

In this part of the activity, you will configure IPv6 static default and floating static default routes for IPv6.

Step 1:   Configure an IPv6 static default route.

On Edge_Router, configure a **next-hop** static default route. This primary default route should be through router **ISP1**.

Step 2:   Configure an IPv6 floating static default route.

On Edge_Router, configure a **next hop** IPv6 floating static default route. The route should be via router **ISP2**. Use an administrative distance of **5**.

Part 3: Configure IPv4 Static and Floating Static Routes to the Internal LANs

In this part of the lab you will configure static and floating static routers from the ISP routers to the internal LANs.

Step 1:   Configure IPv4 static routes to the internal LANs.

    a. On ISP1, configure a **next-hop** IPv4 static route to the **LAN 1** network through Edge_Router.

b. On ISP1, configure a **next-hop** IPv4 static route to the **LAN 2** network through Edge_Router.

Step 2:   Configure IPv4 floating static routes to the internal LANs.

a. On ISP1, configure a directly connected floating static route to LAN 1 through the ISP2 router. Use an administrative distance of **5**.

b. On ISP1, configure a directly connected floating static route to LAN 2 through the ISP2 router. Use an administrative distance of **5**.

Part 4: Configure IPv6 Static and Floating Static Routes to the Internal LANs.

Step 1:   Configure IPv6 static routes to the internal LANs.

a. On ISP1, configure a next-hop IPv6 static route to the **LAN 1** network through Edge_Router.

b. On ISP1, configure a next-hop IPv6 static route to the **LAN 2** network through Edge_Router.

Step 2:   Configure IPv6 floating static routes to the internal LANs.

a. On ISP1, configure a next-hop IPv6 floating static route to LAN 1 through the ISP2 router. Use an administrative distance of **5**.

b. On ISP1, configure a next-hop IPv6 floating static route to LAN 2 through the ISP2 router. Use an administrative distance of **5**.

If your configuration has been completed correctly, you should be able to ping the **Web Server** from the hosts on LAN 1 and LAN 2. In addition, if the primary route link is down, connectivity between the LAN hosts and the **Web Server** should still exist.

Part 5: Configure Host Routes

Users on the corporate network frequently access a server that is owned by an important customer. In this part of the activity, you will configure static host routes to the server. One route will be a floating static route to support the redundant ISP connections.

Step 1:   Configure IPv4 host routes.

a. On Edge Router, configure an IPv4 **directly connected** host route to the customer server.

b. On Edge Router, configure an IPv4 directly connected floating host route to the customer server. Use an administrative distance of **5**.

Step 2:   Configure IPv6 host routes.

a. On Edge Router, configure an IPv6 next-hop host route to the customer server through the ISP1 router.

b. On Edge Router, configure an IPv6 directly connected floating host route to the customer server through the ISP2 router. Use an administrative distance of **5**.

15.6.2 Lab—Configure IPv4 and IPv6 Static and Default Routes

Topology

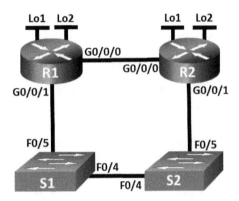

Addressing Table

Device	Interface	IP Address / Prefix
R1	G0/0/0	172.16.1.1 /24
		2001:db8:acad:2::1 /64
		fe80::1
	G0/0/1	192.168.1.1 /24
		2001:db8:acad:1::1 /64
		fe80::1
	Loopback1	10.1.0.1 /24
		2001:db8:acad:10::1 /64
		fe80::1
	Loopback2	209.165.200.225 /27
		2001:db8:acad:209::1 /64
		fe80::1
R2	G0/0/0	172.16.1.2 /24
		2001:db8:acad:2::2 /64
		fe80::2
	G0/0/1	192.168.1.2 /24
		2001:db8:acad:1::2 /64
		fe80::2
	Loopback1	10.2.0.1 /24
		2001:db8:acad:11::2 /64
		fe80::2
	Loopback2	209.165.200.193 /27
		2001:db8:acad:210::1 /64
		fe80::2

Objectives

Part 1: Build the Network and Configure Basic Device Settings

Part 2: Configure and verify IP and IPv6 addressing on R1 and R2

Part 3: Configure and verify static and default routing for IPv4 on R1 and R2

Part 4: Configure and verify static and default routing for IPv6 on R1 and R2

Background / Scenario

Static and Default routing are the simplest forms of network routing and are configured manually. They are fixed, meaning that they do not change dynamically to meet changing network conditions. They are either valid and made available to the routing table or invalid and not made available to the routing table. Static routes have an administrative distance of 1 by default. However, static and default routes can be configured with an administrator-defined administrative distance. This capability allows the administrator to put the static or default route in reserve, and only make it available to the routing table when routes with lower administrative distances (usually generated by dynamic routing protocols) are no longer valid.

Note: In this lab you will configure static, default, and floating default routes for both IPv4 and IPv6, which may not reflect networking best practices.

Note: The routers used with CCNA hands-on labs are Cisco 4221 with Cisco IOS XE Release 16.9.4 (universalk9 image). The switches used in the labs are Cisco Catalyst 2960s with Cisco IOS Release 15.2(2) (lanbasek9 image). Other routers, switches, and Cisco IOS versions can be used. Depending on the model and Cisco IOS version, the commands available and the output produced might vary from what is shown in the labs. Refer to the Router Interface Summary Table at the end of the lab for the correct interface identifiers.

Note: Ensure that the routers and switches have been erased and have no startup configurations. If you are unsure contact your instructor.

Required Resources

- 2 Routers (Cisco 4221 with Cisco IOS XE Release 16.9.4 universal image or comparable)
- 2 Switches (Cisco 2960 with Cisco IOS Release 15.2(2) lanbasek9 image or comparable)
- 1 PC (Windows with a terminal emulation program, such as Tera Term)
- Console cables to configure the Cisco IOS devices via the console ports
- Ethernet cables as shown in the topology

Instructions

Part 1: Build the Network and Configure Basic Device Settings

In Part 1, you will set up the network topology and configure basic settings on the PC hosts and switches.

Step 1:   Cable the network as shown in the topology.

Attach the devices as shown in the topology diagram, and cable as necessary.

Step 2:   Configure basic settings for each router.

    a.   Assign a device name to the router.

    b.   Disable DNS lookup to prevent the router from attempting to translate incorrectly entered commands as though they were host names.

    c.   Assign **class** as the privileged EXEC encrypted password.

    d.   Assign **cisco** as the console password and enable login.

    e.   Assign **cisco** as the VTY password and enable login.

    f.   Encrypt the plaintext passwords.

    g.   Create a banner that warns anyone accessing the device that unauthorized access is prohibited.

    h.   Save the running configuration to the startup configuration file.

Step 3:   Configure basic settings for each switch.

    a.   Assign a device name to the switch.

    b.   Disable DNS lookup to prevent the router from attempting to translate incorrectly entered commands as though they were host names.

    c.   Assign **class** as the privileged EXEC encrypted password.

    d.   Assign **cisco** as the console password and enable login.

    e.   Assign **cisco** as the VTY password and enable login.

    f.   Encrypt the plaintext passwords.

    g.   Create a banner that warns anyone accessing the device that unauthorized access is prohibited.

    h.   Shut down all interfaces that will not be used.

    i.   Save the running configuration to the startup configuration file.

    Question:

    Issuing the command **show cdp neighbors** at this point on R1 or R2 results in an empty list. Explain.

Part 2: Configure and verify IPv4 and IPv6 addressing on R1 and R2

In Part 2, you will configure and verify the IPv4 and IPv6 addresses on R1 and R2. Use the table above for the information necessary to complete this part.

Step 1:   Configure IP addresses for both routers.

    a.   Enable IPv6 Unicast Routing on both routers.

    b.   Configure the IP address for all the interfaces according to the Addressing Table.

Step 2: Verify addressing

    a. Issue the command to verify IPv4 assignments to the interfaces.

    b. Issue the command to verify IPv6 assignments to the interfaces.

Step 3: Save your configuration.

Save the running configuration to the startup configuration file on both routers.

Part 3: Configure and verify static and default routing for IPv4 on R1 and R2

In Part 3, you will configure static and default routing on R1 and R2 to enable full connectivity between the routers using IPv4. Once again, the static routing being used here is not meant to represent best practice, but to assess your ability to complete the required configurations.

Step 1: On R1, configure a static route to R2's Loopback1 network, using R2's G0/0/1 address as the next hop.

    a. Use the **ping** command to ensure that R2's G0/0/1 interface is reachable.

    b. Configure a static route for R2's Loopback1 network via R2's G0/0/1 address.

Step 2: On R1, configure a static default route via R2's G0/0/0 address.

    a. Use the **ping** command to ensure that R2's G0/0/0 interface is reachable.

    b. Configure a static default route via R2's G0/0/0 address.

Step 3: On R1, configure a floating static default route via R2's G0/0/1 address.

Configure a floating static default route with an AD of 80 via R2's G0/0/1 address.

Step 4: On R2, configure a static default route via R1's G0/0/0 address.

    a. Use the **ping** command to ensure that R1's G0/0/0 interface is reachable.

    b. Configure a static default route via R1's G0/0/0 address.

Step 5: Verify that the routes are operational.

    a. Use the **show ip route** command to ensure that R1's routing table shows the static and default routes.

    b. On R1, issue the command **traceroute 10.2.0.1**. The output should show that the next hop is 192.168.1.2.

    c. On R1, issue the command **traceroute 209.165.200.193**. The output should show that the next hop is 172.16.1.2.

    d. Issue the **shutdown** command on R1 G0/0/0.

    e. Demonstrate that the floating static route is working. First, issue the **show ip route static** command. You should see two static routes: A default static route with an AD of 80 and a static route to the 10.2.0.0/24 network with an AD of 1.

f. Demonstrate the floating static route is working by issuing the **traceroute 209.165.200.193** command. The traceroute will show the next hop as 192.168.1.2.

g. Issue the **no shutdown** command on R1 G0/0/0.

Part 4: Configure and verify static and default routing for IPv6 on R1 and R2

In Part 4, you will configure static and default routing on R1 and R2 to enable full connectivity between the routers using IPv6. Once again, the static routing being used here is not meant to represent best practice, but to assess your ability to complete the required configurations.

Step 1: On R2, configure a static route to R1's Loopback1 network, using R1's G0/0/1 address as the next hop.

    a. Use the **ping** command to ensure that R1's G0/0/1 interface is reachable.

    b. Configure a static route for R1's Loopback1 network via R1's G0/0/1 address.

Step 2: On R2, configure a static default route via R1's G0/0/0 address.

    a. Use the **ping** command to ensure that R1's G0/0/0 interface is reachable.

    b. Configure a static default route via R1's G0/0/0 address.

Step 3: On R2, configure a floating static default route via R1's G0/0/1 address.

Configure a floating static default route with an AD of 80 via R2's G0/0/1 address.

Step 4: On R1, configure a static default route via R1's G0/0/0 address.

    a. Use the **ping** command to ensure that R2's G0/0/0 interface is reachable.

    b. Configure a static default route via R2's G0/0/0 address.

Step 5: Verify that the routes are operational.

    a. Use the **show ipv6 route** command to ensure that R2's routing table shows the static and default routes.

    b. On R2, issue the command **traceroute 2001:db8:acad:10::1**. The output should show that the next hop is 2001:db8:acad:1::1.

    c. On R2, issue the command **traceroute 2001:db8:acad:209::1**. The output should show that the next hop is 2001:db8:acad:2::1.

    d. Issue the **shutdown** command on R2 G0/0/0.

    e. Demonstrate the floating static route is working. First issue the **show ipv6 route static** command. You should see two static routes: A default static route with an AD of 80 and a static route to the 2001:db8:acad:10::/64 network with an AD of 1.

    f. Lastly, demonstrate that the floating static route is working by issuing the **traceroute 2001:db8:acad:209::1** command. The traceroute will show the next hop as 2001:db8:acad:1::1.

Router Interface Summary Table

Router Model	Ethernet Interface #1	Ethernet Interface #2	Serial Interface #1	Serial Interface #2
1800	Fast Ethernet 0/0 (F0/0)	Fast Ethernet 0/1 (F0/1)	Serial 0/0/0 (S0/0/0)	Serial 0/0/1 (S0/0/1)
1900	Gigabit Ethernet 0/0 (G0/0)	Gigabit Ethernet 0/1 (G0/1)	Serial 0/0/0 (S0/0/0)	Serial 0/0/1 (S0/0/1)
2801	Fast Ethernet 0/0 (F0/0)	Fast Ethernet 0/1 (F0/1)	Serial 0/1/0 (S0/1/0)	Serial 0/1/1 (S0/1/1)
2811	Fast Ethernet 0/0 (F0/0)	Fast Ethernet 0/1 (F0/1)	Serial 0/0/0 (S0/0/0)	Serial 0/0/1 (S0/0/1)
2900	Gigabit Ethernet 0/0 (G0/0)	Gigabit Ethernet 0/1 (G0/1)	Serial 0/0/0 (S0/0/0)	Serial 0/0/1 (S0/0/1)
4221	Gigabit Ethernet 0/0/0 (G0/0/0)	Gigabit Ethernet 0/0/1 (G0/0/1)	Serial 0/1/0 (S0/1/0)	Serial 0/1/1 (S0/1/1)
4300	Gigabit Ethernet 0/0/0 (G0/0/0)	Gigabit Ethernet 0/0/1 (G0/0/1)	Serial 0/1/0 (S0/1/0)	Serial 0/1/1 (S0/1/1)

Note: To find out how the router is configured, look at the interfaces to identify the type of router and how many interfaces the router has. There is no way to effectively list all the combinations of configurations for each router class. This table includes identifiers for the possible combinations of Ethernet and Serial interfaces in the device. The table does not include any other type of interface, even though a specific router may contain one. An example of this might be an ISDN BRI interface. The string in parenthesis is the legal abbreviation that can be used in Cisco IOS commands to represent the interface.

CHAPTER 16

Troubleshoot Static and Default Routes

The "Study Guide" portion of this chapter uses a variety of exercises to test your knowledge and skills in troubleshooting static and default routes. The "Labs and Activities" portion of this chapter includes all the online curriculum labs and Packet Tracer activity instructions.

As you work through this chapter, use Chapter 16 in *Switching, Routing, and Wireless Essentials v7 Companion Guide* or use the corresponding Module 16 in the Switching, Routing, and Wireless Essentials online curriculum for assistance.

Study Guide

Packet Processing with Static Routes

In this section, you review how a router processes packets when a static route is configured.

Refer to Figure 16-1. PC1 is sending a packet to PC3. R1, R2, and R3 are configured with static routes to ensure full connectivity. For this exercise, ignore the processing done by the switches. In the space below Figure 16-1, describe the process of routing a packet from PC1 to PC3.

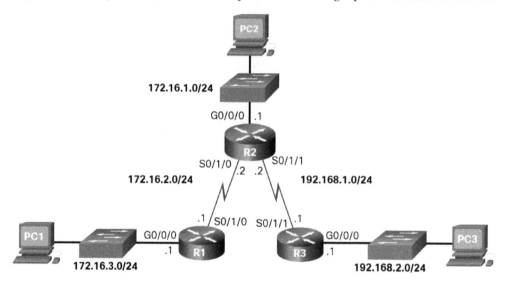

Figure 16-1   IPv4 Static Routing Topology

Check Your Understanding—Packet Processing with Static Routes

Check your understanding of packet processing with static routes by choosing the BEST answer to each of the following questions.

1. True or false: In Figure 16-1, R1 must encapsulate received packets into new frames before forwarding them to R2.

   a. true

   b. false

2. True or false: In Figure 16-1, R2 forwards frames to R3 with an all-1s Layer 2 address.

   a. true

   b. false

3. In Figure 16-1, what action does R3 take to forward a frame if it does not have an entry in the ARP table to resolve a destination MAC address?

   a. It sends a DNS request.

   b. It drops the frame.

c. It sends an ARP request.

d. It sends the frame to the default gateway.

Troubleshoot IPv4 Static and Default Route Configuration

In this section, you review how to troubleshoot common static and default route configuration issues.

By now, you should be very familiar with the troubleshooting tools at your disposal to locate problems in a small network. Common IOS troubleshooting commands include the following:

- ping
- traceroute
- show ip route
- show ip interface brief
- show cdp neighbors detail

Packet Tracer Exercise 16-1: Troubleshoot IPv4 Static and Default Routes

To use Packet Tracer to apply your knowledge about troubleshooting IPv4 static and default routing, download and open the file LSG02-1601.pka from the companion website for this book. Refer to the Introduction of this book for specifics on accessing files.

Note: The following instructions are also contained within the Packet Tracer Exercise.

In this Packet Tracer activity, your job is to troubleshoot the IPv4 static and default route configurations. Two errors in the configuration are causing problems. B1 and B2 should be using a default route to HQ. HQ should be using static routes to the B1 and B2 LANs. Discover and resolve the issues.

This activity is not graded. However, click Check Results and then select the Connectivity Tests tab. All three connectivity tests should be successful.

Hint: Make sure you remove the bad routes.

Labs and Activities

16.3.1 Packet Tracer—Troubleshoot Static and Default Routes

Addressing Table

Device	Interface	IP Addresses
R1	G0/0	172.31.1.1/25
		2001:DB8:1::1/64
	S0/0/0	172.31.1.194/30
		2001:DB8:2::194/64
R2	G0/0	172.31.0.1/24
		2001:DB8:3::1/64
	S0/0/0	172.31.1.193/30
		2001:DB8:2::193/64
	S0/0/1	172.31.1.197/30
		2001:DB8:4::197/64
R3	G0/0	172.31.1.129/26
		2001:DB8:5::1/64
	S0/0/1	172.31.1.198/30
		2001:DB8:4::198/64
PC1	NIC	172.31.1.126/25
		2001:DB8:1::126/64
PC2	NIC	172.31.0.254/24
		2001:DB8:3::254/64
Server	NIC	172.31.1.190/26
		2001:DB8:5::190/64

Objectives

In this activity you will troubleshoot static and default routes and repair any errors that you find.

- Troubleshoot IPv4 static routes.
- Troubleshoot IPv4 default routes.
- Troubleshoot IPv6 static routes.
- Configure IPv4 static routes.
- Configure IPv4 default routes.
- Configure IPv6 static routes.

Background / Scenario

A newly hired network technician is attempting to preconfigure a simple topology that will be delivered to a customer. The technician has not been able to establish connectivity between the three LANs. You have been asked to troubleshoot the topology and verify connectivity between the hosts on the three LANs over IPv4 and IPv6.

Instructions

Step 1: Locate and document the problems.

Record your findings in a table like the one below.

Location	Problem	Solution

Step 2: Repair the problems.

Configure the devices so that full connectivity exists between the hosts on the LANs over IPv4 and IPv6.

Note: Your task is to establish connectivity using the existing static route design. Changing the types of static routes used will result in a loss of points.

16.3.2 Lab—Troubleshoot IPv4 and IPv6 Static and Default Routers

Topology

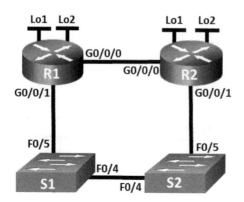

Addressing Table

Device	Interface	IP Address / Prefix
R1	G0/0/0	192.168.0.1 /28
		2001:db8:acad::1 /64
	G0/0/1	192.168.0.17 /28
		2001:db8:acad:16::1 /64
	Loopback1	172.16.1.1 /24
		2001:db8:acad:171::1 /64
	Loopback2	209.165.200.1 /25
		2001:db8:acad:209::1 /64
R2	G0/0/0	192.168.0.14 /28
		2001:db8:acad::14 /64
	G0/0/1	192.168.0.30 /28
		2001:db8:acad:16::2 /64
	Loopback1	172.16.2.1 /24
		2001:db8:acad:172::1 /64
	Loopback2	209.165.200.129 /25
		2001:db8:acad:210::1 /64

Objectives

Part 1: Evaluate Network Operation

Part 2: Gather information, create an action plan, and implement corrections

Background / Scenario

Your instructor has preconfigured all the network equipment and has included intentional errors that are keeping the configured routes from working. Your task is to evaluate the network, identify, and correct the configuration errors to restore full connectivity. You may find errors with the route statements or with other configurations that impact the accuracy of the route statements.

Note: The static routing approach used in this lab is used to assess your ability to configure different types of static routes only. This approach may not reflect networking best practices.

Note: The routers used with CCNA hands-on labs are Cisco 4221 with Cisco IOS XE Release 16.9.4 (universalk9 image). The switches used in the labs are Cisco Catalyst 2960s with Cisco IOS Release 15.2(2) (lanbasek9 image). Other routers, switches, and Cisco IOS versions can be used. Depending on the model and Cisco IOS version, the commands available and the output produced might vary from what is shown in the labs. Refer to the Router Interface Summary Table at the end of the lab for the correct interface identifiers.

Note: Ensure that the routers and switches have been erased and have no startup configurations. If you are unsure contact your instructor.

Required Resources

- 2 Routers (Cisco 4221 with Cisco IOS XE Release 16.9.4 universal image or comparable)

- 2 Switches (Cisco 2960 with Cisco IOS Release 15.2(2) lanbasek9 image or comparable)

- 1 PC (Windows with a terminal emulation program, such as Tera Term)

- Console cables to configure the Cisco IOS devices via the console ports

- Ethernet cables as shown in the topology

Instructions

Part 1: Evaluate Network Operation.

Use Ping and/or Traceroute from the router console to test the following criteria and record the results.

a. Traffic from R1 to R2's 172.16.2.1 address use the next hop 192.168.0.14.

b. Traffic from R1 to R2's 209.165.200.129 address use the next hop 192.168.0.30.

c. When R1's G0/0/0 interface is shut down, traffic from R1 to R2's 172.16.2.1 use the next hop 192.168.0.30.

d. Traffic from R2 to R1's 2001:db8:acad:171::1 address use the next hop 2001:db8:acad::1.

e. Traffic from R2 to R1's 2001:db8:acad:209::1 address use the next hop 2001:db8:acad:16::1.

f. When R2's G0/0/0 interface is shut down, traffic from R2 to R1's 2001:db8:acad:171::1 address use the next hop 2001:db8:acad:16::1.

Part 2: Gather information, create an action plan, and implement corrections.

a. For each criterion that is not met, gather information by examining the running configuration and routing tables and develop a hypothesis for what is causing the malfunction.

b. Create an action plan that you think will fix the issue. Develop a list of all the commands you intend to issue to fix the problem, and a list of all the commands you need to revert the configuration, should your action plan fail to correct it.

c. Execute your action plans one at a time for each criterion that fails and record the fix actions.

Router Interface Summary Table

Router Model	Ethernet Interface #1	Ethernet Interface #2	Serial Interface #1	Serial Interface #2
1800	Fast Ethernet 0/0 (F0/0)	Fast Ethernet 0/1 (F0/1)	Serial 0/0/0 (S0/0/0)	Serial 0/0/1 (S0/0/1)
1900	Gigabit Ethernet 0/0 (G0/0)	Gigabit Ethernet 0/1 (G0/1)	Serial 0/0/0 (S0/0/0)	Serial 0/0/1 (S0/0/1)
2801	Fast Ethernet 0/0 (F0/0)	Fast Ethernet 0/1 (F0/1)	Serial 0/1/0 (S0/1/0)	Serial 0/1/1 (S0/1/1)
2811	Fast Ethernet 0/0 (F0/0)	Fast Ethernet 0/1 (F0/1)	Serial 0/0/0 (S0/0/0)	Serial 0/0/1 (S0/0/1)
2900	Gigabit Ethernet 0/0 (G0/0)	Gigabit Ethernet 0/1 (G0/1)	Serial 0/0/0 (S0/0/0)	Serial 0/0/1 (S0/0/1)
4221	Gigabit Ethernet 0/0/0 (G0/0/0)	Gigabit Ethernet 0/0/1 (G0/0/1)	Serial 0/1/0 (S0/1/0)	Serial 0/1/1 (S0/1/1)
4300	Gigabit Ethernet 0/0/0 (G0/0/0)	Gigabit Ethernet 0/0/1 (G0/0/1)	Serial 0/1/0 (S0/1/0)	Serial 0/1/1 (S0/1/1)

Note: To find out how the router is configured, look at the interfaces to identify the type of router and how many interfaces the router has. There is no way to effectively list all the combinations of configurations for each router class. This table includes identifiers for the possible combinations of Ethernet and Serial interfaces in the device. The table does not include any other type of interface, even though a specific router may contain one. An example of this might be an ISDN BRI interface. The string in parenthesis is the legal abbreviation that can be used in Cisco IOS commands to represent the interface.